The Kept Ones:
The Fame Years

by Bunny DeBarge

This work depicts actual events in the life of the author as truthfully as recollection permits and/or can be verified by research. Occasionally dialogue consistent with the character or nature of the person speaking has been supplemented. The views expressed in this work are solely those of the author. All persons within are actual individuals; there are no composite characters. This is the Bunny DeBarge story.

Book Cover and Copywriting by Sally B. Waller of VocalzMusic & Publishing | VocalzMusic.com | SingingFlat.com

This latest 2023 edition was originally published in 2020 and is the second volume of a series.

ISBN- 979-8-9882366-1-0 (Print)

ISBN- 979-8-9882366-2-7 (Ebook)

PRINTED IN THE UNITED STATES OF AMERICA

I dedicate this book to my greatest legacy—my children, grandchildren, and great-grandchildren.

> *Behold, children are a gift of the Lord; the fruit of the womb is a reward.* **(Prov. 127:3)**

I also dedicate this book to the loving memory of my dearly beloved brother Robert Louis DeBarge Jr. (1956–1995).

> *Like branches on a tree, we grow in different directions, yet our roots remain as one. Each of our lives will always be a special part of the other.* **(Anonymous)**

FOREWORD

Bunny DeBarge offers a captivating revelation detailing her family's near–rocket ship rise to the top of R & B music royalty. Bringing us a degree closer than the usual run-of-the-mill gossip, Bunny intimately navigates through the pitfalls that have haunted her and *DeBarge* for decades. Although they have wrestled with demons that have haunted them since childhood and worked endlessly to destroy their destiny, *DeBarge's* miraculous faith has allowed them to continuously overcome obstacles along the way. What emerges from their struggles is a full-scale portrait of a beautiful, extremely gifted musical family. Their story is as much about each of us as it is about *DeBarge*. Along the way, Bunny untangles the importance of forgiveness, the value of self-awareness, and the importance of recognizing when GOD's Hand is on your life.

Skee Skinner
Film Director, Writer, Producer

ACKNOWLEDGMENTS

First, to my Heavenly Father who remained by my side as I uncovered the pain I carried inside my heart. Thank you, Lord! Without Your Grace and Mercy, I could not have cried those needed tears. You held me in Your Loving Arms as I cried and healed. This has been nothing short of a miracle.

Thank you to my children—Damea, Janae, Tonee, and BuDan—for being with me through my darkest hours and my brightest days. To know we can achieve all things through Christ who strengthens us is a Blessing in and of itself.

To my beloved siblings and second-generation DeBarges, I wrote this book so you will understand where we came from and how far we have grown in love and forgiveness.

Special thanks to Julia Lyons of Elite Press Editing LLC. You are a true GODsend. I could not have made it through without you being there pushing me and believing in how important it was to get my story out. I do not know if you sensed it or not, but many times I had given up. Thank you for helping me edit the *"Bunny-isms."* I love you dearly for your patience, understanding, and guidance. Thank you for believing in me.

Thank you, Nichelle Jackson! You believed in this project for years.

Also, to all the fans who gave to the cause of getting the real story out. Because you believed in me, I will give you the unadulterated truth as I lived it. You have waited patiently. Enjoy! I love you all!

Skee Skinner, thank you for your hard work in taking it to the next level and for just being there for me.

CHAPTER 1

HOLLYWOOD, CALIFORNIA, 1979

I HAD NO IDEA WHAT Hollywood looked like up close and personal. I wondered if it looked exactly as depicted in movies and television. In my mind, Hollywood was this fantasy filled with glamorous people and fulfilled dreams. After months of listening to Bobby "Big Bro" and Tommy carry on about the beautiful scenery, I began to wonder if Hollywood, California, was indeed paradise on earth. Bobby also knew how much I enjoyed growing and tending to exotic plants. I guess to make sure I did not change my mind, he convinced me those same plants grew everywhere in California and everyone planted them in their yards. Now this would be something I had to see!

As I sat on the plane and imagined what California would look like, my mind began to drift. I began to imagine what it would be like to live in Hollywood. What would I say if by chance I met a star? Would I know what to say? What about when *I* became a star? Would this change me? Would I still be Bunny DeBarge? Then there was *Soul Train*. What would it be like performing on the *Soul Train* stage? What would I say to the host? As I grew more and more anxious anticipating what was to come, I decided one of the first places I absolutely had to visit was the *Soul Train* studio. After all, I needed to see glimpses of what I believed in my heart and soul to be my true destiny.

Then there was the weather. Bobby and Tommy had gotten me all excited about the warm sunny California weather. They swore up and down the sun was always shining and the winters were always warm. Coming from Grand Rapids, Michigan, and dealing with unbearable winters, I needed to believe such a place existed where everything was not frozen over for what seemed like most of the year. Although I had grown accustomed to the frigid Michigan winters, it was never lost on me how everything around me appeared dead. The leaves had long fallen, and the naked limbs were seemingly clothed in a fresh coat of snow each day. Cars were buried under what looked like mountains of snow on tree-lined streets. Although as children it was fun to see your breath freezing in midair, as an adult you realized how painful and difficult it was to breathe in subzero temperatures. Of course, there was the wind. The wind in Grand Rapids is quite vicious, and you would easily lose the battle as your body was viciously whipped in different directions. Here I was moving to a place where it never snowed! California felt like it was going to be a whole new world—and different. Not only was I determined to fulfill my destiny, but I also desperately needed a change of scenery for more reasons than one.

Leaving Grand Rapids, Michigan, also meant leaving my spiritual roots and the safety and security of my second home—the church. Our humble beginning as entertainers (and how the music industry worked) started in the church with us singing gospel music. My brothers and I enjoyed performing in church. Through our singing, we were touching the lives of many people. It gave us joy, a sense of purpose, and revealed our destiny. Even with our small "success" as a local gospel singing group, I never forgot the hurt I felt when we received a rejection letter from Light Records after submitting our gospel demo tape: *We don't know where to place you.* Light Records felt our music, even though it was gospel music, was different—and they were correct. We were never meant to sound like other gospel groups. We had our own sound that set us apart from other gospel singers of the day. Still, those words of rejection remained an open wound for a very long time. All our hopes and dreams of becoming gospel artists were shattered. We believed in our heart GOD had given each of us a unique gift to share with the world. Even as our lives at home became increasingly unbearable, sharing the gift of music made us happy. As my mind relived this moment of rejection, I was overcome with a brief bout of depression. The feeling was quickly replaced with new hope as it dawned on me, once again, I would soon be landing in Hollywood, California!

***

Bobby and Tommy met me and my daughters, Damea and Janae, at the airport. The children and I were so excited to see Bobby and Tommy. They were stars (in their own right), but to me and their nieces, they were Uncle Bobby and Uncle Tommy. We walked over to baggage claims with our arms around each other. Even though it was not Christmas, today felt different. Here I was reunited with my brothers, along with my children being with me, in this magical place where everything looked and felt brand-new. As we exited the airport, everything around us teemed with life. You could feel a spirit of happiness and excitement engulfing the city. The sun was shining brightly, and the trees, unlike the barren ones in Grand Rapids, were still in full bloom. To think it was snowing when I left Michigan, yet here I was in California, stepping into summertime.

I could not help but feel anticipation in the air. I looked down at my children as we made our way over to the car. Seeing the huge smiles on their faces as they held tightly to their uncles' hands made me have no regrets about my decision to move to California. A sudden rise in confidence overcame me, and I began to believe anything was possible. I could sing, write, and produce. Moving to California was necessary to achieve my dreams. All I needed was my family, and we would make it big. Oh, what hope I had! What great expectations!

Once inside the car, Bobby and Tommy brought me back to reality. Eager to tell me all about the city and their experiences, they talked over each other. They both wanted to be the Hollywood expert. However, it was hard to hear what either of them had to say because they were so busy going at each other trying to make sure the other told the story correctly. It was pure comedy listening to differing versions of the exact same topic. They were continuously disputing what took place. At first, I was folded over in laughter. This was just another Bobby and Tommy moment—always going at it about something. After a while though, my brothers had gotten on my last nerve and their banter had become insufferable.

"Okay, you guys," I stated, exhausted. "One at a time!"

The intense back-and-forth ended, and the conversation shifted and became very informative as Bobby and Tommy discussed the politics of their music career. As I continued listening to what they were sharing, I could not help but be amazed by the highways. They were expansive. The trees off to the side of the highways were lush and beautiful. California was truly a breath of fresh air. I glanced at my brothers who were now perfect examples of how to become successful. They both looked amazing. They were glowing, and they looked like stars! The California life appeared to be treating them well.

As we were making our way to Cerritos, California, I began to have a strong sense of freedom. Suddenly, it dawned on me: more than anything—the fame, the stardom, Hollywood, etc.—I wanted freedom. *Free!* I thought as my mind drifted again. As I tuned out everything around me, I realized a huge part of me was glad my husband Tony was not with me on this journey. I had so many mixed emotions about being married to him. The freedom I craved so deeply was due to feeling trapped inside our marriage. Now, he was not here with us in California, and I realized that what had been missing from my life all this time was a sense of freedom. Being with my family in a new place gave me a new lease on life. No longer overwhelmed with shouldering a marriage, I soon became high off life.

Bobby and Tommy had a surprise. They took a detour and headed to Hollywood instead. As we exited onto Sunset Boulevard, my eyes became glued to the scenery surrounding me. I rolled down the window so I could take in the sights and sounds of the city. Skateboards zipped across the concrete. Laughter filled the air. Seeing everyone so happy was contagious. The competing conversations sounded like a crowded arena. I slowly exhaled and thought, *we are going to make it happen!*

As we drove on, I looked at the palm trees lining the streets and was amazed at how different they looked from the trees in Grand Rapids. The cars were different too. Untouched by snow and rock salt, they glistened in the sun and were showroom ready. Most of them were convertibles. After seeing all this, I was sure this was the life I wanted. There was not one corner we passed that did not have something electrifying happening.

We stopped on the corner of Sunset and Vine. There stood a tall building that belonged to First Interstate Bank. I looked at Bobby trying to understand why we had stopped. Bobby stated that the Motown offices were inside the building and took up five floors. He pointed out the actual floors where Motown was housed. My excitement could not be contained, and I was eager to see the inside of the building. Bobby stated he had made other plans for today but promised to take me there soon. So off we went to Santa Monica Boulevard.

Once we finally reached Santa Monica Boulevard, there were billboards plastered everywhere. The billboards were promoting upcoming movies and album releases. Only stars who were hot at the time would have their images and names on the billboards. The billboards were so huge they nearly covered the sky. *Wow!* I thought to myself. *I have never seen anything like this before in my life.* We hopped back into the car and drove down a little farther. Bobby then pointed at another billboard. "Look, Bunny!" he stated. "Who is that?"

He pulled the car over to the curb. I could not believe my eyes. Right there was a billboard with a bright light shining on it. On the billboard was a picture of *Switch*! The image was huge, and it seemed to jump out and come to life. Underneath the image were the words: *Up and Coming Soon on Motown Records.* Motown had a billboard of the *Switch* album right there in Hollywood! A huge picture of my brothers was shining bright just like other big-name stars. What a thrill to see! *Big time!* I thought. *Big time!* We all stood there in awe, taking in the moment of this great accomplishment. "Look at you, guys!" I lovingly stated while holding back tears of joy.

I was ecstatic! Like a proud mother, my mind went back to when Bobby and Tommy were little hard-headed boys. Then I thought about everything they had endured at the hands of our Father. To see how far they had come in such a short time was a very cathartic moment. My brothers had grown from little boys to grown men. I guess sensing my emotions, Bobby felt it was time to head home to Cerritos. As he drove off, my daughters and I turned and looked out the back window at the billboard. We could not take our eyes off it. It became smaller and smaller until it finally faded into the distance. It seemed like a dream except it was really happening.

***

We finally arrived at the place we would call home in Cerritos, California. As we pulled into the driveway, I noticed a beautiful light-brown Mexican-style stucco house. It had a huge lush front yard with colorful flowers planted along the edges of the landscape. The other homes on the street were bigger than ours and looked like mansions in comparison. It did not matter because our home was still beautiful.

Before we could make it out of the car, we were greeted by the boys (Randy, Mark, and El), who had been awaiting our arrival. I looked toward the house then at each of the boys. Just as I had figured—the DeBarge boys were having a party, and there was a house full of girls. *Oh boy, here we go!* I thought. Then again, what could I really say or do? They were good-looking boys enjoying the freedom of being on their own. I mentally dismissed their groupies while giving each of the boys a huge hug and warm kiss. "We didn't forget about you!" El shouted. "Look! Come and see the house!"

Once inside, I noticed the boys had instruments. It seemed that in addition to the girls and the partying, they were at least taking their music seriously. The boom box was on full blast, and I could barely make out what they were saying. My brothers showed off their respective rooms. The home still needed to be furnished. I figured we would just take a page out of our mother's book and catch a few garage sales to get the things we needed. For them to be young boys, I was very impressed by how they had taken care of business.

It had been a long day. Damea and Janae were exhausted to say the least. After attending to their needs and putting my girls to sleep, I was on my way back to Hollywood with Bobby. Tommy had decided to join the boys' house party. Bobby, on the other hand, was eager to get to the studio and show me what he had been working on. He began to brag about how Mr. Berry Gordy, the founder of Motown, had shown him favor. Because Mr. Gordy liked him, Bobby said he could do just about anything he wanted in the studio. He always loved the piano. Growing up in Michigan, he spent hours upon hours practicing the piano. All his diligence had finally paid off—Bobby was now a full-fledged producer at Motown. Bobby had a sweetening session scheduled for his new song, "I Call Your Name." I would finally get to see him in action. Bobby knew exactly how he wanted his music to sound. He forewarned we would be in the studio until he got everything just right—even if it took all night. I knew Big Bro and had no problem with how long the studio session would last. The most important thing was hanging with my Big Bro.

Bobby and I headed to the Motown recording studio. The sun had gone down, and the city was now lit up. The nighttime brought out a different crowd of people, and they were just as eclectic as the ones I saw earlier in the day. Bobby talked about the upcoming studio session. He stated there would be a string and horn session going on. The guy orchestrating the session, Clare Fisher, was also from Grand Rapids. Bobby was very fond of Mr. Fisher.

"He's an older white guy and quite the musical genius. Clare went to school at Michigan Universal and studied classical music. Mr. Gordy suggested we work together. Musical geniuses work well together," Bobby proudly stated. He went on to say, "I'll introduce him to you— you'll love him. He's a great guy! Very down to earth. You'll be surprised at how he relates."

Once we were in the studio's parking lot, I noticed the sign on the building that read Motown/Hitsville Recording Studio. I was finally here! Across the street, I noticed a park.

"That's Poinsettia Park," Bobby said. "We go over there a lot during our breaks when we have daytime sessions. You'll see how beautiful it is in the morning because we're going to be here all night."

We entered the building, and a lady was sitting at the receptionist's desk. Bobby spoke to her as he signed us in. She returned the gesture with a warm smile. "Bobby, you're in Studio B tonight."

Bobby knew where to go, and I followed close behind. I had never been in an actual recording studio. When we did our gospel demo back in Michigan, it was in the basement of someone's home. We sauntered down the hallway until we came upon a large brown door with lots of insulation. From its appearance, it looked very heavy. Bobby explained the door was insulated and heavy because it was soundproof. He then pushed the door open with ease, and I could now hear musical sounds coming from inside. Once inside, I noticed it looked a lot like the music room I had visited at the local junior college while still in Grand Rapids. There were two rooms—the room where the console sat and another room where the musicians sat with their instruments. Different sounds were pouring from various instruments. There were flutes being practiced on, chimes ringing for no real reason, and violins screeching as they were being fine-tuned. Behind the console board sat the largest tape player I had ever seen. Bobby explained it was the master tape. It had twenty-four tracks of music he had already recorded.

I was in awe of everything going on around me. Bobby was amused. He introduced me to the engineer who sat behind the console. Before we could exchange pleasantries, a short gray-haired gentleman rushed into the room, flustered.

"Are you ready to work, Mr. DeBarge?" he stated, shuffling the sheet music in his hands, trying to get them organized. He then looked over at me and extended his hand. "Hello, I'm Clare Fisher."

"Bunny DeBarge," I stated. "Nice to meet you. I'm Bobby's sister."

Bobby looked over at Clare and said, "This is her first time here. I have my sister with me today. I'm ready when you are, man."

As Bobby and Mr. Fisher talked among themselves, I remember standing there feeling important because Bobby let everyone know his sister was at the studio. He even bragged to everyone, saying I was a great singer and songwriter. He ended his praise by promising everyone they would hear from his sister soon. With Bobby preoccupied with Mr. Fisher, it was my chance to walk around and check out the place. I went to the window and observed the musicians in the music room. I was surprised to find such a diverse group of musicians from different nationalities, age groups, and even with how they dressed. There was a music stand with sheet music in front of each musician. I could not wait to hear how each person's part would come together and was ready for the session to begin. I looked around for Bobby and Mr. Fisher. They were still engaged in conversation regarding the sheet music and trying to finalize the details. They had minor disagreements, but nothing they could not easily overcome to ensure a successful studio session.

Finally, Mr. Fisher walked back into the music room and took his place in front of the group. Bobby went and sat with the engineer. The big tape began to rewind. Bobby pushed a button on the console board to talk to Mr. Fisher.

"We're ready in here, Clare. We're starting from the top," Bobby stated.

He was now focused and tuned out everything and everyone around him. As I took my seat next to Bobby, he did not pay me any attention. The music began to play, and it sounded amazing. To me, the sound came right out of heaven! I was awestruck watching my brother, along with Mr. Fisher, create the string and horn parts for the song "I Call Your Name." Bobby sat at the console, feeling every sound as it vibrated from the instruments and the musicians played in perfect harmony. At first, I thought he was being overly dramatic until he got up and went to take Mr. Fisher's place inside the music room. I was trying to figure out what Bobby was doing. He had never conducted an orchestra. To my amazement, despite him not having any formal training in classical music, Big Bro knew what he was doing! Mr. Fisher was amazed as well. He loved Bobby's energy and enthusiasm toward music. He would always go out of his way to give Bobby whatever he needed to be creative. Everything Bobby told me about Mr. Fisher was correct. He was indeed a musical genius, and there was a definite musical chemistry between Bobby and Mr. Fisher.

Time passed quickly. When I looked at the clock, I was surprised. It was early morning. Just as Bobby predicted, we spent the entire night inside the studio. The session was long, but I was too hyped after witnessing my brother's musical genius. There's an old saying: Time flies when you're having fun. Well, I had just lived this truth in the studio all night with Big Bro. *Fun! What a concept!* I thought to myself. Fun was not something I had experienced until this very moment. I was having fun—the most fun I ever had in life.

***

El came charging out of the door with my daughters in tow.

"Your husband has been calling all night. Where have you guys been?" he asked with concern in his voice.

Bobby, still inside the car, popped in the cassette tape from our late-night studio session. "Listen to this, El. I did a sweetening session last night."

Just like that, El's full attention was on listening to Bobby's music and taking notes. He handed my girls to me and jumped inside the car. My focus shifted as well, but not in a way that pleased me emotionally. The fun I felt while at the studio was fleeting, and reality set in. Although the arrival to California had been a whirlwind and I was able to witness Bobby in all his musical glory, I was now forced to deal with the reality haunting me from Grand Rapids. Still, I was not sure what to do or how I would face my failing marriage.

I knew as a wife that I should have contacted Tony when I first arrived in California. My intentional oversight weighed on me mentally. As someone who was brought up with traditional Christian values toward marriage, I was not fulfilling my wifely duties by avoiding my husband. I thought about what I would say to justify not calling. Do I tell the truth and just let my husband know I have not felt like a wife for quite some time now? Maybe I should lay everything bare and admit I was no longer happy with our relationship, and this was not something that happened overnight. I wrestled with myself and thought about taking the easy route. Why not just go along with what my husband wanted and perhaps I would not feel so conflicted? But I had dealt with my husband's insecurities in the past and did not want to go down this road again.

My husband Tony's insecurities caused him to become very domineering and possessive to the point he would not let me out of his sight. I thought about how close I was to getting my singing career up and running and subsequently realizing my dream of becoming a star. With his deep insecurities, Tony would become a problem and possible hindrance to my success. I decided against calling him for now. I knew Tony, and simply telling him I was with Bobby in the studio all night would not be good enough. He would make a big deal out of it, and the last thing I wanted to do was allow him to push me into another argument. I wanted to enjoy this newfound feeling of being free as a bird. I wanted to have a career and not feel as if my own husband would sabotage my success. Lastly, I wanted to have fun—the same fun I had last night in the studio watching my brother live out his childhood dream of being a star. I looked back at my own childhood—at my mother's life—and realized how her dreams had gone by the wayside due to her marriage.

My mother, Etterlene DeBarge, dreamed of becoming a professional gospel singer. She was unable to pursue her dreams because she was a committed submissive wife to my father, Robert Louis DeBarge Sr. My father's controlling and abusive behavior stopped her dreams dead in their tracks. I refused to go down this road and sacrifice my destiny. After my relationship with Kevin Murphy ended, I made a promise I would never put my God-given talent on the back burner for the sake of a relationship. Kevin, for all intents and purposes, had been my first love. We shared a deep spiritual connection in the beginning. However, our relationship eventually hit a sour note due to him becoming emotionally unavailable.

Even though it was taught to me while growing up in the church, being a submissive wife never sat well with me. It was a form of control and I did not want to be with someone who wanted to exercise such authority over my life. Though my marriage was suffocating for the most part, I still had feelings toward my husband, which were tender and a heart still willing to make it work. I just did not know how to reconcile being a free spirit and staying married to Tony. The only thing left to do was voice this to Tony and stand firm in my convictions. My only issue was I simply was not ready to face my husband and risk a huge argument. The pressured thoughts morphed into anger and eventually dampened my spirit.

Exhausted from traveling on top of an all-night studio session, I needed rest. Despite everything going on in Grand Rapids, I was with my brothers and my girls in beautiful, sunny California. I felt at home and I felt needed. I decided dealing with Tony would simply have to wait. Therefore, I continued avoiding his calls.

Bobby
& Tommy

Interstate Bank Building
Sunset & Vine
Motown housed the top 5 floors

We could not take our eyes off of it,
It became smaller and smaller until finally
faded into the distance

Me, Damea, Janae

The Streets of Los Angeles

The electrifying streets of Hollywood, photo by Oxana Mells

Electrifying streets

*Outside Motown studio in
West Hollywood*

*Bobby Engineering
in Studio*

Clare Fischer

*Barney Perkins
Engineering*

String session in Studio

CHAPTER 2

SOURCE RECORDS

Bobby picked us up early for a day at Motown. He was excited to be with his family, and it showed in the way he walked and talked. Bobby behaved like a proud father while I, always the mother figure, sat back and quietly cheered him on. The day had finally arrived! Our hearts were united as we walked in total rhythm with each other. We were very close-knit as siblings. Putting on a united front, we prepared to enter our destiny. If joy were a tangible entity, our faces is where it could be seen and measured. The only other time I remember any semblance of joy being manifested in our lives was when we finally relocated to Grand Rapids from Detroit. What a sense of freedom to be living out everything we believed we were meant to be in life—stars.

Today, we were all headed to the Artist Relations Department (A&R) at Motown Records. As we entered the lobby, the energy flowing between us was electric. We were eager to reach our destination, but the building was crowded and the elevator quickly filled with people. Bobby had us wait for the next elevator so we would have it all to ourselves. Once we were on the elevator, Bobby announced we would be going to the fourteenth floor.

We could have never imagined everything our eyes would visualize once we stepped off the elevator. When the elevator doors swung open, there we were in the lobby that housed Motown's A&R Department. In the middle of the lobby sat a receptionist's desk. We slowly inched off the elevator into the lobby in complete awe. Images of great Motown artists from past and present covered the walls of the lobby. There were various styles of photography—some in glossy black and white and others in color. Bobby and Tommy had become accustomed to seeing this unique setup. They remained cool, calm, and collected. For the rest of us (Randy, Mark, El, and myself), we were stopped dead in our tracks trying to take in all the images. Even though we were only looking at pictures, we were completely starstruck.

There were beautiful images of the diva herself, Diana Ross. Then there were (*to me*) the King—Smokey Robinson. The Temptations had images represented that included David Ruffin and other images of Dennis Edwards. Other Motown artists featured about the walls were Rick James, Teena Marie, Ozone, Dazz Band, Switch, the Jackson 5, and Jermaine Jackson. I stared at the image of Switch. It melted my heart to see images of my brothers beautifully framed and displayed among other Motown greats.

Bobby and Tommy checked in at the receptionist's desk. All we had to do now was wait for someone to come from the back offices and meet us. Looking around, I noticed we were not the only ones in awe. The receptionist sat there and stared at us, unable to utter a single word. Perhaps she was trying to figure out who we were—six people who all favored one another in one way or another. Bobby, always sensing when someone had a question, was about to explain everything to the receptionist. Before he could do so, the double doors swung open, and we were off to the A&R Department.

Bobby and Tommy appeared to have a great relationship with everyone. Each person we passed made small talk with them. There were conversations about promotional strategies and marketing ideas for Switch's next album. Some people even joked about their upcoming photo shoot. It felt like the rest of us were walking through a foreign country because we did not understand the terminology being used. They might as well have been speaking in French. I did not allow this to discourage me though. I figured soon enough, the rest of us talented DeBarges would fill Bobby and Tommy's shoes and be able to understand the lingo.

Bobby and Tommy stopped at just about everyone's office to introduce us while giving them a complete rundown of each sibling. Some people knew of our impending arrival while others were surprised. My brothers were indeed happy to show us off and even happier we would become members of the Motown family. Bobby bragged on us incessantly throughout the day. He made sure the powers that be knew each person's musical strengths as well as the part each would play in the group. By the time Bobby and Tommy were done showing us off and bragging about our musical gifts, it dawned on me we would have a lot to live up to at Motown. Bobby and Tommy did not make it easy by the way they carried on. Of course, they were being your typical proud brothers. Still, it was too much. We left Motown with a renewed sense of purpose and with Bobby promising everyone they would be hearing from us real soon.

The boys were already signed to Source Records, and I was getting ready to sign. We had no idea what the contract entailed, and a part of us did not care. Our goal was to sign with Motown. The Source Records deal was temporary. We surmised that once Bobby was ready to showcase us at Motown, we would simply switch companies! Boy were we in for a rude awakening!

When Bobby learned the boys had already signed to Source Records, he was furious. They had somehow managed to keep this information away from him. It was easy to do since Bobby was consumed with Switch and barely found time for anything else. He rarely inquired about what was happening in our day-to-day lives. However, news of the boys signing with Source Records broke his heart. Bobby voiced his concern we may have jumped the gun. When Bobby initially discussed this with me, I was in complete shock because I was sure the boys ran this by him before they made any moves. Bobby was furious mainly because he had lost control.

"How could you let them do this, Bunny?" he asked. "You guys knew I wanted us all to be together at Motown."

"How could *I* let them do it?" I asked, not understanding why he was blaming me. "It was not my idea! I thought you knew."

Bobby stated he knew nothing about the Source Records deal. He did backtrack for a minute and stated he may have heard through the grapevine the boys were already signed to a record label. However, because he did not hear anything directly from me, he simply let it slide. I confirmed with Bobby the boys had indeed signed with Source Records, but I was only privy to this information after the fact. I let Bobby know I was not signed yet. Seeing Bobby upset, I felt depressed and defeated. I knew how important it was to him for us to stick together and be on the same record label. He wanted to know what Bernd Lichters had gotten us into with Source Records.

Bobby was right about us jumping the gun. From the moment El threw the shovel in the snow and walked away from his job, to the day the boys moved to California, and finally when my girls and I joined them, everything was moving under a fog. We had more questions than answers. However, we believed in Bernd and believed his benevolence was a show of support for our burgeoning careers. Bernd had provided us with airline tickets, a place to stay, and instruments for the boys. We were on our way to becoming entertainers. We did not give a second thought to the business side of the deal. Why should musicians concern themselves with business dealings? We were artists, and the business side was not as appealing and ended up a very confusing process. All we wanted to do was make our way into the recording studio and work our magic. We quickly discovered the importance of also understanding the business side.

Frustrated, Bobby gave me a hard-hitting lesson regarding the *music business*. It was a business first, and somewhere down the line, the music mattered. Placing the music above everything else is a recipe for disaster. There were vultures swarming the industry preying on those who did not handle their business. I learned what a contract meant but mostly all it concealed. The contract the boys signed would bind us to Source Records for seven years. Bobby stated we should have known better and used the assistance of a good lawyer to negotiate the terms of the contract. However, since the boys had already signed, it was too late, and they would not be able to get out of the contract. Listening to Bobby, I realized he could have helped us with so much if only we had run everything by him first. He mentioned we should have been provided a salary by the record company. In doing so, we would be able to focus on being creative without having to work a regular nine-to-five job. Bobby then went on to inform me Motown was the only company he knew who placed their artists on salaries. He opened my eyes and helped me understand a lot of the business side. I realized we truly had no clue. Signing the contract was more serious than we could ever imagine.

At this point, I believed there was not much anyone could do to help. The boys were under contract and had done so without any legal advice. Bobby believed if the boys stayed under the contract with Source Records, it would only spell doom. I figured maybe he could talk to Bernd and fix the situation. Bobby became even more frustrated because he was busy in the studio trying to complete his album. He did not want to become entangled in the business affairs of another record company. Bobby stated he hoped the deal with the company worked in our favor, but it was on us to figure it out. I told Bobby I would find out more and inquire about the record company's next move concerning the group.

One thing for sure, Bobby had lit a fire under me. After talking with my brother, I had an idea of what I needed to say to the president of the record company. Bobby and Tommy's record deal with Motown appeared to be going smooth. I wanted the same deal with Source Records that they had with Motown. I hoped after stating my concerns to the powers that be at Source Records, it would happen. There was no time for me to tarry. I needed to figure out how to clean up this mess. I had yet to meet the president of Source Records. My only means of communicating with him was through Bernd. Later in the evening, I put in a call to Bernd and let him know I needed to meet with the president of Source Records, Mr. Logan H. Westbrooks. Understanding my concerns, Bernd promised to reach out to Mr. Westbrooks and get back to me the following day. With this situation squared away (for now), it was time for me to focus on my personal life.

I was still dodging Tony's calls. I felt torn between working on a marriage no longer fulfilling to me versus focusing on my career and trying to clean up the mess the boys had made by signing the contract with Source Records. I was sure Tony must have been unhappy since he had no idea where my head was concerning our marriage. I needed to talk with my husband soon. Before I took the next step, I wanted to be sure about a few things: Did I want to continue with my marriage or let it go? Even though I was one step closer to my destiny, I had not yet signed to Source Records. I did give Source Records my word I would sign once I arrived in California. With everything Bobby had schooled me on regarding the music business, I weighed my options. Do I focus on my marriage and try to make it work? Or do I commit myself to my dream and try to work everything out once I met with Mr. Westbrooks? I began to question who had my best interest at heart—my husband or the record company?

Since the move to California, I busied myself with looking after my brothers and taking care of my girls. I enjoyed caring for everyone. It felt comfortable and familiar. Even though I did not give birth to them, I was their older sister and still felt a responsibility to them. I loved my brothers with my entire heart. From a very early age, I felt as if they were mine to protect. It took many, many years for me to recognize (and accept) my brothers were just that—my brothers and not my responsibility. Anyone could see they were big in my world and I could not help but feel the need to protect them—especially when they make decisions such as signing a record deal that may not work out in their best interest.

Bernd stopped by our home later to tell us Mr. Westbrooks had set up a meet and greet. The boys and I were to meet the president of Source Records for lunch at a Los Angeles area restaurant. He stated he would pick us up the following day and drive us to the location.

The very next day, Bernd picked us up (El, Randy, Mark, and me) and drove us to the restaurant. We were finally going to meet the president of the company. We had planned to share with him the songs we had written and how we were eager to lay tracks in the studio. It was our hope Mr. Westbrooks would make this happen soon. Spending time with Bobby and Tommy gave us an inside view of how the studio process worked. We were excited about the meeting and eager to take the next step.

The restaurant was warm and inviting. After we were seated, Mr. Westbrooks walked into the restaurant with the confident swagger of a successful businessman. The boys rose quickly to shake his hand and give him a hug. He made us feel at ease and gathered our attention by speaking on our favorite subjects: music and its pioneers. I found Mr. Westbrooks warm and approachable. He had a gentle spirit and was very much a teacher. He was well versed on many topics. He was also a great listener and allowed us to express our expectations of the company concerning our careers.

Our lunch meeting with Mr. Westbrooks was sobering. We had to face the cold, hard facts about the seven-year record contract and what it entailed. Mr. Westbrooks explained that Source Records was a small record company and had invested money in a master tape. They needed a group to promote it. For the first year of the contract, the group's obligation would be to promote an album resulting from the master-tape recordings. Apparently, Source Records had purchased a master tape of White Heat's recordings from Bernd. Bobby, Gregory Williams (White Heat/Switch), and Jody Sims (White Heat/Switch), as well as my husband Tony Jordan (White Heat), were former band members. Barry White had produced the album. The tracks had never been released. The one track written and sung by Bobby entitled "Please Don't Let Me Go" would now be our single. Source Records planned to release it under the group named Smash. Unbeknownst to us, the group Smash would consist of El, Randy, Mark, and myself. Bernd had told Mr. Westbrooks that El's voice sounded almost like Bobby's voice, which then piqued his interest. It seemed like only Bernd and Mr. Westbrook were privy to these little behind-the-scene details. No one let the boys or I in on any of the discussions regarding the master tape. To say my brothers and I were shocked and disappointed was an understatement. To add insult to injury, Source Records had already set up promotional tours for us at high schools and radio stations in the local area. The company wanted to recoup the money they invested in buying the master tape. They intended to use us to ensure a return on their investment. We were promised after a year, we would be allowed to go into the studio and record our own songs. Our schedule was mapped out for us with zero input. We also learned the promotional tour would begin right away.

The surprises kept coming. Being a small company, Source Records could not afford to put us on salary. They had rented the house. However, it was our responsibility to maintain it. Mr. Westbrooks reassured us after we learned the album, we could do small gigs to earn money. The rent had been paid three months in advance by the company. We had two months left. Afterward, we were on our own to foot the bills. The more we learned about the nuances of our deal with Source Records, the more our world came crashing down. We thought our contract would at least be like our brothers' contract with Motown. We had hoped to be placed on a salary because we needed money. We had no idea what we had gotten ourselves into with this deal. Even worse, we had no idea how to get out of the deal.

I soon became the focus of the meeting. I knew it was coming, and I dreaded it. Mr. Westbrooks informed me I would be receiving a contract to sign. Even though I was still on the fence, I came to the meeting leaning toward signing with the company. Upon learning the actual details of the record deal, I had second thoughts. Instead of asserting myself and making it known I had no intentions on signing the contract, I politely smiled and stated, "Thank you, sir. I look forward to reviewing the contract."

I thought to myself, *this is crazy! Thank GOD I have not signed!* Even though I was stalling, I had no idea how this would play out in my favor. My brothers had already signed, and I was a member of the group. Who could I go to for help? I had no contacts in the industry. I did not know the first thing about getting an artist out of a contract. The only person I figured could help was Bobby except he was already feeling some type of way about everything transpiring behind his back. He knew Bernd, though. Perhaps he could discuss with Bernd about getting the boys out of such a lousy contract. When I fully explained everything to Bobby, he went off. "I told you guys to wait! I can't do anything right now. Motown is pressuring me every day to complete this album . . . and now, I've got to think about you guys too?" Bobby ranted. "You need a lawyer! The record company is not going to release you. You guys already signed. There's nothing I can do."

Our future in the music business looked bleak. The boys were bound to a seven-year contract that did not have their best interest at heart. All my hopes and dreams seemed to be going up in smoke. I could not help but question the situation. What difference did it make since we had already written our own songs and was just waiting to record them? We were not allowed to do anything with them because of the contract the boys signed. As far as I was concerned, moving to California was a waste of time. I was furious because our hands were tied. Although I had not signed (and had no intentions of ever signing), I did not want to leave my brothers high and dry. We needed a miracle! Although I did not feel close to GOD, I knew He was close to me. My Christian foundation had taught me such: *He's married to the backslider and He promised to never to leave me nor forsake me.*

"Father GOD," I prayed. "We're in trouble. Please help us."

Smash Album Cover *Mr. Logan Westbrook*

cords has signed Smash, according to Logan Westbrooks, presi
t in March, distributed and marketed by MCA. Pictured at the s
(standing) Stanley M. Bethal, VP, marketing-sales; Kenneth C.
ation; and Logan H. Westbrooks, president; (front) Bernd Lich
manager; Stanley Hood, Randy DeBarge, Andre Abney, and Ma

The group Smash,
before El

The group after El
& before me

we walked in rhythm through the bank lobby
to go to motown for the first time

Motown Artist pictures on lobby wall

Marvin Gaye   The Temptations

The Supremes   Smokey Robinson & The Miracles

The Jackson 5   The Marvelettes

CHAPTER 3

A RUDE AWAKENING

THE NEXT MORNING, I AROSE thinking about all the drama going on in my life. So many thoughts were traveling through my mind. It did not make for the best start to my day. I had to get on my grind and straighten out this fiasco we were facing. There was only one problem—I was not quite sure where or how to begin. Not only was I stressed with the thought of my career ending before it began, but I also still had the issue of my husband looming over my head. I figured today would be as good a day as any to finally stop avoiding Tony. The joy I had initially felt about being in California was quickly turning into a nightmare. The thought of Tony going off no longer fazed me. I picked up the phone and slowly dialed home.

Much to my surprise, talking to Tony was not bad at all. It turned out to be just what I needed. They say absence makes the heart grow fonder. Perhaps Tony not having access to me made him a bit humble. Still, he wanted to know what was going on with me and where I was mentally concerning our marriage. Normally, he would have been arrogant in his approach. This time, he meekly approached the subject. It made it easier to be honest as I expressed concerns about why I felt our marriage could no longer work. I did let Tony know I wanted to be free. Of course, Tony was not having any of it. He wanted his family plain and simple, and ending our marriage was not an option he would consider. He promised not to get in the way of me pursuing my music career. Listening to Tony talk about compromising and how our time apart made him realize he needed to change was encouraging. For once, we had a meaningful conversation, which was not domineering and one-sided.

As we continued to talk on the phone, I began to feel comfortable sharing with Tony what was going on regarding Source Records. I explained to him the particulars of the boys' contracts and the disappointment we were all feeling as a result. Tony stepped right in and shared in the regret regarding the contract. He convinced me I could use his help. I was somewhat relieved to have the support of my husband. He was so encouraging, and at this point, I needed his strength to get through this storm.

Tony stated he would be driving to California to be with the kids and me as soon as our home was sold. We made plans over the phone for him to come to California, get a job, and we would move forward with the contract issue. Despite the strain of our marriage, we had lived quite well in Michigan. We both worked decent-paying jobs and was able to purchase a home together. Now, here we were in the final phase of leaving Michigan altogether and starting over in California. *Perhaps this will work out after all*, I thought.

Later in the afternoon, Bobby came by and invited me to spend the day with him. I thought it would be a good way to take my mind off things. He had some business to handle at Motown and wanted me to meet Jermaine Jackson and Hazel Gordy's secretary, Addye. Bobby was very fond of Addye. She helped him with a lot of business dealings, and he felt it would be good for us to finally meet.

When we arrived at the office, Bobby introduced me to Addye. She came off as very kind natured. Addye stated she felt as if she already knew the family since Bobby talked about us nonstop. This day was no different. Still reeling from the record contract fiasco, Bobby brought Addye up to speed about everything going on. He went on to express how he felt the company was a complete joke.

"How sad!" Addye expressed compassionately. "They knew you all were green to the industry, and they used it to take advantage of you! I know for a fact Jermaine and Hazel were interested in you guys."

The more Addye talked, the more it dampened my spirits. We were so close to signing with Motown. Now everything seemed as if it was ruined. As Addye continued to talk, I put on a brave face because I did not want her to notice the hurt I felt now.

"Bobby always talks to Mr. and Mrs. Jackson about how talented his family is," she continued. "Bobby is persistent. They would have listened to you guys and gotten you in for a showcase. The timing is bad right now because they are busy with Switch."

Addye had an expression of pity on her face, and all I could do was scream inside. She made it clear she felt as if we had made a horrible mistake by signing the contract with Source Records. Perhaps realizing I was hurt by the situation, she turned her focus to Bobby and the reason he came to the Motown office today. As sobering and eye-opening as my conversation was with Addye, there was a friendly connection, and we exchanged phone numbers.

Addye and I soon became very close friends. Not a day went by we did not talk to each other—even if to simply check in and say hi. We would go to lunch together often. There were days I went by her office just to sit and talk. What I admired the most about Addye was the relationship she shared with GOD. I loved her spiritual insight and appreciated her willingness to keep my brothers and I lifted in prayer. Not only did she pray for us in her alone time, but whenever we got together, we would always join hands and pray. Addye always had a positive word to declare, and I looked forward to the times we spent together. As our friendship grew deeper, Addye expressed genuine concern about our situation with Source Records. Because she knew how important it was to me for us to follow our hearts and become entertainers, she vowed to do everything she could to help make our dreams come true.

The promotional tour had started. Each morning, Source Records sent the company van to the house to pick us up. We were to arrive at the first high school by 9:00 AM. We would then answer questions and sign autographs. We were so nervous about the promotional tour. We had no idea what to expect or how we would be received. It did not take long for us to find out—the students thought we were stars! Even with all their enthusiasm, we did not feel like stars in the least. We would jokingly say amongst ourselves, *we aren't stars—we're starves!* It was the truth. We were the true definition of starving artists! We would make an appearance at the first school then head off to McDonald's for a quick lunch. After lunch, we would hit up another high school. Sadly, the one McDonald's meal would sometimes be all we ate for the day. During this time, mostly filled with hunger pangs and self-doubt, I looked forward to my husband joining us in California. I knew at least he would come with money we could use to get us through this difficult period.

Every day, I would tell Addye how we were pretending to be stars. We would joke about it and laugh, but Addye knew it was getting to me. She always knew the right things to say, though. She stayed offering encouraging words. Addye knew the Word of GOD just like I did and reminded me of it. "Remember, we've been praying," she would say. "You guys just hold on. Something will come up. You just watch and see." I appreciated her encouraging words.

The day arrived when Tony finally made it to California. He had received half of the money from the sale of our home in Michigan. The realtor assured him we would receive the rest of the money after the closing was completed. The money he brought with him assisted us a great deal with our day-to-day living expenses. We shared what we could with my brothers. However, problems arose when my husband saw the money dwindling and nothing coming in to replace what we were spending. This caused tensions to flare up in our marriage once again. Tony went to look for a job and felt the boys needed to look for a job as well. He eventually found work and frowned upon the fact he was the only one bringing in an income.

One day, while talking to Addye, I mentioned how disgusted I was with Source Records. Speaking out of sheer anger, I told her I felt like just going over to Source Records and giving Mr. Westbrooks a piece of my mind. I still had not signed the contract, and I was dodging him. But now, I wanted him to know I was not happy about his one-sided contract.

"I want to tell him my feelings so bad," I told her. "It is not fair we have to promote an album that isn't even ours. The contract forces us to not be productive. We're much too talented for that. I have the guts to do it, Addye, and maybe he might consider letting us out of the contract."

A part of me was hoping Addye would talk me off the ledge. Much to my surprise, she applauded my assertiveness.

"Girl, what a great idea!" Addye stated proudly. "We're going to pray on this one. Get with your brothers and tell them your plan. Then you all get together and pray."

I went to my brothers and let them know I planned to confront Mr. Westbrooks about the contract they had signed. I told them there was no need to try and talk me out of my plans. I was going to do it whether they agreed with me or not. However, it would mean more to me if I had their blessings. "I need you all to touch and agree with me," I stated.

My brothers did not protest. Rather, we simply joined hands and prayed. Whenever times grew difficult, prayer is what we had turned to growing up. Even though we were out here in the world on our own, we saw no reason not to come together and support one another during this difficult hour. We planned to go to Motown as a family and assure them we wanted to become Motown artists.

My brothers and I prayed. Yet we were so unhappy, extremely discouraged, and wanted out of the contract with Source Records. We were hungry and broke, and there was nothing we could do about it for now. To add insult to injury, we were losing the house Source Records had provided. Yes, an eviction was looming! The boys did not care about losing the house because they were homesick and wanted to return home. They became disillusioned. As their big sis and mother figure, it nearly broke me spiritually seeing them so despondent. I kept praying and believing a miracle would surface. The miracle came in the form of an angel, Mrs. Lantha Byrd.

We first became acquainted with Mrs. Byrd through her daughter Dawn. Mrs. Byrd had two teenagers, a boy and a girl. Dawn took a liking to Mark. You could say Dawn was in love with Mark. She was a senior at the local high school. Nearly every day she was at the house and would bring her friends and other girls to hang out with the boys.

Having Mrs. Byrd enter our lives gave true meaning to "you reap what your sow." Our mother and her family did a lot of sowing into the lives of many people back home in Michigan. They were very giving and loving people who knew nothing except extending kindness to others. Despite my mother having plenty of children of her own, she was always willing to help a child who was less fortunate. Those good deeds my family sowed resulted in us reaping a blessing just in the nick of time. Mrs. Byrd was there and willing to help us in any way possible.

Mrs. Byrd was a beautiful woman inside and out with a compelling spirit. She believed in us and helped us out enormously. We quickly became family. She fell in love with each of us and concerned herself with our well-being. Almost every day, we were at her home to eat. If we did not go to her home, she would bring food to the house. When it was time for someone's birthday, she would bake a cake. She even drove us to various appointments. The boys and I adored her and was so appreciative of her care and benevolence. She was there for us through the struggle. We would not have forged ahead during this time without her compassion and empathy.

I learned that Mrs. Byrd was dealing with a lot of hurt and pain in her personal life. She had confided in me as well as shared the source of her pain. I learned that her first husband died and she remarried. However, her new husband was a very selfish man and did not care for her children. Despite going through what felt like my own private hell, GOD used my situations in life to help her surrender the pain to Him.

Our last month in the house was insane. The boys were meeting new girls and seemed to party every day. They partied into the wee hours of the night. Being married and parents to two small children, Tony and I found their hedonistic lifestyle overwhelming and unbearable. Even though we were trying, our marriage was on the brink. To make matters worse, the utilities in the house were now cut off. We ended up spending a lot of time at Mrs. Byrd's home as a result. Mrs. Byrd was doing everything she could to help us out by taking us in and feeding us each day. We only went back to the house at night to sleep.

Days passed and I still had not gone to talk with Mr. Westbrooks. Even though I initially felt confident and assertive, I was not feeling so bold these days. Needing a little boost, I called Addye. I wanted reassurance if we were released from our contract with Source Records, would it then be possible for her to set up a showcase with Jermaine and Hazel (Gordy) Jackson. I was trying to think ahead and come up with a backup plan. I was adamant and had every intention of calling a meeting with Mr. Westbrooks. After all, it was his one-sided recording deal that contributed to our current plight. I was not about to let him off the hook so easily. Addye stated that her only concern was she did not want to involve Jermaine and Hazel if, by chance, Mr. Westbrooks decided against releasing us from our signed contract. She reiterated we had to be released from the contract before she felt comfortable mentioning a possible showcase to Jermaine and Hazel.

"What are you up to, Ms. Lady?" Addye asked suspiciously.

"I believe GOD, Addye. I must give Him something to work with. I'm going to call and make an appointment to see Mr. Westbrooks today. It's time I follow through," I stated with resolve.

Addye, always an encouraging presence in my life, gave me her blessing. After our phone conversation ended, I immediately phoned Bernd. I voiced to him I needed to make an appointment to see Mr. Westbrooks as soon as possible. I let him know it could no longer wait. Concerned, Bernd felt as if he were the only one who could truly help us out. He wanted to know why I needed to speak with Mr. Westbrooks. I did not go into detail. I let him know that the questions I had only Mr. Westbrooks could answer. Bernd promised he would relay the message and get back to me with an appointment. Now all I could do was wait it out. I did not know how much longer we could hold out without losing our minds. The situation at the house was dire.

In the meantime, Bobby found himself an expensive studio apartment to rent in Culver City. He invited Tony, the girls and me to stay with him. By this time, we were out of the house in Cerritos and had nowhere to go. Everyone was pretty much on their own and fending for themselves. The money from the closing on our house in Grand Rapids came just in time. Tony, the girls, and I were able to find a cheap motel. Therefore, we did not take Bobby up on his offer initially. Mrs. Byrd, Bernd, and Bobby all pitched in to help the boys pay for their motel rooms for a month. We were all situated for the time being. However, it was not lost on us that soon we would, once again, be scrambling to avoid becoming homeless.

We stopped the promotional tour. I guess you can say we were protesting. We refused to promote the song any longer and hoped the company would do us a favor and drop us. Bobby warned us we were breaching our contract and the fallout that could result. Even if we were dropped from Source Records, the company could still make the decision to not release us from our contractual obligations. In other words, Source Records could hold us back from signing with anyone else for seven years. If we were under contract to them, no other record company would pursue us as artists. Addye had shared the same information with me earlier. At this point, we simply did not care how the record company responded to us stopping the promotional tour. We were exhausted and knew we deserved a better contract. If they wanted to play hardball, we were willing to play their game. We decided to pawn all the music equipment Source Records had provided. We were hungry. Period!

CHAPTER 4

DARE TO BE BOLD

TOMMY HAD MOVED FROM Los Angeles to a city called Sepulveda located in the San Fernando Valley. Since we had very little money, it was too far for us to travel, and we saw less and less of Tommy. The only way we were able to "keep in touch" was through information we had gotten from Bobby. He mentioned Tommy had a new girlfriend and had also purchased a new car. We were all surprised and could not wait to see Tommy and meet his new girlfriend.

Tommy must have been just as eager to see us and show off his accomplishments. One day, out of the clear blue, Tommy drove to see us. He pulled up in a fancy sports car smiling from ear to ear looking like a Hollywood star. Tommy had purchased an Alfa Romeo, a very expensive luxury sports car. In the passenger seat was his new girlfriend, Yolanda Payne, whom Tommy affectionately called Duckie.

Between the car and Duckie, it was hard to tell which one he treasured the most! Duckie was very attractive, friendly, and soft-spoken. She seemed passionate about her love for Tommy. Their interaction was delicate, warm, and very intimate. Anyone could see they cherished their relationship and was very affectionate and attentive toward each other.

It did not take long, however, to realize why Tommy named her Duckie. She had a very distinct, yet soothing voice, which was quack-like and seemed to squeak whenever she talked. To me, it complemented her personality—very innocent and bubbly. I instantly took a liking to Duckie and was happy Tommy had found someone to love and who loved him in return. She fit right in with ease and behaved as if she had known us for years! This was not surprising, though. Whenever one of us met someone, friend or love interest, we would always fill them in on the rest of the siblings. By the time they met any of us, they would have a complete rundown of our likes, dislikes, and most of all, our talents. Duckie was very comfortable around us even though we had just met in person. I could tell Tommy had boasted about his family to Duckie.

Now Bobby was a different story. When I shared with Bobby that I thought Duckie was nice, he was somewhat dismissive. It was not a surprise. Bobby was hard on Tommy and would always find something to complain about and criticize. These two always had personality clashes. The biggest personality clashes occurred as we were coming of age back in Michigan.

As children growing up, I was always saving Tommy from Bobby's wrath. Being he was the older brother (and in his mind, the father figure), Bobby felt Tommy was out of control. Bobby relished being in control and maintaining control over his life and others. Tommy was the complete opposite. Growing up, he was a handful—always in mischief because he was so extroverted, outgoing, and talkative. Bobby, on the other hand, was extremely introverted and refrained from expressing his feelings to anyone. He had a quietness and thoughtfulness about his personality even though he was very bold and deliberate when finally speaking his mind. Whereas Bobby could be a mystery, Tommy was an open book. This sickened Bobby and was at the root of many of their dustups.

Bobby was embarrassed by how Tommy engaged those outside his immediate family. He believed Tommy was only seeking pity by being an open book. Tommy often lacked boundaries in what he disclosed to others. As siblings, we understood how Bobby felt. Truthfully speaking, we were all embarrassed by Tommy's lack of tact. Unlike Bobby who let Tommy know of his disdain through bouts of fury, the rest of us quietly endured those embarrassing moments. It was like walking around on eggshells because you could never predict what would come out of Tommy's mouth. I knew Tommy was hurting inside and his spontaneous statements were an outlet for the internal pain he felt. I could never get Bobby to understand this side of Tommy.

Here was Tommy, proudly beaming with seemingly the *loves* of his life—Duckie and his Alfa Romeo. On the flip side, there was Bobby raining on his parade. Bobby believed Duckie was too meek for Tommy—too softhearted with a calm spirit. He felt Tommy did not need a woman whom he could walk all over. He honestly felt Duckie would be unable to stand up to Tommy. Bobby felt Tommy needed a woman who could challenge him and not put up with his out-of-control behaviors. I saw things quite differently. By Tommy being in love with Duckie, he now had someone to confide in—someone who would listen to him and help nurture him through his pain. This was better than him opening his big mouth and blabbering to whoever had a listening ear. Plus, they were such a cute couple! Moreover, Duckie truly had my brother's best interest at heart. Bobby, ever the pessimist, was still not convinced. Therefore, I chose to ignore Bobby's comments. Seeing Tommy happy was good enough for me.

***

Switch was headed to Denver, Colorado, to record at the Caribou Ranch. Bobby had finished "I Call Your Name." However, there were other songs the group needed to finish recording. Due to the financial windfall they were receiving from Motown as a result of the recording contracts, the group was able to live apart from each other. Now scattered throughout the Los Angeles area, it was hard for them to come together for rehearsals. Jermaine and Hazel felt sending them to Denver would allow the group to be in one place and put them in a creative frame of mind. Plus, they needed a break from Los Angeles and all its trappings.

Switch was working against a very strict deadline. Daily, Motown would mark days off the calendar for when they expected the album to be finished and released. The pressure was on, and Switch was off to Denver. The timing could not have been more perfect for me and Tony. We took Bobby up on his offer about staying at his apartment.

The rest of my brothers were not as lucky. Bobby's apartment was small, of course, with only one bedroom. Bobby really did not want the boys staying at his place, and he made me promise to not allow them to stay there while he was away. He worried their hard-partying lifestyle would get him kicked out. They were a wild bunch. Bobby also figured they would tear up his apartment if they stayed. Although they had nowhere to go, neither of the boys appeared too worried. For the time being, they had groupies occupying their time who were willing to help them financially by paying for hotel rooms and food.

Days had gone by, and I still had not heard anything from Bernd about setting up a meeting with Mr. Westbrooks. Time was running out! Even though the boys were getting help from their lady friends, the reality of the situation was they were living from pillar to post. Their tomorrow was being met with uncertainty. I was unable to relax not knowing what would happen to the boys with each passing day. I decided not to wait on Bernd to get back in touch. I surmised if he were going to set up a meeting between Mr. Westbrooks and me, he would have done so by now. I was going to call Source Records on my own. It was do or die.

I knew Mr. Westbrooks had to be displeased with our acts of rebellion. Regardless of the veiled threats, we still insisted on not promoting the song or going on promotional tours. Mr. Westbrooks had every right not to talk to me. After all, I was not even a signed artist with his record company. What could I realistically talk to him about since I technically was not one of his employees? I began to have doubt and wondered if it was even worth either of our time for me to insist on having a sit-down with him. As I thought about the boys and their dire situation, I figured it was worth it to speak to him about releasing them from their contractual obligations with Source Records. The worst he could say was no (although I had no intention of taking no for an answer). *There you go!* I thought to myself. I had finally persuaded myself to pick up the phone and call Mr. Westbrooks's office.

Mr. Westbrooks's secretary answered the phone. I explained to her it was urgent and I must meet with Mr. Westbrooks concerning *my* contract. I figured this would arouse his interest since he was still under the impression I would eventually sign. To my surprise, the secretary set up the appointment for the next day. I was excited because I expected her to put me off. After ending the call with Mr. Westbrooks's secretary, I immediately called Addye at Motown and let her know I had a meeting set up with Mr. Westbrooks. She was elated to hear the good news and prayed for GOD to provide me favor during the meeting.

Throughout the day, I rehearsed over and over in my head everything I planned to say to Mr. Westbrooks. I had to persuade him one way or another to let the boys out of their contracts. At bedtime, I was still anxious about the meeting and could barely sleep. I tossed and turned and prayed all night. My prayer was simple: *Dear GOD, give me the words to say to this man. I need you to go before me and condition his heart.*

The next morning, I arose earlier than usual. Besides not being able to get a good night's rest, I had to mentally prepare myself for the meeting. I wanted to put this nightmare behind us once and for all. I dreaded not knowing how Mr. Westbrooks would respond to my demands. I had no intentions of begging for a release—I intended on demanding and securing a release. As much as I felt emboldened, I still grappled with a fear of the unknown. This uncertainty was killing me on the inside. As I prepared to leave the apartment, the phone rang. I did not have time to answer because I needed to get to Mr. Westbrooks's office as soon as possible. I figured with him being a businessman, he would be quite busy. If I were not on time, he would just go to his next appointment and I would miss out. It was good I did answer the phone. On the other end was Mr. Westbrooks's secretary calling to cancel the appointment. She explained an emergency had come up and he had to leave town abruptly. I began to panic especially when she advised me Mr. Westbrooks would be out of the office until the following week.

"A whole week? No, I must see him sooner," I insisted. Though my tone was a bit harsh, I decided I was not going to let Mr. Westbrooks off the hook.

"I'm sorry, Ms. DeBarge," his secretary began. "There's really nothing I can do about it. Mr. Westbrooks won't return until Friday, and it looks as if next week, he's all booked up. He will be in the office on Friday, but I'm not sure of the time."

I did not care about his other appointments, his schedule this week, next week, or even next year. I only cared about my brothers who were floating from one motel to the next relying on the benevolence of groupies and Bobby (who would send them money here and there to rent a room). They only had two weeks left at their current motel. They were threatening to leave California and return home to Michigan. I could not say I blamed them if they decided to leave. I told the secretary she can reschedule the appointment for the following week. The boys had somewhere to stay for the next two weeks at least. I figured this gave me time to get them out of the contract with Source Records and get us a showcase with Motown Records. If we get the showcase at Motown, I believed in my heart we would be signed to a record deal.

After hanging up the phone, a lightbulb went off in my head: *Wait a minute. She said he would return Friday. She just did not know the time. Maybe I should go up there on Friday morning and sit and wait for him to arrive.*

I knew this would come off a tad bit pushy, but I was desperate. I did not tell Tony my plans right away because he would have thought they were ridiculous and try to stop me. I picked up the phone and called Addye. I shared my plan to camp out at Mr. Westbrooks's office all day Friday. At first, Addye laughed. I knew my plan was a bit over the top. However, I was used to Addye encouraging me during moments like this—not discouraging me. When she was able to compose herself, she let me know she was not laughing at me—she was just enjoying a little laughter because I was being so tenacious. She applauded my tenacity and gave me the encouragement I needed to follow through with my plan. She reminded me to be sure to get everything in writing once the boys were released from their contracts. Her affirmations, as though she believed everything would work out in our favor, warmed my heart.

Addye reassured me that once I had the written release in hand, it would allow her to talk to Jermaine and Hazel. She told me to also make sure the release was typed on the company's letterhead and signed by Mr. Westbrooks. She went on to advise me it was essential for me to have this letter in hand, and I was not to leave the office with just his word. Before ending the call, she promised me she would arrange a showcase for us at Motown as soon as I was able to provide her with the release. I now had the incentive to forge ahead with my plan to camp out all day Friday at Source Records.

The boys continued to talk about going home. In fact, they were trying to secure bus or plane tickets back home. I did not want them to leave. I did not want to be in California pursuing my dreams without my brothers. I wanted to be with my family and I refused to give up hope. To give them a little bit of hope as well, I went to visit them. I informed them of my upcoming appointment with Mr. Westbrooks. They were antsy about their uncertain living situation. The boys listened to what I had to tell them, but they were not enthusiastic. They had lost all hope in believing Source Records would grant them a release. They were hungry and missing home. I felt alone in the fight, but I was hoping I was wrong. If they went back to Michigan, they would be giving up on their dreams—*Our* dreams together. I did not want this for us. I left the motel not knowing what they were going to do, and it was not a good feeling. My heart ached for them but provided me the determination needed to secure releases from their one-sided contract.

***

The next morning, I was ready to go. I could hear my mother's voice resonating in my mind: *Where there is a will, there's a way.* There was no argument—I most definitely had the will. Before Tony and I left Bobby's apartment, I called the boys to make sure they were still around. No one answered the phone. It was still early so I did not freak out. I figured they might have been up all night and were probably just now getting some sleep. The desk clerk assured me they were still at the motel. Satisfied the boys were still in California, Tony and I set out for Source Records to wait for Mr. Westbrooks.

We sat in the lobby at Source Records the entire morning. Around noon, the secretary came to the lobby where we were waiting and invited us to lunch. We told her we would continue to wait for Mr. Westbrooks. She was pleasant and assured us Mr. Westbrooks would be in the office some time during the day. She apologized for not being sure what time he would arrive, but we were welcome to continue waiting in the lobby.

It was now around five o'clock in the evening, and *still* no word from Mr. Westbrooks. His secretary was ending her shift. I was tired and disappointed. It felt as if I had wasted an entire day with nothing to show for it. I had desperately wanted to bring the boys some encouraging news as well as call Addye to set up the showcase at Motown. But where was Mr. Westbrooks?

As the secretary was leaving, she managed to ease my mind. She told me she had finally heard from Mr. Westbrooks, and he was on his way to the office. He knew I was there waiting to see him. She stated he knew I had been waiting for him all day. Apparently, Mr. Westbrooks had been on his way home when he called to check in with his secretary. After she told him I had been waiting all day and refused to leave, he felt he needed to come to the office and meet with me.

"I told him it was urgent," she stated. "I have to go, but you can continue to wait here in the lobby for him. It shouldn't be much longer." She then exited the building.

I sprang back to life! All was not lost, and I let out a huge sigh of relief. My efforts no longer felt as though they were in vain. Not long afterward, Tony spotted Mr. Westbrooks' limo pull up in the parking lot.

"He's here," he stated with relief. "He's getting out of the limo now."

"Oh my GOD! He's here!" I stated anxiously.

The nervous energy was beginning to get the best of me. I had everything I was going to say all mapped out. Just like that, my mind went blank. Like always when under pressure, I offered up a quick prayer: *Okay, GOD, it's on You. I need Your Strength to get through this. I can't go in there acting timid. I must be bold.*

Mr. Westbrooks entered the lobby, and I could see he was tired. As usual, he was well dressed and displayed his trademark humble spirit.

"Ms. DeBarge," he stated, stopping in the lobby to exchange pleasantries. "What can I do for you? My secretary informed me it was urgent that you see me."

Not sensing any frustration in his tone, I faced him with a charming smile. He smiled back and waited for me to speak.

"I believe it is very urgent, sir," I replied.

Mr. Westbrooks then asked me to give him a quick minute to get to his office and get comfortable. He would come back to the lobby to get me and then we could talk.

"I'm not going anywhere, sir. Take your time," I stated.

Once in his office, I did not waste any time getting straight to the point.

"Sir, I am here on behalf of my brothers and to discuss the contract they signed with Source Records," I began. "I realize this was an obligation they have already breached by not fulfilling the promotional tour you set up for them. But understand, they are not happy—we are not happy, sir." I looked him straight in the eyes to make sure he was hearing my heart.

"As you know, I did not sign with the company," I continued. "But I was working with my brothers. It's not fair to pretend to be another group. We've got talent, sir. The boys and I are very talented and being in a contract with Source Records is stagnating our creativity." I felt myself getting emotional but held my composure.

"You must know the boys didn't realize what they were signing. We are young, sir. They don't have a lot of knowledge about the music industry. However, we do have our brothers, Bobby and Tommy, who we believe have a great contract. I know you can hold my brothers here, but we would like to be released to go to another company we feel is better suited for our talent."

It was not my intention to beg and plead for the boys' release from their contract. However, before I could stop myself, I made a last-ditch effort. "Please, Mr. Westbrooks. The boys are starving and need a place to stay. No company will talk to us unless we are released from your company. Please consider releasing them so we can move forward with our career."

As I stood there waiting for his response, an uncomfortable silence lingered. I tried in vain to read his blank facial expression. I was sweating bullets not knowing what to expect. He just stared at me the entire time

I spoke. I did not allow him to intimidate me. I maintained eye contact and presented my point of view. Mr. Westbrooks sat back in his chair as I continued to wait for the silence to break. I felt as if he was studying me the whole time. Finally, he spoke.

"Well, Ms. DeBarge, what a genuine sister you are. As for your brothers? Well, they should be proud to have a sister such as you," he stated.

Okay, I thought. *He started with a compliment and I'm impressed. But what's coming next, Mr. Westbrooks?*

He went on to explain to me how the company purchased the masters and how they had lost so much money. He talked about the promotional plan not being a success. He said he knew we had talent and had plans for us to go into the studio.

"But . . .," he spoke slowly. "I want you guys to be happy. I'm not in this business to hurt anyone. At the same time, I'm not in this business to lose either. I do sympathize with you and your brothers' situation." Then he paused. "Young lady, I'm going to do something I don't even understand myself. I'm sure my lawyers will not be happy with me, and neither will my business managers. I appreciate your honesty and your courage. I'm going to grant your brothers a release. I will get on top of this Monday."

My heart skipped a beat; then I breathed a long sigh of relief. "Thank you! Oh, thank you so much, Mr. Westbrooks! But I need to ask you one more favor," I stated. "I need you to put it in writing today. It's crucial I have it to get some money on Monday. I can't get money unless I have the letter or the guys and I will be out on the streets."

Mr. Westbrooks laughed at my persistence. I pretended to laugh with him, yet I was hardly laughing. I needed the letter with his signature on it today. He told me the office was closed; however, he would have his secretary type up a letter for him to sign on Monday. It still had to go through his lawyer, but the letter with his signature would still be legally binding. He assured me he was a man of his word and I could pick up the release letter on Monday morning. A part of me wanted to demand the letter right now. The other part of me did not want to rock the boat. Therefore, I let Mr. Westbrooks know I would be at his office first thing Monday morning for the release letter.

I did it! I got the release! I left the office so full of myself. I was so caught up in the spirit I almost started speaking in tongues. I was most definitely praising GOD. I could not wait to tell my brothers they were free. It was a huge relief. Half the battle was won. It was all on Addye now. I told myself I would call her in the morning. Tonight, I wanted to just call my brothers and share the good news. I was thankful to GOD for showing us favor.

Tommy Alfa Romeo

Bunny & Tony

Tommy & Duck

CHAPTER 5

HE FOLLOWED US!

I FELT ELATED ABOUT THE outcome of the meeting. The hardest part was behind us, and now I could proudly state, *Mission accomplished!* I reflected on the favor GOD must have bestowed upon me during the meeting with Mr. Westbrooks. *What an awesome GOD!* I thought. I believed my faith, though wavering, allowed GOD to condition Mr. Westbrooks' heart to do what was right by me and my brothers. It blew my mind how GOD intervened on our behalf even though I did not feel completely connected to Him in a spiritual sense. I felt left out of GOD's will. Even with my faith being tested, GOD was faithful and He was still my Savior! I thought back to the words of an old hymn: *He looked beyond my faults and saw my needs.* Mr. Westbrooks could have been stubborn and stood firm regarding the terms outlined in the contract. Our current plight—hunger, discouragement, and homelessness—did not warrant him letting us out of our agreed-upon contractual obligations. The boys, regardless of their level of understanding, signed a legally binding document. Had it been any other record company, they probably would not have budged especially since we had stopped promoting the song and cost the company money. Therefore, while I was happy with the outcome, I gave all credit to GOD's Divine Sovereignty.

It was late when Tony and I returned to the apartment. Exhausted from spending an entire day camped out at Source Records, the only thing I could think about was sleep. I decided to reach out to the boys in the morning. The entire experience had drained me physically and emotionally. As soon as my head touched the pillow, I fell asleep. It did not last long. I began to toss and turn, and eventually the excitement caused me to awaken from my slumber. I decided to call the boys and share the good news. I was sure they were up—most likely partying. Plus, they were notorious night owls. Anxiously, I dialed the motel and asked to be connected to my brothers' room.

The voice on the other end of the phone was El. He was obviously in a silly mood and tried to disguise his voice.

"El," I cried. "Stop playing! I have something important to tell you."

El continued with the charade and tried to get me to playing the guessing game.

"El, I need you to be serious!" At this point, I could no longer disguise the irritation in my voice.

"What's going on, sis?" he finally asked through laughter. "How are you doing?"

"Well, I'm fine now since you've stopped with your silliness," I began. "I was trying to wait until tomorrow to call, but I couldn't sleep. Mr. Westbrooks is releasing us from the contract! I did it, El! I went to talk to him today, and it's final! I got him to release you guys, and I get the letter on Monday. We're free! Now we can go with Motown! Isn't that wonderful?"

"Are you serious, Bunny?" El seemed skeptical. I assured him I was telling him the truth.

"That's great! Praise GOD! This is the best news I've heard all day." El seemed excited and relieved. I overheard him sharing the news with everyone in the room. *"Mr. Westbrooks released us! Bunny said we're free!"*

El was trying in vain to speak over all the commotion in the room. *"Did you hear me? Listen up, you guys. Listen up!"*

After the room had quieted down, El began to pretend as if he was preaching at a Sunday church service or revival. *"Come on, Saints! It's time we put on our dancing shoes! For the time has come!"*

Randy was the first to follow suit. I could hear him mimicking the bass notes from the church shouting music. My brothers were now in a full-fledged silly mood. I would love to have been there because my brothers could be a bunch of comedians. The news sent them over the moon with happiness, and there was a lot of laughter and celebration in the room.

"Pharaoh . . . I said Pharaoh done let GOD's people go!" El continued on.

The spirit was high inside the room. I could hear the table being used as a bongo. Everyone was whooping and hollering and praising GOD. The boys had started out goofing off and being silly. But I felt a shift in the atmosphere. They were now serious about their praise. It touched me. It was a family moment that the boys did not mind sharing with those present in the room. I was praising GOD right along with my brothers.

When El returned to our conversation, I gave him all the details. I told him I would call Addye in the morning and should have more details to share afterward.

"Addye will get us in to see Jermaine and Hazel. Just hold on," I promised him.

After ending the call, I felt a surge of relief knowing that my brothers' hope had been restored. I planned to arise early so I could hopefully catch Addye at the office. It was Saturday, a day she usually did not come to the office. However, she did tell me she would be at the office for a few hours on Saturday in case I had some good news to share.

Later in the morning, I contacted Addye at her office. Although she was happy, she shared she was not surprised at all and knew GOD would deliver us from the contract. I told Addye it was all on her now, and she had to come through concerning the showcase. Of course, it was no small task to get a showcase with a record company. Once again, I relied on my faith to reassure me everything would work out in our favor. In my heart, I knew that if GOD secured our release from Source Records, He would ensure we became signed Motown artists.

Addye stated she had to figure out a way to get us in the office to sing for Jermaine and Hazel Jackson. They were extremely busy with Switch—trying to get the album completed and released by the fast approaching deadline. When she looked at their calendar, Addye told me they were fully booked.

"Don't you start worrying, girl. You let me worry about this end of the situation," she stated. "Just make sure you get me a copy of the release letter. I'm working double-time over here. I can't promise you a date or time but be ready. You're on call, my dear. It could be at any time. You have to be ready and willing."

Her words were music to my ears! We were no longer stuck—the train was moving! "We can do that," I reassured Addye. "We have nothing else to do. Do your thing!"

After the call ended, I could not help but be grateful for all Addye was doing for us. I could barely wait for Monday morning to arrive. Once I get my hands on the release letter from Source Records, I planned to take it straight to Addye. We were racing against time! Even though we had secured the release and Addye was working overtime to get a showcase scheduled, our living situation was still precarious.

I called my brothers and provided them with the latest update. I let them know we were "on call" concerning the showcase and what this entailed. This did little to calm my brothers' fears about their living situation. They only had a few more days left at the motel. I told them if push came to shove, I would sneak them in at night to stay with Tony and I at Bobby's apartment. I knew Bobby would not like it especially since he had already let it be known to me the reasons he did not want the boys staying at his place. However, I had no intentions of telling him if the boys did end up sleeping at his apartment. I figured we would cross this bridge later if needed.

***

Monday morning came, and true to his word, I received the signed release letter from Source Records. I took the release letter directly to Addye. Everything was now on her to get the showcase scheduled. A few days passed, and I had not heard a word from Addye. I tried calling her to make sure everything was still going according to plan. Each time

I called, she was either busy or could not talk. She promised to return my calls. However, a day or two would go by and still no return call.

It was now down to the wire. The boys had only two days left in the motel room. It was breaking my heart to know they were sad and depressed about their living situation. I could only imagine what they were thinking. I hoped they did not feel let down. I felt terrible because I had no way to lift their spirits. I began limiting my calls to them until I had some good news to share. It was time to initiate plan B, which was to bring them to the apartment to stay with Tony and me. As much as I dreaded it—thinking about Bobby's reaction if he found out—I needed to be able to talk to them, hear their thoughts firsthand, and keep them encouraged until we had the showcase at Motown. I did not share with them Addye was now avoiding me—this was the last thing they needed to hear right now. I put on a brave face and let the boys know I would come and pick them up the next day. We would all stay at Bobby's apartment until everything came through at Motown.

I had not convinced my brothers of much over the phone. Hopefully, it was enough to stop them from making any rash decisions. After hanging up with them, I called Addye once again. She answered this time but rushed me off the phone. There was obvious irritation in her tone. I refused to be discouraged by her attitude—especially when my brothers were suffering. I planned to call her every day until we got the showcase. The following morning, I was awakened by the phone ringing. To my surprise, Addye was on the other end. She apologized for her behavior lately. All was forgiven because she finally gave me the news I had been waiting to hear.

She stated apologetically, "I know I've been cranky. But guess what? It's on, my sistah! I need you guys in here tomorrow at three o'clock. Don't be late. In fact, come early. I'm penciling you guys in right now. The Jacksons are in the office tomorrow with interviews. I'll squeeze you guys in with them before they leave the office. Call the guys and get four of your songs together. I know you'll do well. I'm in a hurry and must go but be here. I'll call you if anything changes."

Addye ended the call before I had a chance to thank her and let her know of my excitement. My head started spinning, and I rushed to call the boys. Since the showcase was tomorrow (and I was sure we would be signed), I decided to pay for their room for one more night. After the showcase, they could come to Bobby's apartment with me and Tony.

I called the motel. The desk clerk answered. When I asked for El's room, she informed me they had checked out.

"Checked out?" I was confused. "No, they couldn't have. Are you sure? Maybe they are in another room."

"No, ma'am," she stated. "The DeBarge boys checked out yesterday. I believe they went back to Michigan." She went on to state, "Hold on a minute."

I could hear chatter in the background but could not make out what was being discussed.

"Yes, my boss told me they went back to Michigan," she said sympathetically.

I panicked and screamed through the phone before slamming it down. The devastation I felt caused me to start talking to myself. My emotions were all over the place. I was an emotional wreck! It was a good thing I was not around my brothers because I was very upset with them for what they had done. How could they do this to me? I did all this hard work for what? I asked myself. How was I going to tell Addye they were back in Michigan? How was I going to get them back? We had to be at Jermaine and Hazel's office tomorrow—no ifs, ands, or buts! Once again, I found myself back in the position of getting my brothers out of another dire situation they had created. All I heard was Bobby's words: *They jumped the gun!* I now knew how Big Bro felt because I felt the same way too. As angry as I was, I had no time to focus on what I was feeling. I needed to get the boys back to California *and fast!* I calmed myself down and placed a call to my mother's home in Grand Rapids.

My mother answered the phone, and I informed her I needed to speak to El. I gave her a brief synopsis of what was unfolding. We had to put our heads together and come up with a way to get the boys back to California. According to my mother, the boys had arrived in Grand Rapids earlier in the morning. El was now at her home resting. Mama put El on the phone.

"What are you doing, El? We've got a showcase tomorrow!" I did little to hide my frustration once he answered the phone. "Addye called to tell me we are in tomorrow at three thirty. What am I supposed to tell her, El? I can't tell her you guys went home. She went out of her way to get us in to see the Jacksons. We finally have an audition. You guys have to come back!"

El informed me they had flown to Grand Rapids, Michigan, on the Red Eye—a cheap flight out of Los Angeles—around midnight. They decided to catch the flight and go back home because they were hungry and tired. El also let me know Red Eye had a flight leaving out of Grand Rapids headed to Los Angeles tonight at midnight. It should arrive around two thirty in the morning. The only problem: we had three people to get back to California and no money. The cost of the plane tickets would be roughly five hundred dollars. We had no one left to ask for money. Everyone we knew had spent money to keep the boys in the motel rooms and supply them with food. Our resources were tapped out. Finally, Mark came up with an idea. He had a friend who had bragged to him about a credit card he received through the mail. The limit on the card was one thousand dollars. Mark viewed this as manna from heaven. He had some persuading to do in order to get the guy to buy the plane tickets. I let them know I did not care what hurdles they needed to jump through—they better be in California for the showcase!

***

The plane arrived late. Being on time would have been too perfect. At least we were going to make the showcase. All I could do was shake my head and think about the obstacles one must overcome when seeking fame. Knowing my brothers were on the plane gave me a sense of appreciation for all we had faced thus far—the contract, hunger pangs, homelessness, being broke, and close calls. Each obstacle was preparation for our destiny. We were well on our way to realizing our dreams of becoming stars. I was jolted out of my thoughts by the announcement over the loudspeaker indicating their flight had arrived.

The boys were back in the city! *Mission accomplished*! We were together again, and I had no plans of letting them out of my sight. We would stay glued to the hips until the showcase.

As Tony drove to Bobby's apartment, I lay back and closed my eyes. For the first time in a long time, I felt at ease. I could breathe, relax, and gather my thoughts. The boys were with me, and in a few short hours, we would showcase our gift of music to Jermaine and Hazel Jackson. What seemed impossible a few months ago was replaced with hope and inspiration.

Looking back, it had only been four months since we left Grand Rapids, Michigan, to come to Los Angeles, California, seeking to fulfill our destiny. It had been a time littered with moments that tested our faith and resiliency. To say our road to stardom was bumpy is an understatement—it was downright treacherous. Knowing what would transpire in a few hours made the struggle worthwhile. I learned so much about myself during this time. As someone who struggled with self-doubt, I now knew I could accomplish anything I imagined. My faith was gradually being restored, and I believed I had favor from the Father above. He promised never to leave me, and He was showing Himself as Faithful each day. We were truly *the kept ones*.

CHAPTER 6

GETTING THE FIRE STARTED

I woke up early and cooked breakfast. We all sat around the table discussing the day ahead. We needed to come to an agreement on the four songs we would showcase. El and I made the final call. We went over a couple of tunes we had written while living in the house in Cerritos: "Share My World," "What's Your Name," and "Queen of My Heart." We also included a song by the Carpenters "Close to You." Our musical set was selected, and our harmonies were intact; they were as tight as the tight-knit family we had become. We loved and appreciated one another. You could hear the chemistry between us in our music. It felt like heaven on earth. It was all about blending and swelling musical notes together, which brought about the magic of our unique sound.

We were ready to showcase our magic to Jermaine and Hazel. There was electricity in the air, and we were beyond ecstatic. Our nerves were not too frazzled because we were not going into the showcase as complete unknowns. Bobby made sure to keep our names and talents ringing in their ears. For as much as Bobby hyped us up, the point of the matter was they had never heard us sing. Today was when the rubber meets the road. We were confident GOD had brought us to this point for a greater purpose. Once the couple heard us sing, we felt confident about securing a recording contract.

We dressed in our best outfits and was on our way to Motown. Before entering the building, we joined hands and prayed. We

arrived

early just as Addye had instructed. Because she had anticipated our arrival, we did not have to wait around in the lobby. Once she learned we had arrived, she came and escorted us from the lobby. I introduced Addye to my brothers. She had never met them prior to today. However, she reassured them she already knew them as much as I spoke of them. My brothers exchanged hugs and other pleasantries with Addye. She ended up taking us to an office suite where there was a couch, a love seat, and a grand piano. Jermaine and Hazel Jackson were still in a meeting. Therefore, we waited for them inside the office suite.

"Okay, DeBarges, make yourselves comfortable. The Jacksons shouldn't be long," stated Addye.

Expecting a DeBarge to be seated and wait was like telling a fish not to swim. No surprise, El made a mad dash to the piano while Randy and Marty were intrigued by the gold albums and pictures of the artists hanging on the wall. My brothers were grown now but still very immature and hyper. Witnessing my brothers in their element, I began to reminisce on what led to this tender moment. When we were younger, I would hold a broom over their heads and threaten to hit them if they failed to remember the words and notes to a song. I was a taskmaster and had no problem whipping them into shape when it came to the music. Being at Motown today, preparing to showcase our talents, meant everything was beginning to pay off. Not only were my brothers great people in general, they were also very handsome, talented, and lively with big loving hearts. To me, they had the "it factor" needed to succeed in music.

I reflected on the hardships we faced as children and how we never quite felt accepted by anyone. The shame, humiliation, and rejection were overbearing at times. Growing up, we relied solely on one another for friendship and protection. Being teased and bullied daily because of our multiracial heritage was a painful experience. Since we were treated differently, we began to embrace being different. Once we embraced being different, we set ourselves on a course for having deep-seated issues of discontentment and resentment. We were suspicious of people and never quite sure of their true intentions. Insecurities caused us to let down our guard and allow the devil to rush in. Even through our suspicions, we craved acceptance. Music seemed to do the trick. Growing up, we were able to capture people's imagination using our gift of music. Though we were unsure, people did seem to love us when we sang. As a result, music became a means of acceptance and not rejection.

El sat playing "Beautiful Story of Jesus" softly on the piano. It was an André Crouch song Uncle Bill (the late Bishop William C. Abney Jr., pastor of Bethel Pentecostal Church) would always sing during church service. El was lost in the music and playing as if my uncle was standing right there singing. As he continued playing, he flaunted his gift of stylish chords. It was indeed a beautiful melodious sound. Although he was playing softly, I wondered if the people in the next room overheard him playing and were distracted. I did not want anything to mess up this golden opportunity. I slipped out of the room to ask Addye if I should ask El to stop playing. Addye was seated at her desk swaying from side to side. Before I could say anything, she looked at me and said, "Beautiful. Is that El?"

"Yes," I replied. "Is he too loud?"

"Oh no, I don't think so. He plays beautifully."

Those words brought a smile to my face. "Oh yes," I responded proudly. "But I will stop him if he is disturbing the meeting."

Addye continued to sway while El continued his piano recital in the office suite. "He's fine. The meeting is over. They are just finishing up. I know they are just as fascinated as I am. He sounds great!"

Unexpectedly, the door swung open to the room where Jermaine and Hazel were conducting a meeting. Addye signaled for me to go back into the suite. I quickly sauntered back inside and closed the door. The boys looked at me with anticipation written all over their faces.

"They are finishing up now and should be walking in the door at any minute," I told them.

Everyone took a seat on the couch, leaving the love seat for the Jacksons. We huddled together on the couch and waited. As we attempted to gather our wits, the door swung open. We sat stiff as a board holding our breath. Addye entered the room. We exhaled. She had a tray that carried drinks for everyone.

"They'll be in here shortly," she whispered. "Here . . . I brought you guys some soda." She placed the tray on the table in front of us. "I will be right back with the Jacksons. Are you all ready?" she asked, smiling. "This is it, you know!"

We all smiled and nodded our heads. "We're ready," we answered in unison.

Addye left the room. We were fidgety. We had met Jermaine and Hazel before, but today was different. Mark started making percussion noises with his mouth, and Randy was rearranging items on the coffee table. El had left the piano and was now seated next to me. The door swung open once again, and we were now at the point of no return. Addye walked in with Jermaine and Hazel Jackson in tow. The moment was surreal.

"Okay, you guys, let's get started," said Addye. "Mr. and Mrs. Jackson, as you already know, this is the DeBarges. DeBarge, Mr. and Mrs. Jackson—my bosses."

After we greeted one another with handshakes, Jermaine and Hazel took their seat across from us.

"How's everybody doing today?" Jermaine asked.

"Fine," we answered in unison as we took our seats.

I found it strange seeing Jermaine and Hazel dressed like regular people in street gear. They both had on jogging suits and tennis shoes. I expected them to look as if they had just stepped off the cover of a fashion magazine.

"I see Addye has gotten you drinks," Hazel observed.

"Yes, I have," Addye responded. "And what can I get you and Mr. Jackson? The usual?"

Hazel replied, "Yes, that would be just fine, Addye. Juice for me and bottled water for Jermaine." Jermaine nodded his head with approval.

"Is that it?" Addye asked while looking around the room to see if we needed anything else.

Mr. and Mrs. Jackson both nodded yes and looked to see if we had any requests. Neither of us said anything. Addye smiled and stated, "Then I will be right back."

"We will wait until you come back to get started," Jermaine told her. "After all, you called this meeting today."

Addye giggled as she walked away. "Okay. I'll return shortly."

My impression of both Jermaine and Hazel was they appeared to be shy and needed Addye to start the conversation. I decided to break the ice. "Have you seen or heard from the boys in Switch since they've been gone?" I asked.

"Oh yes," stated Jermaine as his eyes widened. "We hear from at least one of them every single day."

"I know they are busy working on their new album," I stated, trying to keep the conversation going. "I have not heard from Bobby so I thought they probably get very little free time."

Hazel responded, "The studio they work out of is also where they stay, you know. It is fully equipped with everything they need. It's beautiful, and they should feel comfortable to create." Hazel went on to describe the studio. "The Caribou Ranch has a game room, a swimming pool, and a weight room. There's even a theater room. They can call the time they want to go into the studio and record. They are living like kings."

"But fighting like cats and dogs," Jermaine interjected.

We were impressed by the description Hazel had given of the studio. El looked over at Jermaine and shook his head. "Oh boy, it must be Bobby and Tommy fighting."

"Not at all," Jermaine replied. "It's mostly Bobby against the rest of the group. They have a problem with Bobby and the *company* he's keeping."

Not wanting to get off into a discussion about Bobby, I peered at the door and hoped Addye would walk through. I knew the *company* Jermaine was speaking of and how the other members in the group felt about it. Bobby had a male friend living with him at the studio, and this was not going over too well with the other members of Switch. Just then, the door to the office suite opened. What a relief! After handing the Jacksons their drinks, Addye went to sit at the end of the couch. She had with her a pen and notebook. Jermaine asked, "Which one of you was playing the piano?"

Busted, El quietly stated, "That would be me. I'm sorry. Was I too loud?"

"No, not at all," Jermaine answered. "In fact, it was very soothing to the ear."

Relieved, El stated, "Thank you. I was trying to play softly, hoping no one else could hear me outside this room. I hope it didn't interrupt things."

"No," Hazel reassured El. "The only reason we heard you was because *we* had opened the door. Our meeting adjourned, and we were just relaxing and gathering our thoughts. You sounded great. As my husband said, it was soothing to the ears."

We felt at ease because the conversation had shifted to discussing music. Jermaine went on to add, "You have a different touch than your brother Bobby."

El was modest and replied, "Oh, I don't think so at all. I learned *everything* from my big brother."

El had learned a lot from Bobby. This much was true. However, he also had a gift that was just as prolific as Bobby. This was something he did not always embrace. Bobby oftentimes would say El is more melodic on the piano. Sensing him not being sure of himself, I interjected, "Yes, he did learn everything from his big brother. However, I must agree with Jermaine, El. I understand what he's saying. There's a different touch you have compared to Bobby."

I went on to explain the differences in their piano style. "Bobby masters Bobby. He really doesn't venture off into learning a right chord unless it benefits what he is doing at the time. He's not going to learn your song unless he wants to and then that's only to fit it into one of his songs. El, on the other hand, will get the right chord. He will learn and master your song and then make it his song by putting his personal touch on it. They are different, but very much the same. They are truly brothers. I know Bobby respects his little bro as much as El respects him."

El smiled then embraced me while looking over at Jermaine. "Now what can I say to that, man? You answered that very well, big sis. I'm not going to fight you about that anymore. You would know better than me since you studied us both."

Hazel looked over at me and smiled. "Looks like your sister is your number one fan."

El started to laugh. "I just know my big bro is awesome to me. I learned everything I could from him, and I'm still learning from him. I never put myself equal to or even compared myself to him. However, it's good to hear it from someone who really knows and sees it like that. It's good to know my big sister respects me as well. Thanks, Bunny." El gave me a slight hug.

"Wow! You guys remind me of my family," Jermaine commented.

"Oh yeah," El said. "You got a big sister too—Rebbie. So, you know what I'm talking about, man. They can be special. They have a way of explaining things and remembering things too, huh?"

They both laughed and somehow made a joke out of complimenting their big sisters. Hazel, amazed at how much we resembled each other, complimented our looks.

"You all look so much alike," she said. "Such a beautiful family."

The conversation continued with Mark finally joining in. Once Mark feels comfortable in a social setting, he becomes wittier and engaging. Randy has never been one to talk much and just sits back, quietly observing and smiling. Although Randy is quiet-natured, he is also very mischievous. I have always tended to keep a close eye on him because things can change quickly whenever he is around. Engaged deep in conversation with Hazel and Jermaine, I momentarily let my guard down.

In front of the couch was a coffee table. Atop the coffee table lay a magazine and an ashtray made of crystal glass. Also situated on the table was an odd-looking square-shaped cardboard box with ornate designs on the outside. It was quite an interesting piece of decor. Randy seemed fascinated. From the corner of my eye, I saw him pick up the box to examine it closer. When he opened the box, the inside held long wooden matches. They were bundled together with a rubber band. Randy took the matches out to observe them closer.

As we continued with the small talk and laughter, Randy was left to his own devices. He was playing around with the matches and the box and trying in vain to include himself in the conversation. Without realizing what he was doing, Randy took the matches (which were still bundled together) and rubbed them underneath the box. On the bottom of the box was a strike cover. The entire box of matches quickly went up in flames. "Randy! Randy!" we all screamed.

Surprised the matches were set ablaze, Randy quickly threw them onto the shag carpet. The carpet was now on fire. Everyone quickly sprang into action and started stamping the fire. Randy, dazed and confused, began stamping out the fire as well. Addye and Jermaine ran to get water.

"Oh my GOD, Randy! What were you thinking?" I asked as we continued putting the fire out and making sure it did not spread.

We finally managed to get the fire put out before it could cause any major damage. However, we were embarrassed to no end.

"I am so sorry," Randy stated. "Please forgive me. I can't believe I did that!" He was pleading for forgiveness repeatedly.

My emotions were all over the place. We had not even gotten a chance to showcase our talents, and Randy had already caused a major commotion. I was trying in vain to read Jermaine's and Hazel's faces to discern their thoughts. They did not seem upset with Randy, but they did look puzzled.

What a way to make an impression! I thought.

CHAPTER 7

ROOTED IN LOVE

THE OFFICE WAS SO QUIET you could hear a pin drop. To make sure Randy did not feel the urge to touch anything else, I went and sat next to him. Though Jermaine and Hazel were gracious about the incident, I knew what they were thinking: *Not another DeBarge incident!* From Bobby's accounts, they had experienced similar episodes involving him. He shared with me one time the tub overflowed in his hotel room and into the Jacksons' room underneath. Of course, they were not happy about the incident. Yet they always faced Bobby's mishaps with grace. I figured they must be thinking we caused destruction at every turn.

Jermaine spoke up, getting straight to the point. "Do you all have something for us to hear today?"

"Oh yes," El said. Reeling from the embarrassment, he pointed toward the piano and asked, "May I?"

Jermaine stretched out his hand. "It's all yours."

El got up and walked over to the piano, and we all followed. Although the incident with the fire had shaken us up, we had to make the most of this opportunity. Another obstacle we had to overcome involved Mark. We were not used to singing with our brother Mark. Whenever he was involved musically, it mostly involved him playing the trumpet. El and I were worried Mark lacked the discipline needed to be a part of the group. He also was not a good listener and hated taking directions from anyone. While El, Randy, and I were busy honing our skills, Mark was marching to his own beat. He was spending a good bit of his time in Detroit finishing up high school. He had also expressed an interest in going on to college to study music—except with Mark, you never knew his plans from one second to the next. His free-spirited nature irritated the rest of us, and it proved very difficult to keep him focused. Still, we were confident he would know when to come in on a note and contribute to our distinctive sound. Somehow, he always came through in the end. Realistically, it was on Randy, El, and me to carry the songs at the showcase.

We waited for El's cue. He started our set with "Share My World," which we sang in unison. Our sound was polished—a direct result of years of practicing and performing together. We were eager to show off the DeBarge Harmony. The DeBarge Harmony consisted of me harmonizing on top, El and Mark in the middle, and Randy's silky voice harmonizing on the bottom. El began crooning the first verse. He sang softly and sensuously while telling the story in a captivating way. I came in on the second verse, adding in my trademark soprano, which gave way to just a hint of my operatic abilities. As the song continued to build, El and I interacted vocally with each other. Each note fell from our lips perfectly. In our hearts, we believed we left a great impression on Jermaine and Hazel. By the time the song was over, the expression on their faces indicated we had secured the record deal. Our melodic sound captivated the room, causing Jermaine and Hazel to forget all about the earlier fire episode. They asked to hear more of our songs. My mind went back to Bobby saying, "You know you've done well when they ask for more."

We belted out three more songs: "What's Your Name," "Close to You," and "Queen of My Heart." They were thrilled with each song we performed at the showcase. All must have truly been forgiven with Randy. Jermaine and Hazel provided feedback we found to be very encouraging. They stated El sounded very much like Bobby while still maintaining his own sound. They compared my vocals to Minnie Riperton and Deniece Williams. I had heard this often. They also felt that despite the comparisons, my voice was still unique with an innocence all its own. Our melodic sound had captivated them, and the songs were perfect for our vocals and range. I glanced over at Addye who had never heard us sing before this moment. She was impressed as well. She took pride in knowing she was an integral part of our beginnings at Motown. All her hard work, including going above and beyond the call of duty, had not been in vain.

After looking at the clock, I realized it was getting late. We still had not gotten down to business and discussed the recording contracts. I had no intentions of leaving the showcase with our future up in the air. It was no secret the showcase had been a success. I just needed something definitive regarding where we stood with Motown. Addye interrupted the small talk and spoke as if she had just read my mind. "My, how the time has gone by," she stated. "We've been having so much fun I didn't realize we have been here for hours. I just wanted to remind you, Mrs. Jackson, I placed on your husband's desk the paperwork saying the DeBarges are now free from their recording contract with Source Records. I also sent a copy over to our lawyer, Lee Young, for him to review. Bunny, I also have a copy for you guys."

Jermaine and Hazel nodded their heads with approval. "Very well then," Jermaine stated. "I guess you can say everything is a go. Hazel and I are willing to be instrumental in getting you signed with Motown. This will also enable you to have a contract with Motown's publishing company, Jobete, since you are such good writers." He paused for a second and looked over at his wife.

"Now as far as being your managers, we don't feel it would be fair to you, Switch, or to ourselves at this time. You see, we are new to the business of managing, and I must say it is hard work. We aren't skilled enough to take on another act currently. Dealing with *Switch* is more than enough for us. However, we are impressed with what you can do as artists and writers. Therefore, there should be no reason we cannot help you out with a contract here at Motown."

Music to my ears! Jermaine had just confirmed we would be signed to Motown. We could not control our excitement any longer. At last, we were exactly where we always dreamed! "Yes! We did it!" I shouted, leaping to my feet. It took everything for me not to break out in a praise dance. I was not alone. My brothers were on their feet celebrating too.

Our excitement was contagious as Hazel, Jermaine, and Addye joined in the celebration and congratulated us while welcoming us to the Motown family. We could not thank them enough.

"Listening to you guys made me miss my brothers," Jermaine said as his voice began to crack. After composing himself, he stated, "But we all are doing bigger and better things these days."

My heart went out to him, and I truly felt for him in his moment of sadness. I had been performing with my brothers all my life. We had gone through and overcame so much together. I could not imagine being on this journey solo. Jermaine went on to reveal he was working on his album entitled *Let's Get Serious*, which was due to be released by the end of the year.

"I cannot wait to hear it," I told him. "I know it will be great!" Keeping the conversation light, I went on to state, "Like everyone else, I'm a fan of your family. When I was a little girl, as many girls did back in my day, I picked you as the Jackson 5 to put on my wall." I hoped Hazel did not consider my admiration disrespectful.

"So did I," stated Hazel. "However, I married the guy whom I pinned on my wall." We all burst out in laughter while Jermaine blushed.

Getting back to the business at hand, Hazel asked if we had a lawyer. I answered, "No, Hazel. We don't know of any lawyers nor do we know how to get one. We know nothing about the business side of the music industry. That's how the boys got in the mess at Source Records."

Hazel agreed. "Well, the first lesson you should learn is this: do not sign anything without having your lawyer present." We listened attentively as she continued. "Your lawyer will read the documents, which require your signature and explain to you in layman's terms what it all means. You need everything explained to where you fully understand what you are signing before putting your name on it."

"But we don't know any lawyers or where to go look for one. Besides, we have no money right now, and I'm sure we have to pay him up front—don't we?" I interrupted.

Jermaine and Hazel looked at each other and realized they had their work cut out. Our ignorance regarding the business side of the music industry was evident. It was easy to see why we had been taken advantage of by Source Records. I did not want to repeat the same mistake at Motown. However, I was clearly lost on what needed to take place to ensure we got a fair contract this time.

"It will cost you nothing to consult with a lawyer," stated Hazel. "However, make sure the person is an entertainment lawyer who's familiar with the recording industry."

"Yes," Jermaine stated in agreement with Hazel. "Most entertainment lawyers realize new artists do not always have the money to pay up front. They are willing to wait on their payment and negotiate it within the deal."

I breathed a sigh of relief. I was grateful for Jermaine and Hazel giving us a quick rundown of the music business. I wished someone had educated us before the boys signed their contract with Source Records. Even though the contract was (thankfully) a short-lived agreement, it caused a lot of undue hardship for the boys. Jermaine and Hazel were at least taking time out of their busy schedules to ensure we did contract negotiations correctly this time. Hazel wanted us to understand the importance of having a lawyer to represent us and negotiate deals. She went as far as referring us to lawyers outside of Motown. As a group, we decided to go with Mr. Curtis Shaw who used to work for Motown. In our minds, he was already familiar with how Motown contracts were constructed. He could explain to us what we were signing without taking a lot of time reading the actual contract. We needed money—and quick. We were pressed for time due to our day-to-day living situation.

Addye agreed to arrange the meeting with Mr. Shaw. She would make it for the following week. It would be a consultation to determine if both parties liked each other and could agree to work together. Addye then discussed with Jermaine and Hazel about giving us an advance so we could work out our living arrangements. They agreed to loan us the money; however, the necessary papers had to be drawn up to ensure they were repaid. The payments would automatically be withdrawn from our biweekly paychecks until the advance was fully repaid. We were satisfied with this payment arrangement because it meant we no longer had to worry about our day-to-day provisions. Jermaine and Hazel also shared with us how we could earn additional pocket change while waiting for our contracts to be written.

Jobete had an eight-track recording studio on the fifteenth floor of the Motown building. These were songs written by songwriters within the company, which needed to be recorded to tracks. Once recorded to tracks, Jobete would be able to shop the songs to other artists. Jobete was willing to pay people to record the songs. In addition to this, Hazel and Jermaine also wanted us to go into the studio and record a demo of our songs. It would be in a sixteen-track studio the company would secure for us. They wanted us to begin the creative process as soon as possible. The songs that resulted would be featured on our upcoming album. Addye agreed to set up a time for us to record at the Jobete studio as well as begin recording our demo.

The entire day was a success. All we had to do now was wait for the contracts to be written, reviewed by our lawyer, and then signed by the group. Most importantly, DeBarge was getting an advance. We could start looking for a place to call home. We were so thrilled!

"Okay, Addye, I guess we can say this meeting is over," stated Hazel. "You all have work ahead of you."

Standing, Jermaine said, "It was nice meeting you again. Welcome to Motown! Addye will be in touch with you regarding how we're going to work out the advance so you can get straight on your living arrangements." Jermaine and Hazel said their good-byes and departed.

Addye told us not to leave just yet. She had something else to share. Addye then left the room. My brothers had gathered around the piano again singing and clowning. We were euphoric we had a pending contract with Motown Records! It was truly a family affair. First Switch, now *DeBarge*! At last, we were all on the same label. I could not have asked for a more beautiful outcome. I knew Bobby would be thrilled and looked forward to delivering the good news. When Addye walked back in, she extended her arms, and we embraced. We jumped around the room in sheer excitement.

"We did it! We did it!" we squealed.

"Thank you so much, Addye," I told her while trying to catch my breath. "We couldn't have done it without you." The boys came over and hugged Addye and thanked her for everything.

"You people are bad! Oh my GOD, I was so proud of you!" stated Addye.

"That's right, you never heard us, huh?" El replied.

"No," she said. "But I figured if Bobby said you were great, then it must be true. I trust his judgment. I think he's a genius. That boy . . ." We were beaming with pride because to us, Bobby was a genius.

"Okay, you guys, listen up. We have to get to work," Addye said, getting back to business. "There's a lot to be done. Bunny, I need you to be in touch with me early tomorrow. We've got to get on this lawyer situation. Before I forget, I will need all your full names, birth dates, and social security numbers. Give them to me now before you go because I'll need them for your contracts."

Addye looked around for pen and paper to take down our information. Still filled with excitement, she let us know Hazel and Jermaine loved the showcase. She reassured us if they had not, they would have left hours ago. In fact, Hazel was tired and wanted to cancel the showcase until El was overheard playing the piano. She looked at El and began praising his prowess on the piano. He blushed and tried to remain modest. Addye then walked over to her desk and wrote down our information for the contract.

As we were finishing up the day, El leaned into me and whispered, "I was thinking of Uncle Bill today as I was playing. I heard him singing. Isn't that special, Bunny? To hear him while playing that song is to know our uncle Bill." I knew exactly what El meant. We felt Uncle Bill was with us in spirit. El heard him singing, and this provided inspiration for him as he played the piano. The song captured the Jacksons' imagination. While listening, they marveled at the beautiful story El expressed through music. I thanked GOD for our spiritual foundation and Uncle Bill. We were rooted in love—and love is what we envisioned sharing with the world.

Jermaine & Hazel Jackson

Motown Logo

Uncle Bill

CHAPTER 8

FROM SHAME TO FAME

WE LEFT MOTOWN ON CLOUD nine ready to call everyone to share the news. Everyone back home—family members, church members, and friends—knew about the showcase and were anxiously awaiting the outcome. However, I wanted to call Bobby first. Big Bro deserved to be the first to know we would be signing with Motown—especially since he had worked overtime introducing us to the right people at the record company. He truly was a public relations machine! Plus, I had not spoken to him since he left Los Angeles headed to Colorado to work on the Switch album. A part of me missed talking with him so I was eager to hear his voice.

When I finally got ahold of Bobby in Colorado, it was as if World War III was unfolding. I sensed deep irritation in his voice and knew he was not a happy camper. Music was playing in the background, which sounded nothing like one of Bobby's songs. It did not take me long to figure out this must have been the source of Bobby's discontentment. I knew Bobby, who was never afraid to boldly speak his mind, was not holding back any criticisms of the song—constructive or not. As Bobby began to speak, I could sense anger and frustration building in his voice. It was times like these, when Bobby worked himself into a frenzy, I wanted to be with him to calm him down.

"Hey, Bunny. What's going on?" he asked. He did not give me an opportunity to respond. He just laid his feelings bare regarding the song his bandmates were recording. Bobby was brutal in his honesty about the song Jody Sims had written. I overheard his bandmates in the background and was embarrassed for them as I listened to Bobby's tirade. Bobby was not one to wear his heart on his sleeve. However, when it came to music and the creative process, he had a sensitivity that did not seem to match his otherwise calm, suave demeanor.

"My GOD, Bobby," I stated, trying to get him to calm down. "What's happening with you? You don't sound happy at all." Bobby carried on complaining as I tried in vain to calm him down. It was difficult getting a word in edgewise.

"Oh please!" he blurted out while cutting me off. "You wouldn't be happy either if you were around a bunch of *fake people*!" The noise in the background ended abruptly. Bobby continued ranting and raving with little regard for the feelings of his bandmates.

"Bobby!" I yelled into the phone. "Are you talking in front of people?"

"I'm not one to talk behind people's backs *unlike other people I know*!" he yelled out.

Bobby was in a complete uproar, and I needed to calm him down quick. Had I been in Colorado at the studio with him, I would have taken him off by himself and allowed him to tire himself out. When I initially called Bobby, he was Big Bro, the leader of the DeBarge pack. Now, I had to switch into big sis mode, and Bobby never liked when I treated him as a little brother. Through clenched teeth, I put my foot down. "Go into another room so we can talk!"

Bobby must not have heard a word I had just spoken. He acted as if I was not even on the phone. "I'm ready to tell them all *fuck you* and leave! The song is a waste of our time! It will never make the album!"

I tried again. "Bobby DeBarge, . . . I said go to another room . . . NOW!" It got quiet, and I could now hear a shift in Bobby's tone. He let me know he was in another room and explained to me what was going on.

Bobby began to speak passionately about his discontentment regarding the song. "You should hear it, Bunny. It's sickening, and I'm ashamed to put my voice on it. They keep doing the same ridiculous part over and over. There is no need, Bunny—it's not like it's getting any better."

With Bobby a bit calmer, I tried to throw in some encouraging words. Bobby was not done complaining and cut me off again.

"We are wasting all this time and money for it to be canned. Watch what I say! I already told them; they know how I feel." Bobby finally took a deep breath and I took the opportunity to be a calming force.

"Are you done with your songs?" I asked softly.

"Yes, I'm done with *my* songs. I could come home if I didn't have to deal with this mess," Bobby stated. Due to a stipulation in his contract, Bobby had to remain in Colorado and record on the group's songs. However, Bobby did not have to allow the group to record on his songs. Because Bobby did not like the song, he did not want to put his vocals on it. The band members were not happy about Bobby's decision and reported this to Hazel and Jermaine.

"They are so two-faced, Bunny," Bobby continued. "They know they don't want me here with them—as if I want to be here anyway. They asked me how I liked the song. You know I told them the truth. I said *I don't like it!* It's not even a good album cut—to me—and it's not because I've got a problem with them either. Bunny, it's just a waste of time! They want me to save it by putting my voice on it. I told them Aretha Franklin couldn't save it even if she sang it with no music. They can be mad at me all they want. The song sucks! I can't wait to tell Jermaine and Hazel. They better listen to this song first before we go any further. I'm not singing another note until I talk to them!"

Bobby was speaking in a much calmer yet deliberate tone. However, I could tell my brother was still riled up. He had not even stopped to ask the reason for my call. Since he had just spoken on Jermaine and Hazel, I figured this was a great entrance into sharing news we were in the process of signing to Motown. "Speaking of Jermaine and Hazel, we just left them," I stated. "We had our showcase today."

"Oh, for real?" Bobby became curious. "How did it go? Tell me what is happening with you! I called a couple of times, but you're never there." Bobby had calmed down, and I now had his full attention. I recapped everything beginning with Source Records and Mr. Westbrooks. I told him about the release from Source Records and how Jermaine and Hazel were interested in us signing with Motown. I explained how Addye had supported me and worked diligently in getting the showcase scheduled.

"They loved us, Bobby," I stated with excitement in my voice. I knew how much it meant to Bobby for all of us to be signed to Motown. It meant even more to be able to let him know the hard work it took to get the boys released from Source Records and signed to Motown.

"Are you surprised?" he responded. I could tell Bobby was in a much better mood. "I already told them my family was bad. That's good, Bunny! I'm happy for you guys. Finally, we are together under the same label." We talked for a few more minutes. Bobby felt at ease knowing we were out of the dilemma with Source Records. Not wanting to hide anything from him, I shared that the boys were staying with Tony and me at his apartment. I told him Hazel and Jermaine had worked out an advance agreement with us, and we would have our own places soon. I promised Bobby I would make sure the boys did not tear up his apartment. He did not go off even though he was not pleased. I figured he was too preoccupied with the issues he was having in the studio with his bandmates.

"Okay, Bunny, I have to go. I'll call you later. I have to get in touch with Jermaine right now," he told me before abruptly hanging up.

After hanging up with Bobby, I was mentally exhausted. Bobby had a way of taking you through a roller coaster of emotions. His inner turmoil would surface when he became upset and made communicating with him a daunting task. Bobby was not getting along with the other band members. In fact, it was never a good relationship from the beginning and was only getting worse. There was layered conflict within the group, and personalities clashed left and right. At this point in his life, Bobby was not easy to work with for one reason or another. I understood why he had become so assertive. Bobby had had his fair share of being pushed around and let down beginning in childhood— both at home and away from home. Moreover, he felt let down when he was a member of Barry White's band White Heat. When White Heat disbanded, it deeply affected him, especially since he had the lofty goal of making it big in the music industry (part of his goal was also to bring his siblings into the music business). After the White Heat fiasco, Bobby became a different person. He began to assert himself, which meant being blunt and getting what he wanted without consideration for whom it offended. Bobby ultimately decided to be true to himself. The hardships he faced in life meant to break him had the opposite effect.

I shared a painful history with Bobby. What we endured being the oldest (along with Tommy) made our bond stronger. As a child, I wiped away his tears, held his hand, and comforted him whenever his feelings were hurt. I understood his anger and his reasons for distrusting people. He suffered in childhood. He was often referred to as a punk. Because of the way he would act out, he was labeled a troubled soul. Anyone who did not understand his anger saw a loser and a pushover. Miraculously, Bobby gained the inner strength to believe in himself when no one else cared if he lived or died. He went from hiding in the background to walking with a certain flamboyant flair. He became driven and ambitious. His charisma began to shine through brighter than the sun and toppled his insecurities. He had an aura that made you want to believe in him. Bobby fully embraced his musical gifts and became extremely confident and aware about what he brought to the table. Whether at Motown or another record company, Bobby's gifts and talents reached far beyond what any label could offer. He knew it, and others did too.

To me, Bobby was a genius in so many areas—not just musically. In fact, all my brothers described him as a genius. Bobby was the king of the DeBarges! His words meant everything. We listened and considered every single word he ever uttered. My brothers would hang on to his every word as his opinions were both valued and respected. He could be harsh and would occasionally hurt the boys' feelings. They never allowed his insensitivity to draw a wedge between their brotherly bond. Deep down inside, they knew he loved them unconditionally. Sometimes his sternness toward the younger boys seemed unfair. Those were the times I would step in and stand up to Bobby. As Bobby's confidence grew, our roles reversed. He became my big brother as well, and I respected his new role in my life. He was now the one to hold *my hand* and *guide me.* Everything had come full circle; I could now depend on Big Bro for protection and direction. Regardless of how our roles shifted in each other's eyes, I would instantly become the big sis/mama bear when needed. As mentioned earlier, a lot of my dustups with Bobby resulted from any perceived harshness toward our younger siblings.

Simply put, I was proud of Bobby and loved (still do) him dearly. I watched his growth from once carrying the burden of shame to confidently proclaiming, "I'm Bobby DeBarge, and I brought my name from shame to fame!" Bobby was no longer the scared little boy who once sat back and took orders. He was now stuck in a group his talents had outgrown. There was tremendous pressure for him to come through for Motown. Bobby believed he could come through—but he only believed in *himself.* Even though Bobby did not own the name Switch (Greg Williams and Jody Sims did), he would often announce, "I am *Switch!* The sound belongs to *me.*" He had a point and cared less who disagreed. By believing in himself, he was setting an example for all the DeBarges.

The Confident Bobby

A FAMILY OF MUSICAL TALENT

"DEBARGE": FROM GRAND RAPIDS TO MOTOWN

Bunny & Bobby

CHAPTER 9

MOTOWN ARTISTS

I CANNOT BEGIN TO DESCRIBE the thrill of becoming Motown artists. Our names and image would now exist among some of the greatest entertainers the world has ever known. It was a surreal moment. If I were sleeping, I did not want to be awakened. I wanted this feeling to last forever. However, the business side brought me back to reality, and I began to think about questions to ask the lawyer. We had to make sure the lawyer understood we wanted our names to appear as songwriters with Jobete Publishing.

We were still waiting for a meeting with Mr. Curtis Shaw but was confident it would happen soon. Addye kept us busy by scheduling demo sessions while she waited to hear back from him. It was nice not fretting about our next meal. We had steady income from recording demos at Jobete. Our minds were now free to create music. The money we earned from recording the Jobete songs helped us get by until the contracts were signed. Once the contracts were signed, our salary from the artist and writer contracts would kick in. For now, our days consisted of apartment hunting in the morning, Jobete at noon, then rehearsing for our demo at night.

Recording the Jobete catalog was fun, and we learned a lot. It also gave us exposure on how to lay tracks. Once we learned the process from start to finish, we were ready to get into the studio and record our own songs. Addye had set up the demo budget. It just needed to be confirmed first before we could record. Meanwhile, we were taking life as it came and enjoying it. We were happy our lives were on a meaningful path. My girls, Damea and Janae, were happy, healthy, and thriving. I did not need to hire a babysitter. My brothers were great about helping with them and looking after them. The girls adored their uncles, and we all were having the time of our lives!

Bobby and Tommy were heading home soon from Caribou Ranch in Denver, Colorado. The Switch album was now completed. I was hoping we each would find our own living space before they returned. We were looking for apartments near one another but not too far from Motown. I was the only one with a car and was responsible for getting us to and from our appointments. We quickly discovered that the apartments in Los Angeles were terribly expensive. Someone suggested we check out apartments in the San Fernando Valley. Although it was hotter there than in Los Angeles, we did find cheaper apartments. We ran into another hurdle in our apartment search. Unlike filling out applications back home in Grand Rapids, we were now required to undergo credit checks, have first and last month's rent up front, as well as a security deposit. After all this, you would be placed on a wait list until an apartment became available. I was completely blown away. In Grand Rapids, there were no wait lists and no credit checks. All you needed to rent an apartment was your name, employment information, and phone number. The bright lights began to dim. I viewed California as a place where vultures preyed on those in the entertainment industry. We finally located apartments in the Valley close to one another. Tony and I found a two-bedroom apartment to rent on Rayen Street in Sepulveda, California. The boys found a lovely house to rent on Devonshire. They all agreed to split the rental expense. We were on our own at last. No longer did we have to live in and out of hotels or with Bobby.

After learning we had found our own place to stay, our mother packed up and joined us in California. She brought James, Chico, and the twins. They moved into the house with the boys. We were all now residents of California and began enjoying our time together as family. Our mother would cook dinner every Sunday. No matter what we were doing, we made sure to be at Sunday dinner. Every Sunday seemed like a family reunion.

James, now aged seventeen, was a senior in high school. He wanted to drop out and pursue a career in music. As his older siblings, we had set a poor example for him to follow since we had dropped out of school to pursue music. While not particularly proud of our decision, our passion for music clouded our judgment. Music was our destiny, and we allowed nothing to stop us—even if it meant giving up our education. El and I were determined James would not go down the same path. James was relentless, though. Every day, he asked to join the group. Every day, we told him school should be his focus. We had no problem with James joining the group. El and I just felt it was our duty and responsibility to encourage him to graduate high school first. James, stubborn as ever, would not take no for an answer. He had set his focus on becoming a member of the group, and there was no turning back. El and I pleaded with him to focus on completing his education. We reminded him he was already a senior and would be graduating soon. Our words must have fallen on deaf ears. Instead of completing his homework, James was spending all his free time writing lyrics. El and I ran out of options to redirect James' focus. What many people may not know is our song "Share My World" was written for James. James was upset because he believed we did not want him in the group. This was far from the truth. We only wanted him to do things the right way— get an education first *then* pursue music. To make him feel special, we ended up dedicating the chorus of the song to him. We indeed wanted him to share our world.

The time had finally come for us to go into the studio and record the demo! We wanted very much to be in control of our sound. Therefore, we had to demonstrate to Motown we could produce our own songs. Bobby and Tommy had taught us so much about how to develop and produce our own sound. We were a little concerned because Motown was notorious for using their own in-house producers and songwriters. But we had worked so hard honing our skills and discovering distinct melodies as we rehearsed at home and whenever Bobby allowed us to sit in on his studio sessions. Moreover, working at Jobete recording and laying tracks was also helpful. We were ready!

We recorded a song a day. We would do rhythm tracks in the morning and vocals in the evening. It was a grueling process, but we had fun in the studio. It was a family affair! By the time we finished recording the demo, the contracts were ready to be signed. Mr. Curtis Shaw, our lawyer, called us into his office and explained each section of the agreement in a way we would understand. Once we signed the contracts, we handed over the demo. The songs we recorded were "Queen of My Heart," "Share My World," "What's Your Name," and "You're So Gentle, You're So Kind." Listening to our sound and how our ideas had blossomed into full-blown songs were phenomenal! We were eager to continue the recording process. We now had keen insight on the entire recording process as evidenced by the demo we had submitted earlier. Did we think Motown would be impressed? There was no doubt in our minds. Not only had we proven ourselves as artists, but we were also proving ourselves to be producers. We were truly becoming a musical force!

The DeBarges

CHAPTER 10

THE DEBARGES

It was the summer of 1980. The powers that be at Motown called us into the office for a meeting. They wanted to discuss getting started recording our debut album. Bobby, a master negotiator due to his charm and charisma, joined us for the meeting. He was able to convince Motown to allow El, him, and myself to produce the project. I could not believe it! We were finally going into the studio to produce our very first album! Bobby wanted to be hands-on in the production of our first album. However, he was also busy promoting Switch's album. He entrusted El and me with the responsibility to produce the album and would be on standby if needed.

Motown's Artist Relations Department (A&R) assigned Reggie Andrews to overlook the development of the project. We were provided with a recording budget and was adamant about not wasting time in the studio. After all, time is money! We wanted to make sure everything was a go once inside the studio because we did not want to plow through the budget. To ensure our singing would be on point, Reggie took us to a room inside the Motown office to rehearse our parts. Once the harmonies and melodies became tightly woven together, we were ready to work our magic. The first song we recorded was the ballad "What's Your Name?" El and I were a match made in heaven! I ended up writing lyrics young ladies wanted to hear from their Prince Charming. The words came to me effortlessly. After all, I was a woman truly in love with the idea of being in love—a hopeless romantic so to speak. I knew the words I wanted to hear a man profess to me. Respecting my woman's point of view, El would take the lyrics and embellish them. He had a way of knowing the exact expressions to use to bring the song to life.

Recording "What's Your Name?" was quite a learning experience. Up to this point, we never had the privilege of recording with strings or horns. It was challenging initially. Nevertheless, we began to incorporate the respective sounds into our harmony. On the song, we mimicked the sound of the strings and horns meant to be background parts. We did not know any better. However, the way we imitated the sounds worked to our benefit. The *bop-bop-baa* in the background was meant for the strings and horns. Bobby let us know we no longer needed to sing this part. Rather, we could just add in the strings and horns during the sweetening process. We kept the part anyway, and it incorporated into the final version of the song.

It was now time to lay our rhythm tracks, which would become the foundation of the song. Bobby called in Ollie Brown to be on percussion, Paul Jackson to be on lead guitar, Nathan East on bass, and Harvey Mason on drums. El was on keyboards. Some of the greatest musicians in the business would perform on our songs! For El to be performing among some of the greatest musicians made me so proud. Wow! Were we big time or what? The musicians admired as well as respected El's musical prowess. Each musician laid their part on the track separately. Then each part was brought together. The results were amazing!

Once the session was over, we took the tape home and listened to it all night. Even without the vocals added in, the rhythm track sounded like a record. This made us want to practice our background—our sound. El, Randy, and I stayed up all night ensuring our harmonies meshed with the rhythm. We wanted our voices to swell like strings and bop like horns.

We did not record the lyrics right away. We continued practicing and building our confidence. One day while we were rehearsing, a young petite lady peeked into the room. We were taken aback and stopped singing. We had no idea who had unintentionally interrupted our rehearsal session. After seeing the bewildered looks on our faces, she quickly introduced herself as Teena Marie. She then paid a complement to our singing. "You guys sound great—like angels from heaven! I just had to peek in to see who you were," she stated.

We introduced ourselves as the DeBarges. We let her know we had heard so much about "Teena Marie." Imagine the thrill we experienced finally laying our eyes on her presence. It was a surreal moment. Though she was tiny in stature with a big voice, her presence loomed larger than life. She also had a very feisty nature. "Sing some more," she commanded. "Don't let me stop you. I know your album will be great, and I can't wait to hear it." Teena Marie went on to describe how she had met our brother Bobby. She did not realize there were so many "little Bobbys" running around singing. She lingered around until we finished our song then congratulated us on a job well done. From this day forward, she became good friends with me and my brothers. I grew to love her dearly. I learned her birthday was the same day as Bobby's (March 5). I told her my birthday was the tenth of March. We were so excited our birthdays were so close together and decided to celebrate together the following year.

***

Going to Motown/Hitsville Studio was always a treat. We never knew who (or what) we might encounter. A big-name artist was always in a recording session. I remember meeting Lionel Richie and his then-wife Brenda Richie. I also met Sharon Bryant from Atlantic Starr. We got an opportunity to sit in on a Commodores recording session. One of the most unforgettable encounters was when I briefly met Mr. Superfreak himself, Rick James. I was on the elevator going to a recording session when a guy in a red-and-white leather outfit stepped onto the elevator. The outfit was fitted tightly and displayed all his *manhood*. We both knew of each other. I was the first to speak. "It's the fabulous Rick James," I stated while looking him up and down. He was not my type. Therefore, I was not flirting with him—just exchanging playful banter. He looked at me over the top of his glasses and stated, "Yes, . . . the one and only, baby. Have we met?" I shook my head no then told him I was a member of the DeBarges. He then stuck out his tongue and stated, "I know . . . licky . . . licky!" I was glad the elevator dinged and hurried off.

We met Billy Preston when he visited the studio. We were excited to meet him and amazed by his talents. He was excited about meeting us and invited the boys and me to his house to record. Eventually, Billy would become a very close friend of the family. We also met Lee Oskar—the harmonica player from the group War. The studio was filled with people whom we admired and never dreamed we would be sharing the same recording studio. Yet here we were mingling among bona fide stars while creating music and making history. I was so proud of our achievements. We were the new kids on the block and received a warm reception. I was starstruck and wanted to meet Stevie Wonder, Marvin Gaye, and Michael Jackson. This became my secret mission.

We finished our background vocals to "What's Your Name?" and was so proud of what we had accomplished. El still had to do his lead, but Bobby wanted to be there when the time came. El feared following in his big brother Bobby's footsteps—he did not feel his voice was as melodic or he would measure up to Bobby's talents. However, Bobby and I would be there to lift his spirits and let him know *he* was great in his own special way. Although Bobby was not there physically, he approved the song. He just wanted El to add a little narrative in the beginning to introduce the story.

When he returned, Bobby went into the studio and recorded ad libs for the end of "What's Your Name?" with the intention of teaching them to El. Bobby told him the ad libs would bring the song home. When Bobby finished recording his ad libs, El did not want to touch it. He felt the part belonged to Bobby, and he was not alone in his judgment. Bobby was determined to get El into the studio to record the ad libs using his own voice. However, he lost the battle since we all agreed his vocals should stay. Although he continued to protest, his ad libs became a part of the final song version. When we presented the song to the powers that be at Motown, they were delighted with the results and encouraged us to continue recording.

We recorded the remainder of the album with relative ease. We had a system in place and a lot of support within Motown. Basically, we had a machine behind us to ensure the success of the album upon its release. There were a few finishing touches that needed to be added. Bobby knew of several well-known musicians and wanted us to have the best in the business on our debut album. He called in Harvey Mason (once again) and Leon (Ndugu) Chancler for drums, Paul Jackson and Charles Fearing for lead guitar, Eddie Watkins for bass, and Clare Fischer and Eric Butler for strings and horns.

The final two songs we recorded were "Queen of My Heart" and "Hesitate." Again, Bobby was there to fill in anything missing vocally on the songs. At the end of "Queen of My Heart," he sang an ad lib, which only Bobby could sing. Bobby was a master at adding flair to another person's song. He did it naturally and usually in one take. As he was ad-libbing the ending on "Queen of My Heart," I thought it was too much at first. Once it was done and in the mix, I was completely blown away. For a long time, those who did not know any better thought El sang the ad libs at the end. However, those who knew both brothers recognized it was indeed Bobby singing. Bobby's voice was much stronger than El's voice. We later found out El had a pinched vocal cord that did not allow his voice to be as strong. Yet El was still able to reach every note Bobby did, but it took some effort.

We listened to our songs repeatedly to make sure nothing was missing. We still had the process of mixing to contend with later. So far, the songs sounded incredible. "Share My World" was a masterpiece. Once again, Bobby came in and added his flair to the song. It was a love song I envisioned, from the start, to be sung at weddings. "Hesitate" was written while in the studio with Randy playing around on bass. We ended up building the rest of the music track from his bass line. "Hesitate" was a rap song before rap was ever out and became mainstream. Then there was "You're So Gentle, You're So Kind." The song was all on me and featured my songwriting and producing skills! Bobby made me talk on the track—something I was not willing to do at first. I did not mind singing but hated my speaking voice. There was no winning whenever Bobby was involved. He was determined that when it was over, said, and done, the DeBarges would have an awesome debut album.

Paul Jackson
lead and rhythm guitar

Nathan East bass

Ollie Brown
drummer & percussionist

Harvey Mason drummer

Teena Marie heard our voices and
had to see who we were

Leon Ndugu
Chancler drummer

Rick James

Ozone became the group
to play for us on the road

Lionel and Brenda Richie

Harvey Mason drummer

Lee Oscar from the group War

CHAPTER 11

COULD THIS BE TRUE?

BOBBY CAME OFF THE ROAD polished and with even more confidence knowing what he could contribute to the music industry. He had gained a lot of respect within the company including with the chairman himself, Mr. Berry Gordy. Bobby was very pleased with the outcome of our songs. Instead of having the A&R Department submit the finished album to Mr. Gordy, Bobby wanted to do so himself. We were not the only reason Bobby wanted to meet with Mr. Gordy. His relationship with Switch was not getting any better and going downhill fast. It was taking its toll on him mentally, and there were marked changes in his mood.

From the very beginning, Bobby knew *he* was the sound of Switch—whether he owned the name or not. He was the alpha male of the group. It was his songs, his voice, and his physicality that received most of the attention for the group. He had no problem voicing this to his bandmates. This caused friction and animosity within the group. The members of Switch grew weary of the admiration and favor Bobby was shown by Motown including the chairman.

By the time Bobby signed with Motown, he was already larger than life. He was able to negotiate a stipulation in his contract the others were not. In his contract, it left Bobby with the decision whether to allow the other band members to sing on his songs. However, Bobby's voice had to be on all their songs whether they wanted him on them or not. Philip

Ingram was the only band member Bobby would use to sing lead or co-lead on some of his songs. Aside from the times he used Phillip, Bobby sang lead and background on all his songs. He wanted to promote our family's sound, hoping one day we would all sing together.

Bobby had many stories about the group and the jealousy that existed among the members—particularly toward him. The jealousy and infighting started long before the group Switch was formed. Bobby and Greg Williams' trust in each other as friends was tainted after the group White Heat disbanded. When the group was intact, they played nice, but there was mutual dislike. Greg did not want Bobby in either group—White Heat or Switch. He had many talks with other group members, hoping to influence their opinion about kicking Bobby out of White Heat. When Switch was being formed, Greg Williams and Jody Sims were to be the only two members coming from White Heat. Greg had many discussions with Jody regarding why he did not want Bobby in the newly formed group. Yet when the Switch demo tape was completed, Bobby's vocals were on lead. Greg would use the tape to shop a record deal but had no plans for Bobby to become a member of the group. Greg had bad-mouthed Bobby to Jody, and they were both in agreement about Bobby not becoming a member of the group once they secured a record deal. However, the deal was in jeopardy once Greg revealed to Motown he had no idea of Bobby's whereabouts—even though they were friends and both lived in Grand Rapids. Greg intended to use another lead singer in Bobby's place. Motown informed Greg and Jody they needed to find the lead voice on the tape or there was no deal. Greg became infuriated, and the bad-mouthing grew worse.

The core of the group's issue with Bobby had always been they did not approve of his lifestyle. There were a lot of mumbling about Bobby's lifestyle happening behind his back and how this was hurting the group's image. Bobby seemed to not let their disdain get him down. He walked with his head held high and was confident about his position within the group. He was determined to be himself, and the company only cared about him delivering hit songs—not who he was bedding. There was also a lot of talk about Bobby's drug issue and the fact he was using again. While Greg was quick to mention Bobby's sexuality and drug use to Motown, he failed to disclose he was abusing drugs too. Had Bobby known Greg was on a campaign to taint his reputation within Motown, he would have gladly informed Motown about Greg's own spiraling drug addiction. Bobby never made it a secret he indeed had a male lover and was not the least bit ashamed. He refused to hide his sexuality or allow his bandmates to treat him less than a man.

Bobby grew sick of it all. He felt he had outgrown the group as well as his managers, Jermaine and Hazel Jackson. Since he had met the chairman (Mr. Gordy), he went straight to him for advice regarding his career. He did not feel as if he needed Hazel and Jermaine's direction any longer. Mr. Gordy loved Bobby and was willing to listen to his complaints about the group and management. He agreed Bobby should get out of the management contract. However, he was not so lucky when it came to him asking to leave the group. Nevertheless, the idea had been presented, and the seed planted. Mr. Gordy gave Bobby hope by telling him soon the company would look at signing him as a solo artist at the next contract negotiation. Bobby emerged from the meeting excited about the idea of becoming a solo artist. He also informed us the chairman would be visiting us soon. He had no idea when, but Bobby assured us Mr. Gordy would show up.

***

Bobby had to leave town again. He had to do promotion for the Switch album. For the time being, we would be on our own. It was now time to mix the songs for our first album, but we knew very little about the process. El and I had watched Bobby mix a few times but never got the actual opportunity to mix. Mixing consisted of bringing out certain instruments and vocals, bringing the sounds up and down or maybe not using certain parts at all. Mixing was essential. It made the song by putting on the finishing touches. Bobby left us with notes and instructions while promising to be available via phone. He reassured us once we got started mixing, we would catch on quickly. Also, we still had Reggie Andrews to oversee our project. Bobby Brooks, a Motown engineer, was also there to help.

We spent days mixing the songs. It was a tedious process. Many people within Motown came by the studio to see the new kids on the block—the DeBarges. The attention was fascinating, and for the first time, we truly felt accepted. Lost in all the hoopla surrounding us, we had forgotten about Bobby telling us Mr. Gordy would be coming to see us soon. The day came when we were mixing our final song. It happened to be the song I had written and sang entitled "You're So Gentle, You're So Kind." El and I were focused on mixing the song when the door to the studio swung open. A short, slightly balding man along with a young woman and a tall, tough-looking Italian guy came sauntering in. Even though we had never seen him in person, we knew that the short, slightly balding man was Mr. Gordy. He wore a pleasant smile on his face. He then looked over to where we were mixing, nodded his head in our direction as he greeted us, then took a seat and talked to Reggie. El and I continued with the mixing of the song as we watched him bop his head to the track.

Mr. Gordy worked his way over to the mixing board and began sliding the knobs up and down on the console. Only the chairman himself could get away with this because we would not have allowed anyone else to interfere with our work. Our songs were our babies! It was not like we disagreed with what he was doing. We just knew better than to say anything. Mr. Gordy no longer dealt directly with the artists in the company. Therefore, it was a treat to have him come to the studio and visit us. El introduced himself. Mr. Gordy assured El he already knew him. El laughed then introduced me as his sister and the vocals on the song.

"Ah . ..," Mr. Gordy slowly stated as if a lightbulb had gone off in his head. "This is a beautiful ballad, and your voice is beautiful. So, feature the voice." He began moving buttons on the mixing board, bringing the instruments in and out of the song. Then he brought up my vocals and told us where the strings should be in the mix.

"They should complement your voice," he said. "Bring them under your voice, not over it." He made mixing fun and never made us feel inadequate. He was a pleasant man with an uplifting spirit. He doled out praises and compliments on the project. We were surprised because he was so unassuming, and we found him relatable. He had retired from the company he built with much respect given. We knew he had done his job well. It did not matter if he was retired or not—it was a privilege and an honor to have a living legend looking in on us and praising our music. We were happy to hear from *his mouth* that our songs were great!

As we continued to talk, Mr. Gordy told us our musical style was unique. He went on to say even though our style of writing was different than Bobby's, he could tell we were from the same family. He reassured us we were in the right place. It was his belief Motown had what it took to make us stars, and we were among family. Mr. Gordy had our undivided attention. We were delighted to be in the presence of someone who believed we were geniuses. He referred to us as such and made us feel right at home. In all the socializing and rubbing of shoulders, I could see Mr. Gordy was having a great time! We socialized a while longer with Mr. Gordy laughing, joking, and sharing stories about our brother Bobby—whom Mr. Gordy also referred to as a genius. He explained how he had retired from the company. He did want us to know there were people at the company knowledgeable and capable enough to do for us what he had done for so many artists in the past. Spending the day with Mr. Gordy was certainly a treat. We were amazed at where we were within the company. I guess you could say reality hit me. We were family for sure! It was written in stone!

After we finished the mixing of our songs, the master tape was sent for the mastering process. We had completed all parts of the musical process from start to finish. Motown set up a photo shoot. The preparation for the shoot was long as the actual shoot. The entire process lasted two full days—one full day was dedicated to shopping for clothes, and the other day was dedicated to taking pictures. We found the entire process tiring and not glamorous at all. Those assisting with the photo shoot were constantly touching up our makeup, adjusting our clothes, and fixing our hair. We had not had professional photos taken since high school. However, this photo shoot was quite a process and nothing like preparing to take a high school picture. We had to endure many different poses for them to select *one*. Some photos we took solo and others as a group. We had to make it fun or else we would have been miserable. Trying to get us to be still and think on one accord was challenging, but we managed. We smiled for the camera all day long. The photographer had to have taken at least two hundred pictures for the album cover. When it was all over, Motown selected the image of us dressed in soft pastel colors holding a telephone receiver. It was a beautiful image of us as a beautiful family just having fun.

With the album completed and pictures for the cover selected, it was now time to seek out management. The album had to be promoted, and marketing plans had to be put in motion. The DeBarges needed a manager; however, we were unsure of how to go about obtaining one. We knew nothing about the business aspect of the industry. We did learn a lot from our experience with Source Records. Since Bobby had more experience in the industry and seemed to understand the business side, we were not about to do anything without consulting him first. He was glad we did not make any sudden moves without talking to him. He warned us not to sign a management contract with Motown's inside management company, citing a conflict of interest. We figured our brother knew what he was talking about and would not steer us wrong. We took his advice and started looking for outside management.

It did not take long for us to find managers. In fact, we did not have to look far. Management found us, and it seemed like we were heading toward having a great working relationship. A husband-and-wife team had a talent management company called Tiger Flower Productions. Out of the blue one day, they showed up at the studio. How they heard about us was a mystery. However, they expressed an interest in managing us. We did not know how management worked except for the little information Motown and Bobby had shared. The Tiger Flower team said all the things we thought sounded good. They talked as if they knew about the music industry and how Motown conducted business. They assured us they had what it took to handle business with Motown on our behalf. They also shared they knew about marketing and promotion strategies. They made a lot of promises before presenting us with management contracts to sign. Believing we would have a great professional relationship, the group decided to sign. We thought we had done the right thing by securing management on our own. There was no indication we had made a wrong move.

Reggie Andrews, along with other team members from A&R, called a meeting for us to write credits for the album. Finally, the question came up about management. Thinking we had everything together, we shared about already having signed a management contract. After we explained we had entered into a management agreement with Tiger Flower, the room became uncomfortably quiet. There was a look of shock on everyone's faces, but nobody uttered a word. I wondered why there was a sudden coldness in our conversation. We felt maybe it was due to them wanting us to sign with managers inside the company. Since no one was willing to explain their silence, we allowed any potential discussions to fall by the wayside. We would soon have an album to promote and looked forward to working with our management team. More than anything, we were proud to be done with our album. We felt it was a masterpiece. Now, we had to wait and see if the world loved it just as much. Fresh out of the church, we landed in a world we knew nothing about. Now here we were Motown artists, Jobete writers, with a management team who promised to look out for our best interests. Look out, world . . . Here comes the DeBarges!

The DeBarges

CHAPTER 12

TIGER FLOWER MANAGEMENT

THINGS WERE GOING SMOOTHLY—OR AT least as far as we were concerned. You would think we would be floating on cloud nine since we were Motown artists and preparing to release our debut album. Nothing could be farther from the truth. We were homesick and itching to return to Grand Rapids. Having fulfilled our obligations at Motown, we felt now was our golden opportunity to return home. We had accomplished a lot in a short period of time, but home was never far from our mind. We surmised if there was any business to handle, our managers at Tiger Flower would step up to the plate. We looked forward to returning home to spend time with our loved ones.

There was a lot of talk going around the company regarding Mr. Gordy and our management contract with Tiger Flower. The rumor was Mr. Gordy was not too fond of us signing with an outside management team. There were ramblings that Mr. Gordy was considering coming back to work within the company because he wanted to be more hands on with our group. If the rumor were true, we might have jumped the gun—again. Luckily for us, it turned out to be a rumor, and there was no reason for us to be worried we had upset the chairman. Still, I was uneasy, yet hopeful signing with Tiger Flower would not backfire. We dismissed the unconfirmed rumors and focused on returning to

Grand Rapids. With the album completed, our hearts were no longer in California.

Months earlier, our mother had left California and returned home to Grand Rapids. She was missing her church family and wanted to return for a visit. When she arrived home for a visit, she decided to remain. Our mother was one of the biggest reasons we were so homesick. We had gotten used to her being in California along with our younger siblings. Having the family established in one place was a great source of support. Now with her gone, California felt empty. We discussed our plans to return to Grand Rapids with Motown and Tiger Flower. Neither seemed to have a problem with us not residing in California. Therefore, after finalizing our debut single and its release date, we were on our way back to Michigan. The album would be entitled *The DeBarges*, and the single off the first album would be "What's Your Name?"

I phoned Addye to tell her good-bye and thank her for all her hard work. During our call, she confirmed the rumor Mr. Gordy was upset we had signed with outside management. My heart dropped into my stomach. If Addye said it, I knew it must be true. She had always been straightforward when sharing information. I did not know what to do about the situation and looked to Addye for advice. She seemed to be hesitant to provide input. Since we had already signed, we had to honor our contractual obligations. She shared that indeed Mr. Gordy wanted to either become our manager or he wanted us to work with Motown's in-house management team. Either way, he wanted to be instrumental in ensuring our success and was a bit upset about our decision to sign with Tiger Flower. I was sick! Addye shared with me that Motown could give our managers a hard way to go. In other words, if they chose to, they could sit on the album. This meant they could release the album and do nothing to market or promote it.

"Oh really?" I asked, taken aback. "I don't believe they would do that, Addye. Why would they spend all that money on us to do an album and not promote it?" What Addye shared made no sense. She chose not to elaborate further and changed the subject. We talked about my brothers and I returning home to Michigan. I made sure she had an address to reach me and would call her once I had a new telephone number. For the time being, we all would be living with our mother until we found our own places.

***

Word spread like wildfire that we were coming home for good. Several family members and friends waited to greet us at the airport. It was a great feeling to witness the pride and excitement on everyone's faces. They were so proud of us! We gathered at our mother's house to share stories of our experiences and to listen to our debut album. Motown had provided us with a box filled with albums. We split them among each group member then handed them out to family. The house was filled with music again, and our mother was so happy. There seemed to be an endless buffet of food. Throughout the day, people came and went. There was lots of love and laughter being shared. It was such a beautiful welcome-home reception—warm and heartfelt. Our mother was happy to have her children home—except for Bobby and Tommy who were both on the road with Switch.

Tiger Flower Management appeared to be on their job. Not a day passed whereas we did not touch basis. Part of the reason they kept reaching out was they did not want us to get too comfortable being home. They wanted us to realize the hard work had not even begun. With our debut album released, management had big plans for the group. They wanted us to begin rehearsals for a promotional tour. Tiger Flower advised we would be performing live and needed a drummer. El was also considering using a second keyboard player so he could get up from playing the piano and sing. Getting a drummer was not a hard task at all. There were many who lived in Grand Rapids and would have loved the opportunity to perform with our band. However, we chose our childhood friend Freddy Garner. Freddy, who played with us in church, was very familiar with our sound.

Our mother now lived two houses down from where we grew up on Giddings Street. She was my babysitter so I needed a house close by. Not long afterward, Tony and I found a house down the street between Giddings and Bemis. Our salaries from Motown and Jobete were steady now, and we were able to afford the house. I furnished our home and enrolled my girls in school. In the meantime, Motown released our single. It was the responsibility of management and Motown to market and promote the project. Our managers seemed to be performing up to par. They even gave us money to find a place to rehearse. We found an empty warehouse on the southwest part of town and started rehearsing daily.

Finally, our managers wanted us to come to Washington, DC, where they were headquartered. They had already set up several promotional interviews. They wanted us in their city where they could drop in to see how we were progressing with our live-performance rehearsal. This would give them a better idea of what was needed to perfect our show. I left Damea and Janae in Grand Rapids with my mother so they could continue their schooling. The boys, along with Tony and I, left for Washington, DC. We were happy to be on our way to promote our album.

While in Washington, DC, we tuned into the radio station ready to hear our single. We had an idea of how Motown promoted and marketed songs from watching how they handled Switch's releases. We expected the same machine to be behind our debut release. However, this did not seem to be happening at all. The radio stations were playing everyone else's songs, but we did not hear our song being played. We might have heard our song played once or twice a week—if that. However, it was not being played daily like the Switch songs. When we questioned our promotions manager regarding why our song was getting little to no airplay, we were reassured they were working to resolve the issue. Days passed and nothing changed. We barely heard our song on the radio. Again, we questioned the promotions manager who provided us with excuse after excuse. We finally put our foot down and demanded to know why our hard work seemed to be going out the window. Management finally disclosed that Motown was being difficult, and they were receiving a lot of pushback from the company. Motown was not returning their calls.

Motown would make promises to promote the record at radio stations then renege on those same promises. We were reassured that based on the terms of our record contract, Motown had an obligation to comply with their requests to promote and market the song. Tiger Flower tried to put our minds at ease by promising they would be taking legal action against Motown. We were no longer buying anything they were selling. The double-talk was not convincing. Something had to have gone wrong—we could feel it in our spirits. We were convinced our single was not being properly rotated at radio stations. Moreover, we learned Motown was not promoting our song at all. We started to feel like we had made a mistake by signing with Motown. The feeling was worse than when the boys signed to Source Records. It all began to make perfect sense. It was true what Addye had shared with me before I left California headed back to Michigan. Our managers were not getting anywhere with Motown.

A month or so dragged by, and we were ready to return to Grand Rapids. The decision to leave Washington, DC, would not be cut and dry. It was left to El and me to figure out what we were going to do about our career moving forward. It was evident Motown was shelving our album. We had left California, but now realized we had made a mistake. Now, we wanted to return. Unfortunately, we had to get out of Washington, DC, and away from our management. We needed to get a plan together and get in touch with Motown. The group no longer wanted management to negotiate on our behalf—we would do the negotiating ourselves. We had to know what was going on and what was needed to repair our relationship with Motown. Addye was my contact person at Motown, but I had not talked to her since returning to Grand Rapids. I knew I could call on her in my time of need. Although embarrassed about the soured relationship between the group, Motown, and our management, I needed to let Addye know we have now realized our mistake. Motown had a problem with our management company, and they were not promoting our album as a result. We wanted out of the management contract, and I was confident Addye would steer us in the right direction.

Addye was glad to hear my voice. She scolded me for not keeping in touch. I apologized then told her we were in trouble again. We had signed a contract that failed to work in our best interest. Addye stated

Mr. Gordy had been willing to come out of retirement to work in a management capacity. However, we disappointed him when we jumped the gun and signed with outside management. She then explained Motown was always leery about working with outside management—especially when it came to new artists.

"This cannot happen to us, Addye," I said with desperation in my voice. There was no way I was going to allow a bad management deal to destroy everything we had worked so hard to achieve. "We're going to have to find a way to get out of this contract. El and I are looking for a way to void the contract. We realize we made a mistake."

I could tell by Addye's tone she thought it would be impossible to terminate the management contract. I knew we were going to have an uphill battle getting out of the management deal. With Source Records, all it took was a simple request. Tiger Flower would be a bit more daunting. However, I refused to give up. I promised Addye I would be back in touch with her once we were out of the management deal with Tiger Flower.

CHAPTER 13

WE CAN DO THIS

WE HAD RETURNED TO GRAND Rapids, and El was now staying at my house. Together, we studied the Tiger Flower Management contract ad nauseam. We were hoping to find one word in the fine print we could use to our advantage. There had to be an ace in the hole to help void the contract. With our lack of industry experience, searching for a breach in the contract was like looking for a needle in a haystack. Deciphering the terms of a legal agreement was not something we knew how to do.

By now, Tiger Flower was no longer doing their job as our manager. In fact, they were avoiding our calls altogether. It was time to take charge of this matter. We needed none other than the wisdom from the Divine One. As I started to pray, El came rushing into my bedroom, excited. He had found a clause in the contract he felt we could use to make it null and void.

"Bunny," he stated, excited and out of breath. "It says right here in the contract they have forty-eight hours to get back in touch with us *after* we've sent them a certified letter stating our concerns with their management." Since our managers had been avoiding us for quite some time, El felt this could work. "We can send them a certified letter," he continued. "If they don't contact us within the period noted on the contract, then it will be null and void."

At first, I was not sure if he understood the clause. After reading it for myself, I stated, "Let's try it, El. You're right—it might work. I mean, it's our only hope right now."

El and I went on to write the letter. In the letter, we listed our concerns. If they chose to read the letter, there was no doubt in our minds they would take offense to it. We did not concern ourselves with their reaction because the letter was written with the sole purpose of offending. We wanted to know why they had not been in touch. We demanded to be made privy to the conversations regarding Motown's lack of cooperation. We demanded a call immediately upon receipt of the letter. We reiterated once again the importance of communicating all aspects of our career with us. Our concerns were outlined for them in writing. We hoped they would ignore the letter the same way they were ignoring our calls.

We sent the letter via FedEx and requested they obtain a signature upon receipt. Once we were notified through FedEx's tracking system that Tiger Flower had indeed received the letter, El and I kept close track as the hours passed. Just as we had hoped, they failed to respond. A full forty-eight hours had passed, and still no word from our management. It was time for us to follow through with the second part of our plan. The next letter they would receive would be a letter of dismissal. El and I were sure that this time we would get a response. In the letter, we enclosed a copy of the contract and encircled the clause about the contract being null and void since they failed to respond to the previous certified letter within the specified timeframe.

It worked like a charm! Tiger Flower called us, fuming. However, there was nothing they could do at this point except release us from the management deal. The contract also stated they had a certain amount of time to provide us with a release. Two weeks passed before we finally received the papers stating they had dismissed us from the contract. We were thrilled! Just think, all it took was a little brainstorming and a lot of favor from the Lord. We were shooting in the dark, but we had faith it would work. Now it was time to inform Addye. There had to be something she could do for us to help us get back in the good graces at Motown. I was not sure if Addye would believe we were released from the Tiger Flower contact. Thankfully, I had the papers to prove otherwise. It took a minute to get in touch with her, but I finally prevailed.

"How did you guys do that?" were the first words from her mouth. I spoke with pride while explaining to her the steps El and I took to make sure the management team terminated our contract. "Well, it worked," she stated. "I tell you what, the Heavenly Father up there loves you DeBarges."

"Yesssss!" I proclaimed loudly. I could not have agreed with her more. "Addye," I began, changing the subject. "I need to get to Mr. Gordy. Maybe I can write him a letter of apology. Can you make sure he gets it?"

Addye paused for a second then hemmed and hawed for a good minute. I could tell she was not quite sure if she wanted to get involved. "Oh, Bunny, I don't know about this," she stated. "I mean, this *is* Mr. Gordy you're talking about, dear one." Her voice sounded uncertain. Refusing to become discouraged, I kept right on pressing her until she relented. I felt as though GOD had gotten us out of the contract. He did not bring us this far to leave us hanging.

After giving it some thought, Addye stated, "I tell you what, let me pray on this while you go ahead and write your letter. I'm having lunch with Edna, Mr. Gordy's secretary, tomorrow (the late Edna Anderson-Owens). Maybe I can mention you guys to her and see where her head is these days. I want to read the letter first, though. I want to see what you're saying before I stick my neck out there. I will look to the Lord to guide me on what to say. I'm telling you, Ms. DeBarge, you guys are something else. I'll call you after lunch." I could sense the sincerity in Addye's heart. Even though she thought we were a mess, she had become very fond of the DeBarge family.

After talking with Addye, I felt much calmer. I knew once we had her on our side, there was no turning back. Addye was good at getting the job done. She just had to figure out how to get Edna to report back to Mr. Gordy. I rushed to tell El the plan. I would write Mr. Gordy a heartfelt letter explaining we had no idea he wanted to be involved personally in our careers. I would tell him the truth from start to finish—we thought we were making the right move by signing with outside management. Had we known any different, it would have never happened. I had no intentions of mentioning Bobby suggesting we sign with outside management. I was not crazy!

El thought it was an excellent idea. He left writing the letter to me. "You will know how to put it," he said. "GOD will give you the words." El and I joined hands and agreed GOD would give me the right words to say, and Mr. Gordy would have the heart to read and accept our apology.

We wanted so badly to return to Los Angeles—and soon. We learned a huge lesson moving away from California. Signing with outside management was not our only misstep. It was also the wrong move when we returned to Grand Rapids. Our business dealings were in LA. Grand Rapids was too far and complicated our input. Plus, it would be expensive going back and forth between Grand Rapids and LA. We were not established in our careers to venture elsewhere. We needed to be back in California where we could go to Motown on any given day. We did not need to take a group vote to know LA was the place we would call home.

Addye kept her word and called me the following day. Lunch with the chairman's secretary, Edna, had gone quite well. She mentioned to Edna that the DeBarges were no longer under contract with outside management and how I wanted to write a personal letter of apology to Mr. Gordy. To Addye's surprise, Edna responded in our favor. She thought it was a great idea and assured Addye she would get the letter to him. I was elated! Edna was going to help us. However, Addye warned me we were not out of the woods just yet. She kept reiterating Edna could not promise Mr. Gordy would respond. She was willing to put in a good word to Mr. Gordy on our behalf, nonetheless. Edna believed it would be worth a try. If nothing else, the DeBarges were now free from Tiger Flower Management. The phone call from Addye was music to my ears. That night, I sat down and wrote a letter from my heart to Mr. Gordy.

***

Everyone was packed, ready to head back to Los Angeles. The boys were the first to leave. This time, we included James in our travels. There was no way were we leaving him behind. James was adamant about joining the group, and he was not taking no for an answer this time. I could not wait to get back to California—not only to deliver the letter to Mr. Gordy but also to see Bobby and Tommy. Great things were happening for my brothers. Bobby had bought a house in the San Fernando Valley. He invited all of us to stay with him until we found places of our own. This was Bobby's good news. Tommy had even better news. He and Duckie, who lived in an apartment not too far from Bobby, were expecting. I was so happy for them. Mark was the first to *make* me an aunt then El. Tommy and Duckie made me feel like an aunt for the first time. Duckie and I had formed a close relationship. I was determined to be there to support her throughout the pregnancy.

Once again, I was on a roll and making big plans. As soon as I arrived in California, my mission was to get the letter to Mr. Gordy. Upon our arrival, I made an appointment to see Addye the following day. Addye was happy to see me and promised to get the letter to Edna. I gave her Bobby's phone number and told her I would await her call.

Meanwhile, we were all looking for places to stay. Bobby had a big house to accommodate us, but he needed privacy. We all wanted our own space as well. He was now living with his lover—a guy also named Tony. It was apparent they were close—maybe a little too close for everyone's comfort. His personal life and indulgences were much different from ours. Bobby seemed to be living on the wild side. This made me very concerned. Word had gotten out in the family that Bobby and Tommy had started using cocaine. Bobby was able to hide his use a little better than Tommy. He refrained from using drugs until after work. This way, he could still perform while in the studio. Bobby was pretending to be in a happy place in life. He did not fool me. He was my brother, and I knew him very well. I could tell he was struggling with his lifestyle and was again using drugs. Even if I had not witnessed him indulging in the behavior with my own eyes, his demeanor portrayed all the signs of an escalating drug use. Bobby, who was already aggressive, was more aggressive than usual. Every little provocation set him off, and his reactions always seemed to go a little bit too far.

Bobby was a master at camouflaging unlike Tommy. Tommy was the opposite. He was an open book. Basically, Tommy had no shame in his game—what you see is what you get. There were days when Tommy would be out there in the streets using drugs, and no one knew his whereabouts. Duckie would be left home alone and pregnant. I had been in the drug scene during my high school days. Even though I was not there witnessing Tommy using in the streets, I knew enough to be frightened for him. Watching what drugs were doing to my brothers, I did not want to follow in their footsteps. The only thing my husband and I did at this time was smoke marijuana. We convinced ourselves it was a natural drug that came from the earth. I was not a heavy smoker, though. In fact, I would only take a puff then pass it along. Every time I indulged, I ended up with regret. It never mellowed me out. Rather, it had the opposite effect. It reminded me of the day when I was in the park and saw the demon.

I understood why Tommy seemed so self-destructive. Bobby barely used him in the studio, and this bothered him a great deal. Whenever I would see Tommy, it seemed to be the only thing he wanted to discuss. Bobby's rejection was killing him. One might think it was due to his escalating drug problem why Bobby shunned him in the studio. I knew better. Them acting like bitter enemies was nothing new. The problems started long before Tommy's deep descent into drugs and self-destruction. Bobby did not have the level of patience needed to collaborate with Tommy inside the studio. Also, Tommy was better as a live bass player. He thrived and came alive musically during live performances. Rather than take Tommy under his wing inside the studio and train him, Bobby chose to use studio musicians instead. This hurt Tommy to his core, and he who would often cry to me about Bobby's indifference.

Tommy had songs he had written. He just needed Bobby's help to finish them. Bobby always made promises to help him but never found the time. Bobby may not have been ignoring Tommy on purpose. I believed he wanted to help finish Tommy's songs. However, there was a lot of pressure and responsibility placed on Bobby's shoulders from Motown. Bobby also wanted to have a higher level of involvement with our group. He was overextended, and this left little time for anything else. Tommy's songs were subsequently placed on the back burner.

My heart went out to Tommy. After all, he was my brother too. I knew what he said about Bobby's treatment of him was true. Tommy felt cheated. They were brothers, and there was no reason for Bobby to treat him like he treated his other bandmates. Reeling from the hurt because of the relationship he and Bobby shared, Tommy chose to drown his pain by getting high. Tommy was an all-or-nothing type of person. When he indulged in drugs, he went all out. It was a recipe for disaster. The two brothers never resolved their conflict from childhood, and I was always there to stop their arguments and fights. Bobby was very domineering over Tommy; Tommy was always fighting Bobby for his respect. I was determined that this battle was not going to continue and needed to talk to Bobby about how he was hurting Tommy. Something had to change between the two brothers. I had to find the perfect timing, or Bobby would go off. Regardless, confronting Bobby about his treatment of Tommy was bound to result in a heated conversation. It always did whenever it concerned Bobby and any of the brothers for that matter. Nevertheless, I had to decide if I wanted a conversation with him that was heated but he still listened *or* a conversation that was heated and resulted in him exploding. Bobby thought he was king of the DeBarges—above reproach and rebuke. I must say this was pretty much the truth. In the end though, I was tired of how he was affecting Tommy and had every intention of letting him know.

Exploring his bisexuality, Bobby entered a domestic partnership with Tony. Although Bobby cared less what we thought, we were trying hard to understand. Not only was he and Tony an item, but he also had a female in his life he was very fond of and loved very much. We later learned the female was Latoya Jackson. They talked often and sometimes would go on dates. I began to pray that Bobby and Latoya's relationship would blossom. Being raised with a strict religious upbringing, I felt this relationship was better suited for him. I did not agree with nor did I understand the lifestyle he had chosen with Tony. It went against everything we had been taught in church.

Bobby had met Latoya through Jermaine, and it appeared to be love at first sight. He adored her and talked a lot about wanting to settle down and have a life with her. I remember the first time Bobby called and introduced Janet to the family. He was together with Latoya, and Janet was tagging along. Bobby wanted to introduce Janet to Chico who had a major crush on the burgeoning star. Chico was thrilled to be talking to the little girl who played Penny on the sitcom *Good Times*. I applauded Bobby for spending time with Latoya and hoped they would eventually become a couple. The more time they spent together, the more I became hopeful. For now, I had better things to focus on than Bobby's personal life.

***

"I Call Your Name" topped the R&B charts. The success of the hit song caused Bobby to garner much respect within the company including with Mr. Gordy. I believe the success of the song also had a lot to do with the chairman forgiving us so fast. It was not long after I took the letter to Addye we were in his office for a meeting. Mr. Gordy had a new group of people he wanted us to meet. He referred to them as his team. The team included Tony Jones, Suzanne De Passé, and Suzanne Coston. He introduced them as the management team who would accompany him in directing our career. At the time, we knew nothing about either person. We soon learned that Susanne De Passé had played a significant role in building and directing the Jackson 5's career. Tony Jones was Ms. De Passé's cousin, and Suzanne Coston worked alongside them both. Ms. De Passé and Mr. Jones would serve as our managers while Mr. Gordy would oversee everything else concerning our career. As we signed the new contract, it was a good opportunity to pull James into the group. With everything falling into place, we changed our group name from the DeBarges to DeBarge.

Mr. Gordy was ready to get back to work. He wanted new material from us. Our first album was a bust and indeed a learning experience.

Mr. Gordy wanted to put it all behind us and start anew. We did not dwell on our first album failing. We were just glad to be back in the good graces of the company. We were set up with the best in the industry to guide our careers—the chairman himself and De Passé-Jones management. We trusted Mr. Gordy wholeheartedly with our careers. Being under new management, things began happening fast. It was like a whirlwind. Management kept us busy and moving in the right direction. It was great because DeBarge had lots of energy and needed something constructive to take up our time. We were blessed to finally be able to do what we had prayed for all this time—to sing and have careers as Motown artists. Now it was time to go back into the studio to work on our second album!

Suzanne DePasse management   *Berry Gordy*

Call Your Name   *Bobby & Latoya Jackson*

Suzanne Coston management

CHAPTER 14

DEBARGE

My husband Tony and I found an apartment on Coldwater Canyon Avenue in the well-known Sun Valley area of Los Angeles and enrolled my girls in school. They were growing up fast. Damea was now eight years old, and Janae was six years old. Neither had the slightest inclination they were living a life most children could only dream. I often took them along with me to many DeBarge functions. Their after-school activities consisted of viewing our rehearsals, accompanying us to the studio, and going to photo sessions instead of traditional play dates. Along with us, they were meeting various stars in the industry. The only difference was they were too young to be excited about these opportunities. Yes, being among the stars became a normal way of life for my girls.

The first song we worked on in the studio was entitled "Stop! Don't Tease Me." Even though we were known for our ballad writing, El wanted to show Motown we could produce up-tempo songs as well. It was crazy because all they heard was the rhythm track to the song and loved it! Amazed by the production quality of the track, Mr. Gordy entrusted El to produce the remainder of the album. However, it was a formality for a Motown music professional to be involved in the creative process of all signed artists. Though we had been given creative control, we were still new artists and new to the industry. Motown felt it was best to have a knowledgeable Motown representative readily available

for consultation whenever El needed their expertise. He was bound to get stuck when it came down to the business aspect. They sent in Iris Gordy, the chairman's niece, to assist El. Iris listened to what we had already created. She believed we needed to go in a different musical direction on this album and hired two songwriters—Curtis Nolen and Raymond Crossley—to produce one of their songs for us entitled "Can't Stop."

I was so proud watching El work his magic. There was no doubt in my mind my brother had a God-given musical talent that would bring this project home. In fact, neither of my brothers had any formal training in music. They all learned to play their respective instruments by ear. We did not even know how to read music! It did not matter because they proved their ability to play with the top musicians in the industry.

With the help of Iris Gordy, El was able to hire studio musicians whom we had long idolized. Musicians such as Russell Ferrante for keyboards and Benjamin Wright for strings were among those selected to accompany El inside the studio. We held these musicians in such high regard and never thought in a million years we would have the pleasure of meeting and performing with them. We had become fans of theirs after hearing their undeniable talent on many other artists' albums. Another talented musician joined El in the studio—Ready Freddie Washington, a bass player who played with Patrice Rushen. It was amazing to watch El in the recording room interacting with the musicians. He proved himself to be a self-motivated keyboard player and earned much respect for his abilities. Although he was now playing and producing with big names in the music industry, El remained graceful and humble. I must say my brother was a natural. They soon discovered that "Little El DeBarge" was a master at his craft.

The guitar players made up the rhythm section. They included Charles Ferring and Robben Ford. Ricky Lawson was on drums, and Ollie Brown was on percussions. They were the ones to hold the beat. I knew Ricky Lawson (the Yellow Jacket Klan) personally. I had met him at Cooley High School in Detroit, Michigan, where my cousin Joanie attended. Ricky and Joanie were in the school choir together. When I visited her school, I got the chance to meet him and watch this talented young man play the drums. Now here he was contributing drum tracks. What a small world! After the rhythm tracks were approved, Motown was eager to hear our vocals, and we were prepared to get back into the studio and prove ourselves. We were given a second chance and intended to make the most of this opportunity.

The new sound on the rhythm tracks would be a challenge for the group. We did not work in the typical harmony. We heard the notes differently, which led to our own unique sound. We kept this in mind as we wrote lyrics for the rhythm tracks. It was important for us all to play a part in the creation of the songs that graced our album. Everyone was required to bring a song to the table. If it was not finished, El and I made sure we had the right musical concept and lyrics to help complete each song. It did not matter to us about the credits or who contributed what to the song. Each person just had to have their own song on the album.

El and I worked diligently to make sure everyone contributed to the creative process. Of course, it was a task keeping Mark focused and ensuring he contributed. It was not as if Mark lacked the talent and ability to create hit songs. However, his free-spirited nature caused him to become easily distracted and drift off into his own little world. With this in mind, it was important for us to maintain a positive attitude when recording. Bobby taught us that our mood while recording would show up on the tracks. "No matter if you're mad, sad, gloomy, or glad, your listeners will hear it," he often stated. At this point in the game, DeBarge had unity based on our strong family bond. Plus, we were on one accord as it related to the vision for our career. Our love for one another showed up as magic on our tracks.

Mark's contribution to the album was a song entitled "I'm in Love with You." He had the foundation set, the title of the song selected, and the lyrics for the hook. The concept was there lyric-wise but needed further development. It was quite jazzy at first since Mark was very much into jazz music. El commercialized the melody, and I helped Mark with the lyrics.

Randy came to the table with a song entitled "I Like It." Being the bass player of the group, he had pretty much developed the bass line and melody. Again, the concept was there, but he needed help developing the lyrics. I would eventually bring the song home lyric-wise. After discussing the direction of the song, we felt it needed a bridge. El and I came up with the melody for the bridge. I went on to write the bridge lyrics to go with the melody. Little did I know the lyrics to the bridge would go on to be quoted and sung by many to this very day: *I like the way you comb your hair. I like the stylish clothes you wear. It's just the little things you do that show how much you really care*, and so on. We had no idea the magic we had created with this song but would soon find out.

James, the baby of the group, contributed "I'll Never Fall in Love Again." Unlike Mark and Randy, James had written his song from start to finish. It meant so much for James to present himself as being just as capable as his big brothers Bobby and El to produce. He wanted to prove himself as a great producer. All the song needed was the background added. His persistence and the time spent writing songs had paid off, and we were all proud of his contribution to the album.

I presented a song inspired by GOD entitled "Life Begins with You." It was a story straight from the heart and had a lot to do with what I was going through in my personal life. I wrote from the experience of a woman coming out of a bad love affair and finding someone who made her life feel brand-new. El loved the melody and produced the song. I loved how as a family we could work so well together. We added little nuances to each other's song. It was the DeBarge Sound, and it was magic! After the background was completed, it was time to do the coloring of the song, which was adding the strings. We sang a rough vocal so Benjamin Wright could arrange the parts for the strings and horns. The way he arranged the music, the strings would play around our vocals and compliment the song. We learned that making a hit was like telling a story and that the instruments helped to accentuate the story.

The creativity poured into each song was done in a loving manner. As the creative process unfolded, we become comfortable working in the studio in various capacities. Any insecurities we felt were replaced with confidence in our God-given talent. It was magical! We loved the hard work put into creating our music and all it entailed. We still found time for fun while recording. Working on our second album made us almost forget about the songs we lost on our first album. Although we loved those songs and wished we had a better outcome with the album, we refused to cry over spilled milk. There was no reason to look back. We forged ahead, and our growth on the second album was evident. The album communicated how we had many other songs inside of us just waiting to be released.

Iris Gordy fell in love with us, and the feeling was mutual. She was a very inspiring presence in our lives both inside and outside of the studio. She helped us improve in numerous ways especially when it came to work on our vocals—including our lead vocals. There were times we needed a little encouragement. Iris had the uncanny ability to pull out of us what was needed on a song. El still was not confident doing ad libs even though Bobby was still teaching them to him. He did not want to duplicate what he felt Bobby did so well. Motown already had a Bobby DeBarge, he reasoned. El, wanting to carve out his own lane, wanted to sound different. Iris just laughed at him and said, "Boy, you're Bobby's little brother. Be *glad* you sound like him! Hit those high notes, boy, because you can! Now you get in there and bring these songs home!" This put El at ease and gave him the confidence needed on each song.

Once the songs were finished, they were taken to Mr. Gordy and Artist Relations for approval. Now it was time to pick a single. Mr. Gordy thought the song "Stop! Don't Tease Me" was the one. I was shocked because either "I Like It" or "All This Love" were my choices. Who was I to say anything? At this point, it was all on the company. They wanted this album to act as our first. Mr. Gordy had big plans for introducing DeBarge to the world. Feeling as though the song needed a little more lyrical work, Mr. Gordy called in a guy named Bruce Fisher to help. El returned to the studio to sing his lead again, and they worked the song until Mr. Gordy felt it was a hit.

Our managers were very much involved in the day-to-day process of getting us ready for the song's release. They took us to different places to eat so they could monitor our table manners. They practiced mock interviews with us so we would feel comfortable with public speaking. They also watched how we carried ourselves overall and provided feedback to help polish our image. What they failed to realize was DeBarge refused to be tamed. We acted silly and cracked jokes. Once we caught on to what they were doing, we got a kick out of making them think we had no table manners. Whenever we ate chicken, we picked it up with our fingers. We refused to cut it with a knife and fork. Our mission was to watch them sweat—and boy, did they sweat! It was not an easy task for them to deal with DeBarge as they soon discovered.

Then there were the interviews. Mark was the unpredictable one. No one knew what was going to come out of his mouth. It seemed as if he relished getting on everyone's nerves. He would make the wildest and weirdest statements just to watch the facial expressions of those around him. Whenever Randy and James were asked a mock question, they would immediately turn their heads toward me and El. The managers decided El and I would do the interviews. We seemed more at ease than Randy and James and able to follow the script unlike Mark. Even though we got a kick out of being a little passive with our stuffy management, we loved working with them. It was much different than working with Tiger Flower.

Things seemed to be rolling right along. We were dubbed "Berry Gordy's Little Protégés." There were rumblings around the office we were the next Jackson 5. The only thing I knew was things were happening way too fast. Susanne De Passé worked closely with us the same way she had worked with the Jackson 5. She was a taskmaster. Tony Jones kept in close contact with us almost daily. If he did not call us, someone else from the management team did. They wanted to be sure we did nothing to taint our public image. We were reminded how important the public eye was to our success. DeBarge was on their way to the top!

Raymond Crossley   *Ricky Lawson Drummer*

Curtis Nolen   *Iris Gordy*

Charles Fearing guitar player

Debarge in studio

Bobby

Switch on Soul Train - The Best Beat in town!

CHAPTER 15

THE START OF SOMETHING BIG

WE WERE AMONG THE LEGENDS! Being in the mix of Motown stars we grew up admiring was a mind-blowing experience. Not only were we meeting established stars—we were forming relationships with the newcomers as well. Bobby was so proud of all the positive things happening for the group. Even though he was busy with Switch, he kept a close eye on his brothers and sister. Like always, Big Bro was very protective of us and wanted the best for the group. After a few false starts, our lives looked promising, and careers were finally on the rise. We were grateful our younger siblings—Chico, Carol, and Darrell— had something positive to look up to and follow.

You could not tell us we had not arrived. Our images now hung on the walls in the Motown lobby, being admired by those who visited. What an achievement! DeBarge was in the music industry and making waves. As for Switch? Well, they were not missing a beat either. "I Call Your Name" was climbing the charts, and nearly every R&B magazine in publication featured Switch on its cover or within its pages. The best part was getting together as a family, turning on the television, and watching Switch perform either on *Soul Train* or another television dance show. Our homes were filled with lots of laughter during this time. GOD knows we deserved it after all we had gone through. Bobby was a stride ahead of us, but he unselfishly showed us the appropriate steps to take in our next phase. Our big brother might not have been in our group, but he was leading the way. We followed him with hopes of one day banding together as one larger group.

***

Switch was preparing to go on the road again. Bobby decided to throw a farewell party. I was at his home the night before, helping prepare for the festivities. It was going to be epic! Bobby always threw the best parties. He had invested in a soundproof two-car garage. It was the perfect place to blast music and dance without disturbing the neighbors. I knew the perfect album for the occasion. Michael Jackson had just released *Off the Wall*, and I needed to get to Tower Records to pick it up. I also needed to make a run to the store to get some last-minute items Bobby forgot. He told us he needed to make a run to the city, so we decided to ride together. We had no idea why Bobby needed to go into the city nor did we question it. We were all in party mode, which meant anything goes. Besides, it was another opportunity to hang with Big Bro before he went on the road.

Bobby suggested we take his car. Tony (my husband) and I glanced nervously at each other because we were no stranger to Bobby's driving. In fact, we were downright terrified of his driving. If Bobby drove, it was bound to be a very wild and dangerous ride. Tony volunteered to take the wheel, but Bobby insisted he had everything under control. We whispered a quick prayer underneath our breath then braced ourselves for what was about to come. Bobby, already a hyperactive person when he was not driving, became worse when he was behind the wheels of a car. There were many times when riding with Bobby my feet would cramp up from subconsciously slamming on imaginary brakes I wished were on the passenger side! It was already rush hour before we left, and Bobby was completely void of patience. It would be nothing for him to move onto the shoulder of the freeway and ride it the entire way until he reached his exit. He would be cursing and blowing the horn the entire time. Tony and I knew we had a dramatic forty-five-minute roller-coaster ride ahead of us.

Bobby was driving like a madman! I closed my eyes and braced myself as he sped past cars and moved in and out of traffic with inches to spare. People were blowing their horns, and he was hurling insults in response. As part of our training at Motown, we were taught deep breathing exercises. They were not working! I was in panic mode so my breathing was shallow. I could barely catch my breath and just wanted the ride to be over. As I think back to the many times I endured Bobby's erratic driving, I can only laugh. It was classic Bobby DeBarge, and he never changed.

Once we arrived in LA, I figured out we were on one of Bobby's drug runs. We exited the freeway in the heart of the ghetto at Crenshaw and Adams—an area known for its drug activity. You could sense a spiritual shift in the atmosphere as we continued down the street. The streetscape became very sketchy. Whereas we had experienced people having fun and full of life on Sunset, the people we were seeing now were different. They appeared guarded and suspicious. A spirit of fear swept over me, and I knew we had to watch our backs and be on guard. It was not long before Bobby parked his car and said, "I'll be right back." My eyes stayed glued to our surroundings, but I dared not make eye contact.

As Bobby approached the house, people were seen leaving. Bobby entered the house along with a few other people. Thankfully, it did not take long for him to cop what he needed. Before long, he was back in the car and driving like a bat out of hell to our next destination. I wanted to go ahead and get to Tower Records and the grocery store. However, we needed gas and cigarettes and ended up stopping at a nearby gas station. Bobby gave Tony money to pay for gas. He told me to remain in the car, which was fine with me. I did not need the aggravation of sticking out like a sore thumb. While Tony was in the store paying for gas, Bobby dug into his pocket and pulled out a small packet. "This shit is supposed to be *the shit*," he told me, shaking the packet. "Hold this."

Bobby handed me the packet then proceeded to exit the car and pump the gas. The packet held a powdery substance with little lumps.

Right away, I knew it was cocaine. I had never gone on a drug run with Bobby before and had never seen him do cocaine. What I did learn of Bobby's drug use came from Tommy. Bobby and Tommy were always accusing the other of heavily using drugs. They would confide in me and tell what was going on in the other person's life. Telling on each other stemmed from our childhood. Between Bobby, Tommy, and myself, there was never a secret between us.

Bobby started the gas pump then jumped back into the car. Tony entered after him. I watched as Bobby pulled down the sun visor, took out a mirror, and set it on the seat between us. "Bunny, look in the glove compartment and hand me the little straw and razor," he commanded. As I proceeded to do as he asked, Tony hopped out of the car again to hang up the gas pump. When he returned to the car, Bobby drove to the other side of the gas station and parked near the bathrooms. "Watch for me," he stated.

As I looked around to see if anyone was watching, Bobby poured out some of the white powder onto the mirror and started separating it into lines with the razor. He then sniffed the cocaine through the straw and held his head back. "Here," he stated, pinching his nose as he handed me the mirror and the straw with his free hand. "Just sniff one line—half up one nostril and half up the other."

I took the mirror from his hand but did not indulge right away. My eyes were glued to Bobby. I needed to see his reaction first. It was not like I had never done drugs before—cocaine was not one of them. Therefore, I had no idea what the high would feel like. "Go on, try it. It's only going to numb you up. You will like it," Bobby promised. I could see his mood changing, and he was much calmer now than earlier. I put the straw to my nose and snorted. Afterward, I handed Tony the mirror.

"You will feel it drain in a minute," Bobby stated. "It's going to make you sing like never before. It's a happy, uplifting high. You will like it." As Bobby was talking, I felt the cocaine draining in my throat. It had a numbing effect as it dissolved. It did not take long for paranoia to set in. I began thinking to myself: *Oh my GOD! Has it numbed my vocal cords? Can I speak? Can I sing?* Fearful I would not be able to speak or sing, I started talking for the sake of talking. "How is it supposed to make me feel, Bobby?" I asked. "Just numb? Is that it? Is that all I'm going to feel?" I was spitting out question after question and going on and on about nothing, really. "I don't like this. I mean, shouldn't I be feeling something else?" I realized I was talking to myself. Bobby and Tony were not answering back. I did not even realize the car was now in motion. Bobby, fully engaged in his thoughts, ignored my rambling. He put a tape in the car stereo and started bouncing to the music. He then began to sing and sounded better than the music he was playing! Every note he sang was crystal clear. *Okay, this is it,* I thought. *I'm supposed to be able to sing my butt off, let Bobby tell it. So, let's try this.* I started singing along with him, but it felt as if the numbness in my throat was preventing me from hitting any notes. It started to feel awkward, and I was not proud of the way I sounded.

"Hey, Bobby," I began. "I thought I would be able to sing like never before. I can't sing at all. My throat is numb." Tony just laughed. "What's so funny?" I turned around and asked him, a bit perturbed he found my dilemma amusing. "Can you feel it? Is your throat numb? Hit a note, Tony. Come on, let's hear you sing." Tony could tell I was serious, and it tickled him even more.

"Yes, baby, I'm numb. Believe me, you are singing like never before," he stated while folded over in laughter. "Now could you be quiet for a minute?"

Bobby began to laugh as well. "That's what I meant by *singing*, Bunny. Listen how you are running your mouth. You are singing, nut!" I felt silly—but not silly enough to stop talking. Maybe it was the high making me run my mouth incessantly—except no one else seemed to have diarrhea of the mouth.

Not understanding I was experiencing a cocaine-induced high, I continued to badger Bobby because I wanted him to hear me and feel exactly what I was saying. "I don't feel nothing but numb, Bobby."

Bobby looked over at me and said, "You feel it, Bunny. You just don't know it, and you probably won't know the difference until you come down." I did realize I was high based on my behavior and racing thoughts. I had many questions running through my mind—specifically about where my brothers were in their addiction. Tommy had been gone for days. We were not sure if he would show up in time for the band to leave. Bobby lamented about Tommy's addiction. Whenever he complained of Tommy's addiction, he suggested having his own addiction under control. This could not have been any farther from the truth. Sadly, both of my brothers were in deep trouble. Bobby was just better at disguising his than Tommy.

I began questioning Bobby about what he liked so much about this drug to keep coming back for more. I suppose my curiosity got the best of me. I promised myself once I came down off this high, I would never use cocaine again. One of my biggest lessons in life is learning to never say *never*!

During the ride home, Bobby began speaking to me with candor. "As for me, Bunny, tonight is my last night. I'm cracking my pipe. It's controlling my life. I figure being on the road will be a good thing for me. I can concentrate on my music, my work . . .," his voice trailed off. I knew snorting cocaine was not Bobby's preference. He preferred smoking it. Snorting cocaine was something he did until he could cook the powder into rock form. He started singing as I sat back and closed my eyes. I listened to the angels dance on his vocal cords. My brother truly had the voice of an angel.

We stopped at Tower Records, and I bought new music for the party. Bobby snorted more of the coke in the parking lot as he waited. He offered Tony and I another line, but I did not indulge. My high was over, and I did not care for snorting the drug. On the other hand, I was curious about the drug. A part of me felt the need to know how he smoked powder—or freebase as Bobby called it.

By the time we returned to Bobby's home, I felt back to normal. The numbness in my nose and throat had worn off. I ran straight to the garage to play my *Off the Wall* album. The party was supposed to start the next night. I guess you can say it started for us as soon as the needle hit the record.

***

It was getting late when Tony and I decided it was time to depart. It dawned on me that Bobby had pretty much been antisocial since our return. He had secluded himself in his bedroom. The process of cooking the cocaine and turning it into rock form took a while so Tony and I thought nothing of Bobby isolating himself. We simply left him to his own devices. I did not mind him becoming distant since I had Michael Jackson's newest release to keep me company. When we were younger and Bobby expressed not wanting to be bothered, I usually just left him alone. However, I decided to interrupt his melancholy mood to check in with him and announce we were leaving for the night.

From the outside looking in, Bobby seemed to have it all. He was at the height of his career. His voice was known inside many households. He was favored by Mr. Gordy, making him one of Motown's most beloved artists. To me, he was simply my brother albeit one who was deeply troubled and trying hard to deal with his internal torment. He had accomplished so much and overcome so many obstacles. For this alone, I looked up to him and turned a blind eye to his self-destruction. In fact, we all did. Perhaps viewing Bobby solely through the lens of his professional achievements caused me to believe he was in total control of his life—even though it was apparent he was overindulging in drugs and had a spiraling addiction.

I noticed Bobby standing in the kitchen gazing out the sliding glass door. A feeling of uneasiness swept over me. Although his back was turned, Bobby's demeanor did not radiate confidence. I knew where this was headed. My heart started breaking for my brother because I could sense he was suffering tremendously. He seemed tortured. I knew the feeling all too well. Bobby felt I was the only person he could talk to without fear of judgment. When he noticed me standing in the doorway, for the moment, we both reverted to the abused siblings in Detroit—the siblings who knew each other's thoughts without a word being spoken. The same demon we fought so hard to get rid of was the same demon we now shared. It first appeared in the form of our father. Now it had transformed itself into drugs. Bobby knew I could sense his anguish without knowing all the details.

"I'm sick of this," he stated, beginning to cry. His back was still turned to me. "This is destroying my life." When I looked in his hand, he was holding a glass pipe. Before I could respond, he slid open the glass door and stepped into the yard. He flung the glass pipe as far as he could. "Be gone from my life, Satan!" he cried out. "Go back to hell where you came from!"

Bobby was serious, and he was tired. He could see his reflection in the sliding door. I could see his reflection. He had to be unhappy with what was staring back. My emotions were all over the place. I hated seeing my brother desperate and sad, yet glad to witness this moment of awakening. I hoped he was finally serious about giving up drugs. Believing Bobby would be okay—and at least not using any more drugs for the night—Tony and I left.

Before driving home, Tony and I visited Duckie. She ended up spending the night at our place. Knowing we had a long day ahead of us because of the party, we slept in late the next morning. I was glad Duckie decided to come with us. She did not need to spend another night alone. It had now been three days and not a word from Tommy. I was beyond worried. My sentiments had no effect on Duckie. She seemed genuinely unbothered. I got the feeling she was used to Tommy's disappearing acts.

It was hard to fathom why Tommy seemed ungrateful to have Duckie in his life. She was a beautiful girl—inside and out. In fact, she was stunning. Duckie had beautiful medium-brown hair and hazel eyes, which complemented her auburn skin complexion. More than her outward appearance, she had a genuine and warm personality. Duckie had this natural charm that drew you in. She was personable and loved to talk. Duckie talked endlessly about Tommy and Bobby leaving to go back on the road with Switch. She was looking forward to it and felt it would be good for them to get away from the city—away from the drugs and influences holding them back. She felt unfamiliar territory would reignite their creative energy, and they could then concentrate on music and not getting high.

Duckie changed the subject and began talking about the baby. "If I have a boy, I'm going to name him after his father," she proudly stated. "We can call him Lil' Tommy." Throughout our conversation, she made no mention of Tommy's disappearance. Duckie was always a happy-go-lucky person and very easygoing. I did not mind her following me everywhere in the house talking about Tommy and making plans for the baby. I assumed she had a lot on her chest and needed someone to confide in. Regardless of what she was going through, she had big dreams for Tommy, herself, and their unborn child. Still, it made little sense why she was not at all concerned about Tommy knowing he could possibly be in trouble.

"Aren't you worried about Tommy at all, Duck?" I asked. Many people referred to her as Duckie, but I called her Duck.

My question must have caught her off guard. She took a second to consider her answer. Looking away, she shrugged her shoulders and stated, "Not really. Tommy knows he is leaving tomorrow. He'll be ready. He's not going to miss it. It's the only time he gets to play bass, you know." I was not sure if Duckie was trying to convince me or herself. She talked as if she were the only person who understood Tommy. I could feel the love she had for him and knew the feeling was mutual. Tommy may have had major problems in his life, but he was crazy about Duckie. Bobby was a different story altogether when it came to Tommy and Duckie's relationship. He could easily get himself worked up about a relationship that for all intents and purposes was none of his concern.

Bobby had major problems with Duckie's gentle handling of Tommy. He felt she was way too passive and often let Tommy off the hook too easy. In King Bobby's mind, he believed if Duckie only had a backbone and gave Tommy an ultimatum, he would straighten up *just like that*. I thought to myself, *Oh, the irony*. Who was Bobby DeBarge to talk anyway? He had zero patience with any and everybody—especially with Tommy. If Tommy even hinted at making a misstep, Bobby would fly off the handle. Inserting his constant unsolicited opinions into Tommy and Duckie's relationship was exhausting. I made up in my mind that at the right time, I was going to tell Bobby to have mercy on his brother. Coming from me, he would probably handle it a whole lot better than if Tommy simply told him to mind his business.

The party would be starting soon so I needed to head back over to Bobby's place. I gathered up the girls' belongings for the night, and off we went. When I pulled up to Bobby's home, I heard a heated discussion coming from inside. Upon entering the home, Bobby and Tommy were engaged in a full-blown verbal combat. Duckie rushed over and embraced Tommy. She seemed oblivious to the fact that Bobby and Tommy were at each other's throats. She was just happy to be reunited with Tommy. Bobby was scolding Tommy, and I listened for a minute, hoping to figure out the cause of their latest dustup.

"You're a fool!" Bobby yelled, getting in Tommy's face.

Tommy was not here for Bobby's verbal tirade. He decided to unleash on Bobby. "I'm not a kid anymore, Bobby! You refuse to see that, bro! That's my car and it's my business!" At this point, Duckie had questions written all over her face. I could see from the look in her eyes she really did not want to know the truth. Bracing herself for disappointment, she slowly asked, "Where's the Alfa Romeo, Tommy?"

"I loaned it to my friend, Duckie," he quickly replied. "I know what I'm doing. I'll get it back later." Duckie shut her eyes and slowly shook her head. She tried to speak but seemed at a loss for words.

"*Friend*, Tommy?" Bobby was incredulous. "You don't even know the man! He's a dope dealer, Tommy, and you did it for drugs!" Bobby looked around at us for approval.

Tommy was embarrassed. "Stay out of my business, Bobby! I'm a grown man!"

Duckie looked concerned. Even though she was emotional, she remained calm. "Is the car coming back, Tommy?" she asked.

Bobby was not letting up, and Tommy was doing his best to ignore him. He turned to Duckie. "Yes, Duckie. I told him to have it back in a couple of hours. He'll be back. I trust the dude."

Tommy's eyes caught mine, and I could tell he was embarrassed by the entire situation. Although I was fuming inside, I chose not to beat up on him any further—Bobby had done enough. Because of my disappointment, I did not have the right words to say to Tommy. Had I chosen to address the situation regarding the car, it would have come across all wrong. Therefore, I quickly changed the subject. "Tommy, you need to be getting yourself together to get out of here tomorrow," I stated, not batting an eye. I tried to be Tommy's *big sis* during these times. However, he made it quite difficult—if not impossible—to treat him like a grown man. I am sure my tone came across like a mother figure by how Tommy responded.

"I know, sis. That's why I'm here." He seemed defeated.

Duckie interjected. "Don't worry, Tommy. I packed your things already."

Tommy seemed relieved. "Good. That's my baby." They embraced each other and kissed.

Duckie took Tommy at his word. If he said the guy was returning the car in a few hours, she believed him. As a matter of fact, she was not upset about anything that had gone down. It did not seem to bother her that Tommy had loaned out his car in exchange for drugs. Maybe this was why Bobby felt she was too weak for Tommy. Her focus was on the fact Tommy had returned home safely and in one piece. She was with her man, the love of her life, and only this mattered. Duckie did not leave Tommy's side. She just followed him around the party the entire night.

Partygoers started arriving. The mood was set, and the tables overflowed with food, the drinks continued to pour, and the music was on full blast. Tony (my husband) had the meat going on the grill. Bobby had appointed me as the DJ for the night so my focus was on the music. I always had a passion for recording music to cassette tapes. As we prepared for the party, I recorded the music onto various cassette tapes. It was all planned out. I was saving the *Off the Wall* album for when the house filled up. It was the hottest new release, and I knew it would be appreciated. As soon as Michael Jackson's "Get on the Floor" started playing, the whole party erupted! Everyone was on the dance floor!

By now, the boys had arrived. Like always, they had their special way of bringing life to a party and attention to themselves. They were also trailed by a slew of groupies. The party was live. I went back and forth all night between Michael Jackson and Switch. Bobby had invited many influential people from Motown. The other members of Switch were also in attendance. We ate, drank, and danced all night.

Alcohol would not be the only indulgence of night. At some point in the evening, I looked over at Bobby, and he was torn up off something more than liquor. He had a cheesy grin plastered on his face. I was a bit jealous. Here I was DJ'ing, keeping the music going, and Bobby was sitting there mellowed out and laid-back. I caught him nodding off then scratching his nose. As the saying goes, curiosity killed the cat. I wanted to know what was up with Bobby. "What did you take?" I asked. "Why are you so out of it?"

Bobby looked up at me and tried to keep his eyes open. His words were slurring. "I needed something to calm me down. You know I've been up all night. I took some pills to relax me. I got Tommy some too. I think it will keep him out of trouble." I looked at Tommy who was behaving the same as Bobby. They both looked quite relaxed. "You want to try it?" Bobby offered. "I'll give you and Tony a pill. I took two, but all you will need is one. It will calm you down."

"A downer? Of course. That's more my speed. I need something to relax me." I accepted Bobby's offer. He reached into his pocket then handed me two pills. I walked over to Tony and handed him one. "Take it," I stated. "It's a downer. It will relax you." Tony and I had taken downers before and liked how they made us feel. We put the pill in our mouth and downed it with our drink. For the remainder of the night, we were relaxed. It could not have come at a better time. The party had me hyped up, and I needed to settle down. I never thought in a million years this would be the start of something big.

I was now on a destructive path whereas I ended up struggling with profound addiction for many, many years. In my mind, taking one little pill was just a part of the party atmosphere. It relaxed me. What harm could possibly come from being relaxed at a party? A party was thrown to either celebrate a milestone or to relax and wind down, right? Except *this* party changed my life in ways I could never have imagined. I was aboard a runaway train and was powerless to stop the conductor—Satan himself.

The party kept going until the wee hours of the morning. Eventually, the partygoers started leaving one by one. The music on the cassettes had ended, but those of us who remained broke out in chorus, singing "I Call Your Name." I enjoyed spending time with my brothers. Now, it was time to bid Tommy and Bobby farewell. They would be leaving the city in a few hours. I agreed with Duckie—my brothers needed a break from Los Angeles. Basically, they needed a break from the drugs controlling their lives.

Switch - I Call Your Name

Michael Jackson - Off The Wall

DeBarge - All This Love

CHAPTER 16

SOUL TRAIN, THE PROMOTIONAL TOUR, AND AMERICAN BANDSTAND

DeBarge was set to appear on *Soul Train*! Exciting, huh? Motown had dropped our single "Stop! Don't Tease Me," and it was doing well on the charts and on radio stations. The chairman (Mr. Gordy) and our management team (De Passé and Jones) had a strategy for how they planned to present DeBarge to the world. Wanting to give us a pep talk, Mr. Gordy contacted management and requested a meeting at his home. Our managers alerted us beforehand that Mr. Gordy would probably have us lip-synch the tracks so he could see how well we would perform. Our managers would be bringing video cameras so we would have actual footage of the meeting and feedback from Mr. Gordy recorded. The video moments would eventually become precious memories for us to view in years to come. It was never lost on us what a definite privilege it was to be invited to Mr. Gordy's home. Our managers made sure to drill this into our heads. There were artists within the company who had never met him in person—let alone be invited to his home. DeBarge, which was new to the company, was apparently getting special treatment beyond the norm.

It was early morning when the limo arrived to pick us up for the day's happenings. We had a long drive before we would arrive at Mr. Gordy's home. He lived in the hills in a mansion overlooking the city of Los Angeles. Upon our arrival, we were met by a tall iron gate that reminded me of medieval times. Our driver pressed a button on a big box to gain access. Wow! It felt as though we were entering another world. A voice transmitted through the intercom and gave us clearance. Once the gates opened, we proceeded along a long, winding road leading to the mansion on top of the hill.

Our eyes were overwhelmed at the sight of Mr. Gordy's home! We had never seen such a place. His home was breathtaking to say the least. Not only was there a main house, but there were also a beach house and guesthouse. We were led to the deck and captured views of the city. Afterward, we were led down to the yard. I spotted a pond filled with the most beautiful goldfish I had ever seen! There were many lush trees and beautiful flowers throughout the landscape. However, one tree stood out to my brothers and myself. The tree had two gorgeous parrots perched on its branches. I became fixated on the tree and the parrots. As I spent my time gawking at the parrots, the boys ventured off to the game room to play Donkey Kong on an arcade machine. I am pretty sure we could have spent all day exploring Mr. Gordy's mansion. However, we had work to do and had wasted enough time being mesmerized by our surroundings.

We made our way to the beach house to have our makeup done. The beach house was outfitted with a locker room where we got dressed. Our managers had gone out the day before and purchased a host of brightly colored outfits. As we were getting ready for what we later learned was a photo shoot, a decision was made for the outfits to be worn at our upcoming performance on *Soul Train*. Beginning at the pool, we posed for several pictures in designated areas throughout the mansion and landscape. Every area where we posed was exquisite and elegant—and we felt beautiful! The photos captured a talented, fresh young group full of energy.

The photo shoot was a long-drawn-out process. For the most part, we took everything in stride. Eventually, everything became a bit tedious and tiring. After all the touching up by the makeup artist and moving to different locations throughout the compound, we were physically and emotionally exhausted. Our energy had been depleted, and this was unlike any of us to get tired—even after a long day. The DeBarge clan was known for having lots of vigor. The managers could tell we were clearly exhausted. However, they wanted us to do one more picture scene. They promised we would be done afterward. I guess in order to get us to agree, they said this was *the chairman's idea*. According to our managers, Mr. Gordy wanted a picture of us in the tree with the parrots. We could have cared less about anything except not taking another picture! We had already taken what seemed to be a thousand pictures. Even though we were not happy campers, we did as we were told. However, we were fresh out of smiles. It is funny because the photo of us in the tree with the parrots was later chosen as a poster!

The cooks prepared lunch, and by this time, we had worked up quite an appetite. To our surprise, Jermaine and Hazel arrived and joined us for lunch. Mr. Gordy was pleasant but somewhat flat and monotone as he discussed plans for our *Soul Train* appearance. He wanted Jermaine to introduce us to the world. Jermaine would speak as if *he* had discovered *DeBarge*. We were a bit taken aback at first but chalked it up as simply a marketing strategy. However, this marketing strategy would later become a source of irritation for Bobby. He felt since we were his siblings, he should have been given the credit. As those around us made plans for our world debut, I could hear Bobby's voice playing over and over in my head: *How is Jermaine going to say he discovered MY brothers and sister?* It was a good thing Bobby was on the road during this time. We did not have a dog in the fight, and a final decision was made by Mr. Gordy and our management—Jermaine would be at *Soul Train* the following day to introduce us to the world.

Lunch was prepared and hit the spot. Shortly after we were done eating, Mr. Gordy wanted to see us perform. Now, DeBarge was not a dancing group, and we hoped there would be no expectations around this issue. We were not sure what management had shared with Mr. Gordy. However, if they had indicated we were singers *and dancers*, they were in for a huge surprise. Mr. Gordy wore a stoic look on his face. Therefore, we were unable to discern how he was feeling. I guess sensing that everyone was on edge, he finally broke through the nervous tension. He encouraged not only us but also management. "It's okay," he stated. "They'll do just fine. The world can watch them as they grow. Do your thing, DeBarge!"

DeBarge performed, and Mr. Gordy observed. It did not last long. The next thing we noticed was Mr. Gordy performing alongside the group! All the nervous tension disappeared, and we began to enjoy ourselves. It was the greatest part of the day—interacting musically with the chairman of Motown. He demonstrated some key moves he felt would work for us onstage, and the video camera captured every moment. Our day ended on a high note, and our confidence level was boosted. We were on our way to board the *Soooooul Train! Chicka! Chicka! Boom! Boom!*

***

Our first experience on *Soul Train* was a success. Mr. Gordy was correct—the audience loved us! Here we were, all dressed up performing our song "Stop! Don't Tease Me" on *Soul Train*. It was hard to believe, yet it was really happening. My wildest dreams and imagination were being played out right before my eyes. Most importantly, I had my brothers alongside me to share in those memories. Next, we performed "I Like It." Everything was going according to plan. Jermaine introduced us to the world, and Switch fans finally received clarity we were the siblings of Bobby and Tommy DeBarge.

Soul Train was only the beginning of all the exposure to come. We started hearing our songs on the radio, and *oh, what a feeling*! I remember driving down the street one day and hearing "I Like It" blasting from someone's car. Although "Stop! Don't Tease Me" was the debut single, deejays were getting more requests to play "I Like It." When both our vehicles were stopped at the red light, I started scrambling to find the station playing our song. The other driver had turned the music up louder and was bouncing in their seat while singing the words to our song: *"I like it. I like it. I really, really like it."* It was so overwhelming to witness a total stranger enjoying our music. I could not contain my excitement any longer. I leaned out the window and stated loudly, "Excuse me. That song you're listening to is my brothers and me. So glad you *like it*!" Then I sped off just as the light was changing. Did they believe me? I did not know and was too excited to care. I just found it hard to hide my excitement.

We rarely heard our single "Stop! Don't Tease Me" being played on the radio. For the most part, whenever we would hear our song on the radio, it was always "I Like It." Once Motown caught wind of the song's growing popularity, they did not hesitate to release the song as our next single. It did not take long for "I Like It" to climb the Billboard charts. Motown was ecstatic with the response the song was garnering from the public. Before we could catch our breath, Mr. Gordy requested the group (along with our management team) to reconvene at his mansion. This time, the meeting included representatives from the A&R Department. This must be a very important gathering because our managers were listening intently and taking meticulous notes.

Before getting down to business, Mr. Gordy congratulated the team as well as DeBarge on all our hard work thus far. He went on to reveal he had big plans for DeBarge and wanted to keep the momentum going. He felt we were ready to go to the next level. With a huge display of enthusiasm, Mr. Gordy announced that DeBarge would be going on a promotional tour starting on the East Coast. We would do radio interviews, in-store autograph signings, and in some venues, we would perform our tracks. "It's time we test the waters," Mr. Gordy stated. "Let's see what noise we can make out there and who wants to see DeBarge."

Certainly, Mr. Gordy did not get to where he was without a few calculated risks involved. We believed he knew exactly what he was doing and would not steer us wrong. We were in the care of the best hands in the business so there was no need to fear. One thing we could all agree on was Mr. Gordy knew his business and how to run it. I was just glad he had decided to come out of retirement to help the group get established. He spoke many encouraging words to keep us focused. It was a great opportunity to learn from the creator of a mega music machine. As eager students, we soaked up every morsel of knowledge he shared. We began to feel confident within ourselves. It was easy having Mr. Gordy on our side with our best interest at heart. He was adamant about making DeBarge a household name. The Jacksons were long gone, and Mr. Gordy had come out of retirement to establish another musical family on the Motown roster. He had the same energy and excitement when he worked to establish the Jackson 5 group.

Our lives were moving at breakneck speed. We did not have time to process everything unfolding in our music careers. When we left Mr. Gordy's mansion, we were hyped beyond measure and ready to put Mr. Gordy's plans into action. We were on a mission with goals to achieve. Management and the promotional department did not bat an eye. They were attentive to their notes and worked together to get the ball rolling. There were airline tickets to buy, hotel rooms to book, and clothing to purchase. We had a month to get everything together. As a working mother, I had even more on my plate. I wanted my husband to go on the road with me. Therefore, I needed someone to keep my girls—Damea and Janae. My mother was back east in Michigan, and I did not want to take them out of school. They had adjusted well to the recent changes in their lives, and I did not want to disrupt their routine. Moreover, it would be our very first time being away from each other. I was not looking forward to the separation—even if it was a brief separation. I already began to miss them terribly, and the promotional tour had not even started. Nevertheless, it was my job, and I had to provide for my family's needs. I began the search for a full-time babysitter. Fortunately, I found a relative willing to stay at the house with my girls. I agreed to pay them with promotional funds from the budget.

***

The day of the promotional tour arrived quickly. We were given an itinerary from our managers. Our first stop would be St. Louis, Missouri. The promotions department had meticulously laid out our daily schedule. Based on the agenda, we would be kept quite busy and barely have any time off. Upon reaching the East Coast, the remainder of the trip would mostly be done traveling by bus. We would use this time to rest. From the time we awaken until the end of the last event, we remained busy.

We woke up early to do radio interviews. By noon, we ate lunch. Afterward, we were off to different stores for autograph signings. This usually lasted until dinnertime. Then it was back to our rooms (or the bus) to rest for the following day. It was a very tight schedule, and all this was so new to us. At the last minute, we found out another artist named Bobby Nunn would be accompanying us. He was a new Motown artist, and his single was called "She's Just a Groupie." We knew nothing about this artist except he was associated with Rick James, and Motown was pushing his newly released single.

We arrived in Saint Louis at night, and a limo was there to greet us. We went straight to our rooms and rested until early the next morning. Our managers woke us up for breakfast then off we went to make our rounds at various radio stations. All the deejays were pleasant, full of life, and made us feel welcomed. The interviews were a time for fans to learn about our musical beginnings. El and I did most of the talking. The phone lines were then opened so our fans could call in with their questions. It was a lot of fun, and surprisingly, we were at ease when answering the questions. We were then shuffled off to various stores for autograph signings. The turnout was phenomenal! There were lines as far as the eyes could see! The record stores played our entire album over loudspeakers as we signed promotional pictures. Saint Louis had been selected as one of the cities where we would perform our songs. After dinner, we got dressed and headed to a local teenage nightclub.

When we reached the club, security was there to greet us. They escorted us to the back of the building into a dressing room. We were to wait there until it was time to go onstage. It had been announced on radio stations and at record stores we would be performing later. We could hear the excitement of the audience as we waited inside the dressing room. Finally, security came to get us, and we could hear the emcee hyping up the crowd. The crowd was enthusiastic and cheering us on before we even reached the stage. As soon as we hit the stage, the crowd went into a frenzy!

We sang "Stop! Don't Tease Me" and "I Like It." When the music for "I Like It" began, the audience went wild. The teenage girls became frantic and tried to push through security and rush the stage. There was a look of pure fear on the faces of security. *Maybe they cannot handle the crowd*, I thought. This caused me to become a bit frightened for my brothers and myself. We were used to performing in front of an audience. However, we had never experienced this type of audience behavior. Nevertheless, we continued smiling and kept on singing. As if things could not go from bad to worse, El hit the high note at the end of the song. The crowd was now completely out of control! They broke through security and made their way to the foot of the stage screaming and reaching for El. Before we knew it, fans were on the stage grasping at us and screaming our names! We were naïve and thought the audience's behavior was innocent and they were simply being friendly and showing us love.

Suddenly, I heard someone yell, "*Get some of her hair! Snatch an earring!*" I began fearing for our lives. This was not a friendly gesture. The audience wanted a piece of us—something they could take with them! We needed to get offstage and out of the club as quickly as possible.

Suddenly, security was hovering over us to protect us from the crowd. They then grabbed us up and rushed us to the back of the building straight to awaiting limos. The crowd was following closely behind, still trying in vain to grab a piece of us. As security tossed us into the limos, my dress almost flew over my head. My nylons were ripped, and I had lost an earring. Peering out the window of the limo, I could see that the crowd was still very much out of control. They had surrounded the limos screaming our names and banging on the windows. We had been divided up between two limos—El and I were placed in one limo while Randy, Mark, and James were placed in the other limo. People were everywhere! They were at both limos tugging at the handle trying to get the doors to open! I looked back at the limo behind us to make sure my brothers (Randy, Mark, and James) were safe. Then it happened! Randy leaped out of the limo smiling at the crowd with his hands in the air. What possessed Randy to do this no one will ever know! The only thing his actions did was turn up the notch on an already frenzied crowd. Security rushed to get him back into the limo safely. He was lucky to have escaped with his life.

I sat in the limo thinking, *oh my GOD, this is only the first show!* I wondered if it was going to be like this in every city where we performed. What I hoped would be a fun experience quickly morphed into fear and anxiety. All I could think about was the crowd wanting a piece of my hair! The audience's obsession seemed dangerous and was certainly not my idea of fun. I thought, *How crazy!* Unfortunately, I was the only one who felt some type of way about the whole ordeal. My brothers, along with management, seemed to relish in the crowd's reaction. I figured perhaps my brothers really did not know any better. After all, they were young, handsome, wild, and loved the attention of females. Still, what were our managers thinking basking in the glow of the audience's behavior? They kept stating the reaction from the audience is exactly what they had hoped to see. Yet I found the audience's reaction downright scary.

The managers' thoughts regarding the incident were a bit nonchalant in my opinion. As far as management had determined, the crowd's reaction only proved we were stars. After I protested a bit, management agreed there was a definite need for stronger security. They vowed to immediately work on finding better protection to control the crowds. Even though my nerves were shaken, I had to come to terms and accept that this was our life now—the unforeseen price of fame. I also could not lose sight of the fact there were people out there who *loved* us! Word got back to Mr. Gordy about the "success" of the show, and he was pleased with the feedback. DeBarge was making a lot of noise out there in the music world, and this was the goal of Mr. Gordy and the Motown machine.

In every city we performed, the audiences' excitement grew. DeBarge received warm reception after warm reception, and my brothers loved every single moment. Girls, girls, and more girls! Poor Randy was beside himself with excitement and fell in love with a girl in every city we visited! He would meet a girl then ask to take her along to the next city. It was so hilarious, and I began to tease him by saying, "Randy, remember there are more girls to come." Randy, always very softhearted and kind, would then have to break the news to the girl and let her know she could not accompany him to the next city.

Mr. Gordy had Motown and the group working overtime promoting the singles. Amid the promotional tour, the record label decided to drop another single entitled "All This Love." It seemed as if the fans were deciding which of our singles would be the next one released. We would now be performing "I Like It" and "All This Love" on our city stops. We had one more city left on the promotional tour—Detroit. Before our stop in Detroit, we would have to head back to Los Angeles for a day. Dick Clark wanted us on *American Bandstand!* Mr. Gordy wanted us to cross over from R&B to pop, and *American Bandstand* would introduce us to a pop audience. Once we performed on *American Bandstand*, we would be flying straight to Detroit. Rumor was that a surprise would be awaiting us. Going to Detroit was a mixed bag. Of course, the city was our birthplace. However, we did not have great memories of our lives in the city. It was emotionally triggering to even think about Detroit much less visit. In fact, seldom did we even mention we were from Detroit during interviews. It just came natural for us to say we were from Grand Rapids. The thought of returning to Detroit felt awkward. But for all intents and purposes, we were going "home."

CHAPTER 17

THE FIVE FINGERS
(MY UNCLE BILL)

In Motown's eyes, sending us back "home" to perform would be a bonus for the group. It was supposed to be a special day for DeBarge, and Motown went all out for the occasion. However, they had no idea what bad memories lingered for us in Detroit. I could not speak for any of my brothers. However, my last days in Detroit represented the darkest period in my life thus far. I was harboring pain and agony that had been tucked away for years. Being back in Detroit caused everything to resurface. I was feeling anxious and overwhelmed. I constantly reminded myself that DeBarge was returning to Detroit on a positive note. It was all I could do to manage my emotions. The fact we had beaten the odds and survived an extremely abusive childhood and rose to fame should have been the only thing that mattered at this point. So why was I being emotionally triggered on such an important trip?

Our itinerary outlined quite an adventurous day. We would begin by visiting the Motown Museum, which was Mr. Gordy's original home. It also housed the infamous Motown Studio. A lot of music legends had their beginnings at this very studio including Diana Ross and the Supremes, Mary Wells, Smokey Robinson and the Miracles, the Temptations, Marvin Gaye, and Stevie Wonder among others. Touring the Motown Museum was a privilege and of great interest to us. We thoroughly enjoyed our visit and took many pictures. Afterward, it was back to business as usual. We hit the radio stations and record stores throughout the Motor City. As expected, our reception from the radio hosts and fans were warm and inviting. At the record stores, there were lines of excited fans waiting to meet the new family group signed to Motown Records. The remainder of the day was spent resting up for the performance later in the evening. This performance would not be open to the public. Rather, it was strictly for the Motown executives who still resided in Detroit. Only the VIPs were invited to the pool house that now belonged to Anna Gordy, the chairman's sister. The primary focus of the evening was to welcome DeBarge to Motown. Mr. Gordy wanted to speak on the success of the promotional tour. There were also plans to outline our future with the label. They had great ideas in store for us, and this was only the beginning of our career.

Among those on the VIP list was our father, Robert DeBarge Sr., and Reverend William C. Abney or Uncle Bill—both of whom we had not had contact with for a while. We had become accustomed to Daddy being out of our lives. Our relationship with him had become somewhat estranged. However, we missed Uncle Bill dearly and waited for the moment to see him again. He meant the world to us in so many ways and for so many reasons. Not only was Uncle Bill an extraordinary uncle and pastor, but he was also our spiritual father.

Uncle Bill was invited to speak as one who knew us as children and could accurately define our history. We had great love and respect for our uncle. Knowing how he personally felt about our success meant the world to us. The anticipation of Uncle Bill's speech swelled up as sadness inside my heart. The sadness had little to do with Uncle Bill and more to do with my father. I was feeling overwhelmed as I wondered if Daddy had been invited to speak in addition to Uncle Bill. I could not imagine what he would have to say about our success. Yet despite horrific memories of the abuse we had suffered, I really wanted our father to be proud of what we had accomplished thus far. Still, I did not think he deserved an opportunity to speak on behalf of our success.

I began to experience a burden of guilt about the way I felt toward our father. Some would argue he was still our dad and deserved to say a word or two. I felt differently. As usual, I found a way to stop ruminating over what may happen or might be said by whom—I simply focused on the here and now. We were being honored and officially inducted into the Motown family. No bad memory could dispute this fact! *Look where we are today and where we came from*, I thought to myself. *At least we did not allow our lives with Daddy stop us from making it.* Yes, the good outweighed the bad. Still, I could not shake this feeling of uneasiness. Like always, I suppressed those feelings and prepared for the celebration.

Uncle Bill's presence would be the highlight of the evening. I knew we could count on him to say something inspiring and uplifting. I became teary-eyed the more I thought about his love and devotion to us. His warmth as an uncle and pastor always gave me a sense of hope growing up. Memories of our troubled childhood began to flash through my mind. However, I knew once Uncle Bill began to speak, his words would be precious, and all the cares of the world would fade away. His uplifting words would solidify our monumental journey, having come from the life we suffered as children. Yes, his words would become little golden nuggets I would cherish throughout my life!

The time had come for us to head to the evening's festivities. A limo arrived and carried us to the location. As soon as we arrived at Anna Gordy's home, we were ushered directly to the pool house. The guests were seated adjacent to the pool. An area flanked by a podium and makeshift stage was where we would perform. As we were walking into the room, the emcee took to the microphone: "Ladies and gentlemen, welcome Detroit and Motown's own . . . DeBarge!"

We walked up to the stage as the crowd stood to its feet and applauded. As we took our places onstage, I quickly scanned the crowd to see who was present. I saw my mother and my dad along with some of my cousins in the crowd. The other attendees appeared to be strangers. I did not see Uncle Bill. My heart dropped!

The track for "All This Love" began to play, and we started to lip-synch on cue. I will never forget the look of pride on Mama's face. It was her first time seeing us presented as celebrities, and she seemed genuinely happy. As our eyes met, she gave me a quick wink. One thing was true, Mama has always been very proud of us her children and our musical gifts and talents. When I looked over at Daddy, he seemed equally as proud. Mama and Daddy were not sitting together. This was of little consequence to me. I was just happy they were both there to support me and my brothers. We finished our performance with "I Like It" and received a standing ovation!

After our performance, we were seated in an area marked RESERVED in front of the stage. It was time for the speakers to share how they were connected to our success as a group. As each person approached the podium, they announced their job function and the role they would play in our journey toward success within their respective region. We were surprised they knew more about us than we knew about them.

As the night wore on, I kept wondering when Uncle Bill would arrive. He was supposed to be present but was nowhere to be found. The boys began to worry as well. Just as we were getting antsy, the emcee introduces Reverend William Abney, our uncle Bill! As he strolled up to the podium, my brothers and I were there to greet him with open arms. Our managers had kept him hidden in another room out of everyone's sight. The audience must have seen our hearts skip a beat as we hurriedly approached the *little man with the big heart*. We had tears in our eyes as we watched our uncle begin to cry. We gathered around him and held him tightly. The crowd could not help but feel the undeniable love we had for this true man of GOD. Removing a handkerchief from his pocket, Uncle Bill dried his eyes and walked to the center of the stage.

All eyes were glued to Uncle Bill. I must add he was impeccably dressed for the occasion. He always has had a classy taste in clothing and certainly wore it well. As the audience looked on in admiration, I could tell they were also in agreement. Regardless of the occasion, Uncle Bill always presented himself with so much grace and wisdom. To me, he was truly an anointed pastor. Tonight, however, he was not there to preach. We listened intently to his words, and our eyes beamed with pride. We wanted Motown to appreciate just how special Uncle Bill was to us. It was important they knew the roots of our spiritual inheritance. Uncle Bill represented royalty and was the stock from where our blessings flowed.

"I want to apologize for being so emotional on this evening," Uncle Bill began. "However, . . ." Tears began to well up in his eyes again as his voice trailed off. Now everyone in the room could feel the warmth of his sincere heart. He took a moment to compose himself then proceeded to speak again. "I am crying because I know where these kids came from."

I looked around in curiosity, searching for my father. I wanted to see for myself the expression on his face as Uncle Bill spoke. What I witnessed left me utterly amazed. Daddy sat there with the unbelievable ability to hold a straight face as if he had never done any wrong to his children. I could not help but think Daddy had to have known my uncle was placed as the highlight of the evening because he had earned a special place in our lives. I wondered how it made him feel as a father. I knew Uncle Bill would not mince words and could have cared less Daddy was in the room. He spoke confidently as he held his head high.

"I know what they have been through—and the beginnings were quite hard. For them, I do not have to elaborate. They know what I am saying. It is good to see where they are today." Then he turned to look us straight in the eyes. "Bunny, El, Mark, Randy, and James—this night is for you. Uncle Bill wants you all to know I'm proud of you. You have come a long way, and I know firsthand it was GOD's grace that brought you through. This time, Uncle Bill comes to the city not to rescue you, but to honor you. While driving here today, I reminisced on the turmoil of your youth. I prayed and asked GOD to give me just what to say to you." His words were forceful, yet gentle.

"I struggled with you leaving from under my guidance," he continued. "I have made this known to you. Nevertheless, you all know where your help comes from. You know who your GOD is, and He lives inside each one of you. Therefore, no matter where you go in life, how big you become in this world, or who might love you along the way, remember GOD loves you first and most of all. Remember, only what you do for Christ will last. You are a long way from home, but I am confident in knowing GOD is with you. Be encouraged and stay together."

Holding up his hand, he stated, "Look at my hand, kids. It takes four fingers and a thumb to make up this hand. If anything were to happen to any of the members, the hand could no longer function at its best. You five children represent this hand. Each of you symbolizes a finger and the thumb. Every member is just as important as the other and makes the hand whole."

Before continuing, Uncle Bill came closer so he could look us all in the eyes. "If something happens to the thumb, the pinkie, or any of the members, the whole hand suffers. It misses the member and struggles to do what the hand is supposed to do. I want you to keep this in mind, kids. Stay together, encourage one another, and lift each other up in prayer. Take to heart Uncle Bill loves you, and I am proud of you. Keep up the good work and stay together as GOD would want you to do. GOD bless." We leaped from our chairs then grabbed and embraced Uncle Bill as the audience stood to their feet and applauded. Uncle Bill then stated, "Now I would like to have prayer with you all before I leave here tonight."

As he requested, everyone joined hands and prayed. It was a very sincere, intimate, and heartfelt moment for those who knew us. It was a great day I would always remember. To have Uncle Bill's blessings on our lives meant the world to us. So much happened for us on this day— some we were aware of, and others we had no clue. Many people took to the podium as the night wore on to speak to us in various capacities. What I remember the most—and what stays near and dear to my heart to this very day—are the precious words spoken by our uncle Bill.

CHAPTER 18

LIVING FOR THE WEEKEND

THE PROMOTIONAL TOUR WAS A huge success. Not only was our single "All This Love" climbing the charts, but our album by the same name was also rising on the charts! We were interviewing for features in different magazines such as *Right On!* and *Black Beat*. DeBarge mania was in full swing! Radio stations—not just in the United States but also abroad—had our music playing in heavy rotation. There was huge demand for our single "All This Love" as well as other cuts from the album. It was thrilling to watch the Billboard charts as we crossed over from R&B to pop. Yes, just as Mr. Gordy had predicted, DeBarge was quickly becoming a household name.

Our success made us extremely popular in the neighborhood as well as at my children's school. Management suggested I remove my girls from public school and place them into private school. It made perfect sense to both Tony and me so we began searching for the right school. Regardless of the issues in our marriage, Tony was a great father. He helped tremendously with our girls during this busy time in our lives. He was there to fill in the gaps by cooking, cleaning, and ensuring the girls got back and forth to school.

I was kept busy by the demands of the group. Further, Bobby would often call upon me to assist him with writing lyrics. He strongly believed in my songwriting abilities. Bobby also wanted my assistance in the studio singing background vocals. Whenever an occasion arose to work with other artists, I could always count on Bobby to summon me to the studio. At this time, he was working with a new Motown group called High Inergy. The group consisted of three young ladies the chairman had taken a lot of interest in promoting. He wanted Bobby to write and produce a song for the group. Bobby wanted and needed my assistance to write lyrics for a song he had composed entitled, "Hold On to My Love." He would faithfully pick me up each day to go into the studio, and I was honored to work so closely with him on this project.

I was so proud of Bobby for many reasons. He appeared to be doing so well in all areas of life. Since he had come off the road with Switch, he seemed to be a man of his word with regards to his drug use. His cocaine habit was a thing of the past as far as I knew, and this made me very happy for my brother. I prayed Tommy would soon follow in Bobby's footsteps and kick his own drug habit. Bobby seemed content and to be holding up well—at least I was led to believe. The only thing I witnessed was him popping a pill every now and then. He justified this by stating it helped him deal with the pressures of life and his career. The pills helped him cope with everything troubling him. I learned he was taking Tussionex in pill form, and it did seem to have a calming effect. He just seemed to be in a good mood more often. This was a welcome relief from his wild and unpredictable mood swings. However, I had no idea how deeply he had come to depend on these pills. Working closely with him, I was about to find out firsthand. Each day we spent together in the studio, it became more and more apparent that my brother had a spiraling pill addiction.

Like any day, Bobby picked me up, and we drove to the studio. As we were driving, I could not help but notice that Bobby did not seem his usual self. He was very quiet, his skin was pale, and he was withdrawn. He was also quite edgy and appeared physically sick. "What's wrong with you?" I asked, concerned.

"I don't feel good," he softly replied without elaborating.

I did not push the issue. I simply let it go, hoping the music would bring him out of his funk. However, it did not happen. Something was consuming Bobby, and his mind was far away from the studio and music. He was not concentrating at all during the session. I noticed he had reached into his pocket and pulled out a prescription bottle. He looked at the bottle as if contemplating whether he should take one of the pills. He then placed the bottle back into his pocket. Bobby began to hem and haw then huff and puff until finally reaching into his pocket again and pulling out the same bottle. He opened the bottle then proceeded to swallow a handful of pills. I was initially taken aback, thinking he may have taken too many. It did not take long for me to see a dramatic change in his appearance and demeanor. Bobby was "himself" again. I was amazed with how the color had suddenly returned to his face. His mood was now pleasant, and he became talkative. Finally, he was back to normal. "I need a favor from you, Bunny," Bobby stated directly.

I looked at Bobby in a questioning manner. What favor did he need from me? Then he revealed his answer. Bobby asked me to go to the doctor and get a written prescription for him. I was puzzled. "Me go to the doctor, Bobby? You have pills. I saw you take them. Plus, I have no idea how to do that." I had heard of people doing such things, but it was not my cup of tea. Bobby began to explain he had a white girl who knew a doctor who would write out the prescription. "Then there you go," I replied, a bit irritated.

"That's just it." Bobby began to sound desperate. "I can't go myself. I've been already. I can't get any more prescriptions. However, you can because it will be your first time in the office. All you have to say is you're from out of town. Tell him you haven't been to a doctor here yet and you have respiratory problems. Say you have bronchitis and the doctor you had in Michigan prescribed you Tussionex."

I searched Bobby's face and realized he was dead serious! He had everything mapped out in his head. I could tell he was well rehearsed as far as this was concerned and adamant about me doing this for him. Knowing my brother, he certainly had no intentions on taking no for an answer. Bobby was on a roll and made it sound so easy. "Just like that?" I asked, looking Bobby square in his face. "That's all I have to say? What if he asks me for the doctor's name? What if he wants to call him?" I was hesitant. I had never done anything like this before. Bobby continued to reassure me the doctor would not resort to fact-checking.

"He's a crooked doctor, Bunny. I have just gone as far as I can go with him. He can only write three prescriptions for a person. It must be someone new. No more prescriptions for me!" I could see Bobby was desperate. Everything made total sense now. Bobby was running out of pills. It was crucial for him to get someone new to go to the doctor—*and soon*. As his sister, I felt obligated to help him, but I was apprehensive.

"I don't know, Bobby," I said, shaking my head. I felt sorry for my brother and was hoping there was a better way to handle the situation. For a moment, my mind flashed to my children. "Are you sure about this? I don't want to get in trouble." Bobby had always been a master at convincing people to go along with his plans and schemes. He could talk sweetness out of sugar then sell it back to you. He finally succeeded in convincing me everything would be fine. He was adamant he would never ask me to do something if he felt I would get into trouble. I knew this was something I had to ask my husband first. I managed to put Bobby off by telling him I would have to first ask Tony. If Tony approved, then I would do it. Bobby reluctantly agreed and handed me a few pills.

At the time, I did not believe Bobby was intentionally manipulating me. However, looking back over the situation, manipulation was exactly what he was doing. My memory of the pill was from the going-away party we had at his house. My mind recalled the mellow feeling the pills gave me, and I wanted the feeling again. Therefore, I broke the pill in half and proceeded to take it. I began to feel the effects of the pill almost immediately.

It was a vocal day, and *High Inergy* was in the studio completing background vocals. Bobby wanted my vocals on the background of the song along with the group. I needed to meet the girls first and at least feel comfortable singing with them. In addition, I was working on finishing up the lyrics to the song, "Hold on Baby to My Love." After finishing the lyrics, Bobby had me do a rough lead. It did not take long to record the song for the lead singer of the group who would in turn listen to and study it for our next studio session. Time went by very fast, but we had a lot of fun in the studio. It had been a very productive day. Before nightfall, we were heading back to my home. As we walked up the stairs leading to my apartment, Bobby reminded me to talk with Tony about going to the doctor.

"You can go in the morning to the clinic with me. It's in Ventura—a little ways from here. So we toned to leave early. I need to know tonight, Bunny, so I can call the girl and tell her to expect us."

I began to plot in my mind how best to present this scheme to Tony. Not completely sure if Tony would go along, I handed Bobby the pill he had given me earlier. "You give the pill to Tony first, and I will ask him about going to Ventura later on tonight," I stated, still not sure how my husband would respond. It was all I could come up with now. Hopefully, I would be able to get Tony to agree with Bobby's scheme to get access to more pills. I convinced Bobby the pill would soothe Tony and it would not be hard for me to convince him afterward. I knew Tony had enjoyed the high as much as I did at the party.

After taking the pill, Bobby, Tony, and I smoked a joint. It was evident Tony was feeling good, and Bobby saw this as the best opportunity to hit him with the scheme. Surprisingly, Tony had no problem going along with the plan. Of course, Bobby had to reassure him over and over I would not get into any trouble. He also wanted to know how long it would take to go to Ventura, see the doctor, and return home. Tony did not mind me being away from him and the kids to work. However, when work was not involved, he wanted his wife at home. After Bobby let him know it would take most of the day, the scheme became a problem for him. Bobby was a master negotiator, and before the night was over, he had persuaded Tony to allow me to go to Ventura the next day.

***

Early the next morning, Bobby drove to my apartment and picked me up. Ventura was at least an hour away on a good day. By now, I had become accustomed to everything being far apart and spread out in California. It was also very crowded on the freeway and Bobby was getting worked up. "We cannot miss this appointment," he kept stating, clearly frustrated. "Why is this traffic at a standstill? Move! Move!" he yelled out the car window. "I hate it when it gets like this. Yoo-hoo! Move, people!"

I could sense Bobby's patience had run its course and hated when he had these meltdowns—especially while driving. Enraged, he floored the car and drove over to the shoulder of the freeway and proceeded to drive at full speed! Horns blew and people began yelling profane words from their vehicles. Bobby leaned out the window and cursed back at the other drivers. Scared nearly to death, I sat in the passenger's seat with my hands covering my ears and my feet pressing down on the floor as if there were brakes underneath them. "Bobby, what are you doing?" I screamed. "We're going to jail!" Bobby paid me no mind as he continued driving wildly and having verbal altercations with the other drivers. I was beyond furious with him, but he did not seem to care. The ride to Ventura was dangerous and extremely stressful. Bobby's foot must have remained pressed down pedal to the metal until he saw a sign that read, *Ventura City Limits.*

"I can ease up now," Bobby stated with a huge sigh of relief. "We're here now."

Fury was all in my eyes. "I cannot believe you did that!"

"Believe it, Bunny. We had to make this appointment today, or we would have had to wait until next week," Bobby stated contemptuously while not batting an eye.

There was a brief and uncomfortable silence lingering between us. I knew there was no point in arguing with Bobby. We had arrived and at least in one piece. Once we pulled into the parking lot of the clinic and parked, a young white girl stepped out of her car and walked hurriedly over to Bobby's car. Bobby introduced us, and we both went into the clinic together as he waited inside the car.

"This shouldn't take long," the girl stated. "Everything should be smooth sailing. You know what to say, right?"

"Yes," I quickly replied, not really wanting to make small talk. I was coming off a stressful ride and jumping into another one. Anxiety and nervousness were written all over my face. At this point, I would not have to do much convincing with the doctor about feeling sick.

"There's nothing to be afraid of," she stated nonchalantly while repeating everything Bobby had rehearsed with me earlier. "The doctor knows you aren't really telling him the truth. He can only do so many prescriptions for one person, and I'm afraid your brother has reached his limit."

She strolled casually up to the receptionist's desk, signed in, then took a seat in the waiting room. I followed suit then sat next to her and patiently waited to see the doctor. Before long, her name was called by the nurse. She went into the back office, leaving me to sit by myself and get lost in my thoughts. Bobby had really taken me for a ride, and my stomach was still turned upside down from the experience. One thing for sure, I wanted the day to hurry up and end. I was eager to get back to the safety of my home, my husband, and my children. What had these pills done to my brother to cause him to drive like a bat out of hell with no regard for his life or the life of others?

It did not take long for the same nurse to call me to the back to see the doctor. I was very flat and monotone as I recited the script. My indifference seemed to float straight over his head. He had very little to say as he listened to my heartbeat and asked me to cough. Then I watched as he scribbled out a prescription and handed it to me. "You have three refills, Mrs. Jordan. Take them as prescribed," he stated then walked out of the room.

Mission accomplished! I was so eager to leave and grateful the appointment did not take long. As I walked back out to the reception area, I then noticed the sheer number of people waiting to see the doctor. It seemed as if the clinic was overflowing with addicts in need of a prescription for their fix. The young girl who I came in with had already exited the building. I proceeded to the parking lot where I found her sitting in the car chatting with Bobby. "I got it, Bobby. Now what? We have three refills," I stated, unenthused. Bobby seemed ecstatic. Now we would proceed to the pharmacy to get the prescription filled. The girl agreed to meet us at the pharmacy. In addition to the prescription Bobby was receiving from me, he was also buying her prescription.

Once we pulled up to the pharmacy, Bobby informed me we would wait until we were back in the Valley to fill my prescription. We were only getting the young girl's prescription filled at this time. It took a minute before she came back out to the car. Bobby passed her some money, and she handed him the bottle of pills. "We need coffee," Bobby stated then drove to the nearest convenience store.

Bobby seemed quite anxious. I could tell the monkey was on his back. He purchased coffee for the both of us then returned to the car. He opened the bottle of pills and counted out six pills for himself and one for me. "Here, take it with your coffee. It will hit your system faster." Still feeling the effects of the pill, I had taken the day before, I simply stored the pill away for another time. I wanted to be wide awake for the ride home. I felt the pill could be something to enjoy with my husband later.

We were back on the freeway, and I must say the ride home was much more pleasant. Bobby had his pills thus we were able to enjoy the ride while listening to music. Before dropping me off at home, Bobby stopped by the pharmacy to have me fill the prescription. He then shared some of the pills with me.

When night fell and the kids were off to bed, Tony and I took the pills. All I kept talking about to Tony was the ride to Ventura. Probably because of the pills, we managed to laugh about my experience. It was strange because although I was all too familiar with the level of my brother's impatience, I still could not believe Bobby! He had driven on the shoulder of the freeway most of the way to Ventura. My heart was in my big toe! In retrospect, I witnessed how risky Bobby's behavior had become due to him becoming hooked on those pills. Sadly, I had unwittingly fallen into the misery of his addiction as well.

I was weak when it came to Bobby—plain and simple. Maybe I should have said no to him knowing he had gone too far just by his actions alone. Alas, I had become dysfunctional and sick myself. At the time, I had convinced myself I had a cap on the situation. Perhaps it felt I was playing it safer than Bobby since I had a husband who could keep me on track and from spiraling out of control. I believed I could never get down to where Bobby was with his pill addiction. In hindsight, I am confident Bobby felt the same way once upon a time. Every drug addict has an innocent starting point, and no one wants to believe they will ever become addicted. During a moment in our conversation, Tony and I took a vow we would only indulge on the weekends.

"When we finish these few pills, no more, Bunny—for a while. We can't start doing this every day. We must put some days in between taking them. You and I cannot afford to get a habit anyway. We have the kids and you have a career," he stated emphatically.

"Okay," I responded, relieved he would take the lead and keep us on track. "I'm with you, and you're absolutely right."

I knew Tony was looking out for our best interest. We figured once the few pills were gone, we would be done for good. Nevertheless, we had no idea we were already emotionally hooked on the pills. Tony and I *loved* the high. Whenever we indulged, it became our leisure time— something to look forward to on the weekends to relax and escape. Unfortunately, we were now *living for the weekend*.

ROCK OUT WITH MENUDO!

April 1984

Right On!

VPS 35825
$1.50 U.S.
1.95 CANADA
£1.25 U.K.

**EDDIE
MURPHY
CREATES A BAD
"IMPRESSION!"**

**OLA RAY:
HOW SHE BECAME
THE P.Y.T. OF
"THRILLER!"**

WEBSTER:
MICHAEL
JACKSON'S
NEW BUDDY!

DEBARGE:
THEY'RE BACK IN A VERY
SPECIAL WAY!

15 Dynamite Color Pinups Just For You!

MORE News·Gossip & Interviews

$1.50
WPS 35359
April '84

BLACK BEAT

THE JACKSONS
40-City "Victory" Tour
A Family Affair

Non-Stop To Success On The Motown Express

DEBARGE
They Have A Special Way Of Loving You

OLA RAY
Michael's Girlfriend In "THRILLER" Video

PRINCE
Special In Concert Poster

Special Anniversary Issue

Up-Close & Personal
Four Fantasy Favorites To Take Home

Andre Cymone   **O'Bryan**   **Howard Hewett**   **James Ingram**

0   70989 35359   04

CHAPTER 19

MY HEART IS BROKEN, MY SOUL CRIES OUT

WE WERE ALWAYS A LOVING, compassionate family and very much involved in one another's day-to-day lives. Not a day passed I did not see at least one of my brothers. Even our mother found it hard to stay away. She had moved back to Los Angeles and enjoyed being involved in our day-to-day lives once again. Although most of us were fully grown, to her, we were still little children who needed her nearby. It was also a great time for her since she was expecting a new grandchild. She kept stating that Duckie was "ripe" and due to have the baby soon. She wanted to be there to assist Duckie with her first child. We had also planned a baby shower for her, and Mama wanted to help. She also wanted to check in on Tommy's well-being and keep a close eye on him. He was back to living on the wild side after seemingly slowing up for a moment. Moreover, Tommy and Duckie did not have a phone, and I did not want her to be left alone so close to the baby's due date. Therefore, I kept Duckie close by my side.

Everybody in the family was worried about Tommy and Duckie. He had finally lost the Alfa Romeo. As if this was not enough, they were also losing their apartment. Unlike Bobby, Tommy was struggling hard trying to give up smoking cocaine. It was not long after the tour he picked up his drug habit again. Along with those actions came the same behaviors of staying out all night and sleeping all day. Mama was deeply troubled by this and believed her presence would help bring Tommy back to his senses. She felt the urgent need to try and talk some sense into him. I knew it would not do any good. However, my mother (like so many mothers who have children struggling with addiction) had blind faith in Tommy. Somehow, she felt her words had influence over his addiction. I was simply his big sis, and from my perspective, Tommy was unreachable and too far gone.

Tommy constantly lived in a bygone era and used his past experiences as an excuse to remain high. However, his turbulent childhood was not Duckie's fault, and neither was it the fault of their unborn child. Mama would often say Tommy was much like our father, and she looked at Duckie as being much like herself. Just as Mama had hoped and prayed Daddy would change for the better, Duckie also put the same level of energy behind her loyalty to Tommy. Mama admired the blind faith Duckie had in Tommy, but it was severely misguided. I also admired Duckie's faith in my brother. Unlike Mama, I felt Duckie's faith enabled Tommy to continue in his destructive lifestyle. Perhaps her faith would have been better directed at making a statement in her and Tommy's relationship as opposed to coddling him—especially at such a crucial stage in their lives. An innocent child would soon be brought into their chaotic world. I constantly reminded her it was no longer about herself and Tommy. My nephew would need love and stability from both of his parents. She could not allow Tommy's unstable lifestyle of drug addiction to monopolize her and her unborn son's lives. Admittedly, it was a very touchy subject for me. As much as I loved Duckie, sometimes her nonchalant attitude reminded me of my childhood, and this sickened me to my core. I simply wanted her to become assertive and stand up for herself. Her refusal to do so brought me to a place where I felt hopeless and insecure. Sad to say, I was not the only person who thought Duckie should stand up to Tommy's behaviors and not make excuse after excuse for his indiscretions. Bobby felt the exact same way. We tried in vain to convince Duckie that Tommy loved her enough, and if she would only take a stance against his destructive behaviors, perhaps he would look at himself and change for the better. I then questioned Bobby and myself: *Who were we to look down on and scrutinize Tommy and Duckie's life? I had my own growing addiction as did Bobby.* In some way, we were all agonizing over our abusive childhood. We were all silently living in hell and being overtaken by the demons from our past. Our reality was sobering—everyone would have to learn to live their own lives and get through it the best way they could.

The entire family showed up in force for Duckie and Tommy's baby shower. It was wonderful to see Duckie shine in her hour. The day belonged to her, and she was all smiles because Tommy was right by her side celebrating. Spurred by the presence of her children, Mama insisted we all go to church the next day. It had been quite a while since we had gone to church together as a family. After the baby shower was over, we had a little discussion to work out the final details. We came to a mutual agreement we would attend church in the morning as a family unit. Mama was going to stay the night with El but promised she would be everyone's wake-up call the next morning.

Mama left Peaches (Carole), my baby sister, to stay the night at my apartment. Damea and Janae were thrilled since they had not seen their auntie in quite a while. Peaches, who was thirteen years old at the time, was closer to my daughters' ages than she was to mine. Therefore, she related to my girls much more than she related to me. Damea and Janae adored their auntie. Even though she was only five and six years older than them, Peaches made sure Damea and Janae respected her as their aunt. All throughout the day, the girls were nowhere to be found. Whenever I located them, they were glued to their auntie Peaches' side. With the baby shower over, it was time for the girls to head to bed. After getting their clothes together for church the next day, the girls fell right to sleep. They must have been very tired. It was unusual for them to fall asleep so fast. On a normal night, the girls would be up giggling and playing. Nevertheless, I counted it a blessing. I was exhausted from the day and had to get up early in the morning for church. I was looking forward to going with my family. It felt like old times.

***

The next morning, Mama was prompt in calling to make sure we were up and getting ready for church. We planned out our day. I was to drive over and pick up Tommy and Duckie then meet her at church. The plan was for all of us to meet outside the church then walk inside together. "Let me speak to Peaches," Mama stated. "She called me." I yelled for Peaches to come to the phone and then went to get myself and my girls dressed. Even though I tried to prepare myself the night before, I found myself still rushing to get ready. At last, we were all dressed in our Sunday best and ready to leave. Out the door we went to pick up Tommy and Duckie. To my surprise, they were already waiting outside. They jumped into the car, and we headed to West Angeles Church of GOD in Christ. Once we had arrived at the church, the rest of my family was waiting for us outside.

The church service had already begun. As we prepared to walk inside, Mama stated, "Bunny, come here for a minute. I need to speak with you. Peaches, you come here too. I want you to sit with me." Thinking nothing of what Mama was stating, I looked over at Tony and told him to gather the children and I would be in shortly. Tony turned and walked toward the church building while Peaches and I walked over to where Mama was standing. She stood there and seemed a bit uncomfortable

"What's wrong, Mama?" I asked, concerned.

Mama glanced over at Peaches and stated, "Peaches has something to tell you." Then she pushed Peaches next to me. "Go on, Peaches. Don't be afraid. Bunny is your big sister, and she loves you."

My heart began to beat fast, and thoughts in my head began to race. My concern turned to fear as I noticed that my baby sister's demeanor had changed. "What's wrong, Peaches?" Avoiding eye contact with me, she looked down at the ground. Looking at Mama, I insisted she tell me what was going on. "What is it, Mama?"

Peaches, still looking down at the ground, finally spoke. "Last night while I was asleep, Tony came into the room and touched me between my legs. It woke me up, and when I asked him what he was doing, he just put the cover over me and walked out. It scared me, Bunny."

I could not believe what I was hearing. My heart was broken, and my soul cried out. I had to hear it again just to be sure. "What did you just say?" I began to break out in a sweat. I became hot, then numb, then sick to my stomach. I did not hear anything afterward. I needed to go somewhere and throw up. I looked at my little sister who stood in front of the church in utter confusion. I knew in my heart she was not lying. I thought about the times I tried to protect her from our father and the unimaginable fear I lived with day to day not knowing if Daddy had touched her and caused her any harm. Yet it was my own husband who had the audacity to violate my baby sister. The same man I stood before GOD and made vows to love, honor, and cherish had violated my baby sister in the worst way. Not only was my heart broken and my soul crying out in pain, but I was also furious!

With an utter disregard I was at a place of worship, I turned and walked swiftly toward the building. My mind was racing, and my heart was beating a mile a minute. At the time, I did not know how to respond to Tony. I had to see him and get this straightened out right then and there! Mama and Peaches were right on my heels. Mama was trying in vain to reach me both physically and emotionally. However, I had tunnel vision and could only barely make out what she was saying. Perhaps I did not want to hear anything Mama had to say. "Bunny, what are you getting ready to do? Come here, Bunny," I heard Mama pleading in the background.

I blocked her out! With tears trying desperately not to fall from my eyes, I started to run. I felt alone. The world became a silent blur around me. No one else existed in the world except Tony and me. I ran up the steps of the church and into the building. Upon pushing open the church doors, I looked around at the strangers standing in the hallway waiting to enter the sanctuary. I had hoped Tony would be among those waiting, but his presence was nowhere to be found. My heart was still rapidly beating as I pushed my way through the crowd and to the glass window. I could now see inside the sanctuary. Finally, I laid eyes on my children, and next to them sat my husband. They were sitting toward the back of the church. I immediately opened the sanctuary door and ran to sit next to him.

I tried in vain to compose myself. However, what I had just found out was too much for me to contain. "Did you touch my sister?" I blurted out with no regard to how loud I was talking. At this point, it was between Tony and me and I did not care who overhead our conversation. The look he gave me sickened me to my stomach. I did not give him an opportunity to even respond. His look said it all. Before I knew it, I slapped him. I did not stop there. I proceeded to ball up my fist and punch him as hard as I could in his face. "How could you—you dirty bastard!" Suddenly, my family was behind me. Besides Mama and Peaches, my family had no idea why I was viciously attacking Tony. They began to restrain me. Thankfully, the Spirit was high in the church, and people were into the service and not concerned with the commotion I was causing. The congregants sitting on the same row with us and behind us were the only ones to witness the altercation.

"Get yourself together, Bunny," Mama kept saying. "You're in church. Let's leave. Come on, let's go."

I looked at Mama in utter disbelief. At this very moment, everything from my past came charging at me and hit me like a ton of bricks. I broke down and began crying uncontrollably. "Get it together, Mama? Get it together!" I asked, screaming between the tears. My brothers, still not knowing what was happening, carried me kicking and screaming to the back of the church. "Get my children from that freak!" I cried. Tony looked bewildered as Mama took my children's hands, and we all left the church in a hurry.

The ride home was quiet, yet tense. I was numb as flashbacks of my childhood abuse kept playing over and over in my head. Overwhelmed by the memories, I cried continuously. No matter how hard I tried to comfort myself, the tears would not stop falling. One thing I knew, I did not want to see Tony. Though hardly her fault, I could not even look at Peaches. My emotions were so mixed up, and all I felt was shame and humiliation. I believed my sister—she had no reason to lie. I was her big sis, and I knew she looked up to me and would never say or do anything to hurt me. I felt incredibly guilty for not knowing what Tony was capable of and having failed to protect my sister from such a vile act. *At least he was caught,* I thought to myself, *and she had sense enough to tell.* I was happy she was brave enough to come to me—it could have been much worse.

I decided to stay at Tommy and Duckie's apartment and got some pills from Bobby. I did not want to feel the pain my heart and soul was experiencing. I knew the pills would numb the agony I was going through. I hated Tony more than anyone on this earth and refused to even talk with him. There was nothing he could say to me or my sister. I was determined to keep distance between us—for my sake as well as his. My mind kept reflecting to the look on his face when I approached him, and it sickened me all over again. My heart was broken, and I sat there in a stupor. Soon, I began to feel the effects of the pill. It was numbing and allowed me to fall sleep and escape the anguish of the day.

The next morning, I was awakened with Tony standing at the door of Tommy and Duckie's apartment. He seemed contrite and wanted to talk. His apologetic mood did nothing to move me. I refused to see him, let alone listen to his excuses. I guess one could say I was afraid of what he would say. Perhaps he would deny what I truly believed about the situation. I believed he had indeed violated my baby sister. Any denial would cause me to act out in a way I would surely regret. It was too soon for me to listen to his side of the story. Everything that had transpired the day before left me feeling dazed and confused. I had lost total control of my emotions. They were unsteady, and the world became an overwhelming place. There was no way mentally I could deal with the sight of Tony nor could I bare the sound of his voice.

Duckie was caught in the middle of my unwillingness to talk with Tony. She did her best to communicate to him how I was feeling. He played it cool and did not force me to tear down the wall I erected between us. Knowing he did not stand a chance, he left and went back to our apartment. I had a lot of thinking to do about our future together. Tommy and Duckie welcomed my girls and me into their home for the time being. I promised them my stay was only until I could figure out my next move. I would take this time to weigh out all the havoc in my life. I had no intentions of ever returning to my husband.

I needed to head back to the apartment and pack up some belongings for me and my girls. All I could think about were the pills lying inside my purse. Without much thought as to how the pills could impact my judgment, I reached inside and grabbed one. *There's no need to go to GOD*, I thought. *I'm not walking the walk nor talking the talk. Why would He hear me? I'm not in His Will.* Shame began to consume me, and I felt perhaps I had brought this whole ordeal on myself. As a result, I downed one of the pills, aware that the pain would be numbed in minutes and I could then dwell on better thoughts. Once the pill took effect, I gained a level of faux-confidence. I decided to call Tony to let him know I would be coming by to pick up some belongings for the girls and me. I knew he wanted to talk. I psyched myself into believing I would remain calm once we encountered each other again. Further, I convinced myself it was time to listen to his side of the story.

Bobby picked me up from Tommy's and drove me over to my apartment. The ride was quiet as if he were afraid to say anything to me about what was going on. It was strange witnessing my brothers' reactions. Even though I knew they supported any decision I made, it still felt as if they did not want to choose sides. Was it a man thing? I did not know, and I was too afraid to peel back how they must have been feeling. I was incredibly heartbroken and did not want to enhance my heartbreak by obsessing over their wounds.

When I entered the apartment, I went directly to retrieve what I came for—my children's clothing. Avoiding any eye contact with Tony, I continued to quickly pack. "Baby," he began, "don't you want to hear *my* side of the story?"

I bit my lips and fought to maintain my composure. I let out a brief sigh then stated without making eye contact, "As a matter of fact, I do Tony. Just what do you have to say?" Tony began to speak, and all I could hear was one excuse after the next. His words sounded like a well-rehearsed script.

"Baby, I know your sister feels something happened, but all I did was put the cover over her. I was checking on the kids and saw she was uncovered. I covered her. In doing so, I might have touched her leg. She did wake up, and maybe she felt something totally different. I swear to you that's all it was. Nothing more," he stated, almost pleading.

With everything inside me, I wanted to believe my husband. However, knowing what happened to me as a child and how it made me feel, I could not bring myself to believe my baby sister was lying about what had taken place. I finally gathered up the strength to look at Tony. I looked him directly in his eyes and boldly stated, "I believe her, Tony. I believe *her*, you dirty dog! Now what do you have to say?" My heart began to hurt once again as I began to replay the details in my mind. "I believe *her*, not *you*! My sister is not lying!" As much as I tried to stand strong, the tears welled up in my eyes. My soul was crying, and my heart was broken.

Realizing my pain, Tony reached out to hold me, but I pushed him away. I did not need nor did I want him to console me. "Don't you touch me!" I yelled. "I hate you!" I had never spoken those words before in my life, and I do not believe it was Tony whom I hated. No, I hated the act! My emotional wounds were opened again. I felt naked and vulnerable. My heart was bleeding fast, and I wanted the pain to go away. "I'm ready to leave," I stated defiantly. "I don't want to talk anymore." Tony reached out to hold me once again then pleaded for me to stay. I was so disgusted to the point I could no longer look his way. "I'm ready to go, Tony. Now!"

"I will apologize to Peaches and tell her I'm sorry she felt that way." His words upset me even more. The damage caused by my own sexual abuse at the hands of my father caused one flashback after the other to resurface. I was being triggered by his need to apologize to my sister. *Why would he want to talk to my sister?* The audacity of him to think I would allow him anywhere near Peaches. "Don't *you* dare talk to my sister. You stay away from her!" I had had enough. I could not allow my emotions to spin further out of control. Without uttering another word, I simply turned around and left the apartment.

As soon as I entered the car, I asked Bobby for more pills. By now, he was aware I was in a lot of pain. Concern was written all over his face. "You don't need any more pills today, Bunny. Maybe tomorrow . . . but not today, sis." Then he reached over and hugged me and continued soothing me with his tender words. "It's going to be all right. You're strong, Bunny. You can handle this." I fell into Bobby's arms and tried desperately to hold on to what little composure I had left. I could no longer contain the tears, and there I was—being vulnerable in front of Big Bro. I finally felt safe with Bobby holding me in his arms. *What a familiar place*, I thought.

Deep down inside, I wanted to believe Tony. I truly wanted to believe my husband was a man of honor and would never hurt my baby sister. Perhaps it was just as he had stated, and Peaches took it as something else. How could I think in a healthy way when I was struggling to separate this incident from my own history of sexual abuse? I had been damaged as a child. It was all very confusing, and I did not know how to process everything and move forward. I figured when Mama left Daddy, I had walked away from those problems. However, they were still very present. It was an ongoing disturbance within my soul. It would take many, many years for me to learn how to properly address my sexual abuse trauma.

I continued to stay at Tommy and Duckie's apartment. In addition to ignoring Tony, I was also avoiding my mother's calls. At this point, I did not wish to talk to anyone. Realistically, I did not know how to deal with her either. Even at this point, I was still unable to have a healthy conversation with Mama about the sexual abuse I experienced as a child. I could not find the words to tell her how I was feeling inside. However, I knew what I was thinking. Why was all the past pain from my childhood resurfacing? Why was I feeling so much shame and so much guilt about what happened to Peaches? The only thing I cared to do at this point was curl up and hide from the world.

Unfortunately, my pill popping had already morphed into an active addiction. I used pills to help me get through tough emotional experiences and to numb the pain. My quick descent into pill addiction mirrored DeBarge's meteoric rise to fame. They both happened so fast. After going back and forth a couple of days, I made the decision to return home to Tony. I could no longer voice what I felt about the situation nor what I believed as it related to him. All I knew was I wanted to be with my husband. I accepted my husband's recollection— maybe Peaches believed something that did not actually take place.

CHAPTER 20

THE EARLY '80S

DUCKIE FINALLY GAVE BIRTH TO a baby boy and named him Thomas Keith DeBarge Jr. Not long afterward, Mama returned to Grand Rapids. Little Tommy, as he became affectionately known, was the first grandson in the family. There was now a total of five grandchildren (though many more were to come): Damea and Janae (my girls), Keisha (Mark's daughter), Adris (El's daughter), and Little Tommy (Tommy's baby boy). Little Tommy had a head shaped just like his father while his eyes and lips were like his mother. He was a beautiful baby. We were all so proud of him!

Tommy had a son and seemed motivated to get his life together. Motown came to his rescue by providing him with a pay advance that took a load of worry off everyone. Tommy and Duckie were now able to catch up on past due rent and keep their apartment. We all were steadfastly praying these two blessings would give Tommy the incentive to overcome his struggle with drugs and proceed in a better direction with his life.

Tommy surprised me when he chose to buy himself a new bass with some of the money. I knew how hard the decision was for my brother who was easily controlled by his addiction. This sudden financial windfall could have easily sent him spiraling back down the road of addiction. However, this did not appear to be the case. Tommy was appreciative of the kind gesture from Motown, and his reaction was filled with gratitude. He was motivated to do right. I am sure he had his moments. However, because of his newborn son, he was no longer drowning in his addiction. Tommy fought the urge to continue using and focused on playing his new bass. Whenever I visited, he would be playing it and writing songs. This made me very happy. It was a refreshing change from seeing him sleeping all day until the effects of the previous night's drug binge wore off.

Tommy was back to writing songs with the hope Bobby would step in and reassure him at least one of his songs would make the album. Tommy's newfound motivation also spurred me into action. I became adamant about staying on Bobby to make this happen for Tommy. Tommy was working on a song entitled "I Finally Found Somebody New." It was indeed a beautiful song. I loved it and was doing everything I could, including working on the lyrics with him, to ensure Bobby paid it some attention.

We were all in our own individual spaces in life now. For the first time, each of us were living our own lives separate from one another. The only time we came together was to create songs or do interviews. Despite the many girls who flocked to my brothers, it seemed that each of them had finally agreed to settle down and choose one girl to be the lady in their lives. No one had said "I do" as of yet, but they definitely had said "I will." Bobby still had his male roommate, and he was also seeing Latoya Jackson every now and then. James was dating Janet Jackson, who was now starring in the television series *Fame*. James would be on the set with her, and when he was not, they were on the phone with each other. Yes, love was in the air, and DeBarge was high off life. Randy had met an Oriental girl named Gee-Gee, whom he doted on. Mark was spending his time with a girl named Kim, and they had moved into an apartment together. El was living between my place and my friend Jackie's place. As quietly as it was kept, I believed they were an item behind closed doors.

Despite all the disputes Switch continued to have, they were in the studio working on another album. Bobby worked on all his songs with his family. This presented me another opportunity to work side by side with him on yet another project. I wrote two songs for the *Reaching for*

Tomorrow album with Bobby: "My Friend in the Sky" and "Power to Dance." I was proud of both songs, but "My Friend in the Sky" was my favorite out of the two songs we worked on. It was the first song I had worked on diligently from start to finish.

Bobby and I reached way back into our childhood and remembered a song from a children's album Mama had bought for us. On the album were two songs that stuck in our memory: "GOD Bless the Postman" and "The Best Things in Life Are Free." Oftentimes during our troubled childhood, we would begin humming the songs to ease our pain. I recall countless times standing at the living room window singing the songs. The tune stuck with us, and now we were reworking the melody a bit to make it our own. This is what we referred to as writing a melody within a melody. We captured this method and created "My Friend in the Sky."

Bobby wanted his family to participate on the song. We had no problem agreeing to do so. Bobby was still king of the DeBarges, and we were there whenever he summoned us into the studio. It was such a thrill to work with Bobby. To me, he was a musical genius! I can say our time in the studio was an absolute blast, and we all shared background vocals on the song. My favorite part, besides the background work my family did, was the day Bobby added the strings. I was amazed with how Bobby orchestrated the string part on the end of the song. It was something my brother loved to do and did very well. I would even go so far as to say he mastered this creative element. The string part beautifully and melodically enhanced the story the song had to tell. How GOD had inspired us to write songs way before their time was truly amazing! "My Friend in the Sky" would go on to mean so much to me in the years to come.

Out of all the songs Bobby and I worked on together, "My Friend in the Sky" was the one I most remembered. It forced me to reminisce about those sad moments we shared together as children. However, the melody moved the memories to a place of redemption—a joyful time in our lives. Every section of the song fell right into place. Bobby would often say, "Hits make themselves." We were in awe at the outcome of each part of the song. Many times, during the creation of the song,

Bobby and I would give each other high fives. We were extremely pleased with the outcome of the song, and we both called it our masterpiece.

There was always so much joy in my family when we were working with one another. It was nothing for us to bring fresh ideas to one another for a song we were individually working on. It was a teamwork approach, which stemmed from our childhood and was instilled in us by Mama and her family. We watched as Uncle James Abney would come to our home and bang out a song on the piano. He would say it was a song GOD had inspired him to write. We were all there to witness his creativity and to master the harmony he had just created. Mama would often join in and creatively move the melody to something she was hearing in her head. Yes, it was something special to see, and we were carrying their creative legacy into our generation.

I listened to Bobby and El as they were immersed in writing a song. They would be at the piano going over the song endlessly. Both were so expressive in their movement and mastery of the piano. They were intense in their desire to strike the right chords. It was akin to watching a concert pianist play. Sometimes they would play the same song for hours, creating the intro and making a bridge to the song. If you were around their creative space for any amount of time, you would know the song by heart in the end. If you were musically inclined, you would hear a part of your own melody being played. Tinkering around with the piano chords led to the creation of "Share My World" and "Time Will Reveal." It started right at the piano with El just playing around with various chords. Not having the whole concept of the song in place, I would listen and be inspired to take what he had to the next level. We would spend hours working together. Before we knew it, the day would be long gone. However, by the end of the day, we would have a song completed from start to finish!

We were tapping into each other's musical vibe. The patience to listen and understand each other is what brought about a classic hit. Those times were very special, and there was never an argument about who received credit. It was truly a collaborative effort. Bobby was a great mentor to El and me as far as teaching us about the creative process inside the studio. It would be fair to say while I was the first one whose musical gift was discovered by Uncle Bill, Bobby was the first one of us to learn and master the creative process. He was never selfish when it came to imparting knowledge he had gained with his family. It was important to Bobby for his siblings to prosper in the music industry. Many times, Bobby could have asked more established writers to work with him. However, Bobby loved his family and believed in creating from our natural gifts.

Bobby's dream was for all of us to work together and turn the DeBarge name into a musical empire. He was working relentlessly to do his part to make sure this happened. Switch was the path Bobby was using for a bigger purpose. His heart was never in the group from the very start—he longed to perform with his family. Bobby relished in his role as the big brother and was all about family. No one could take this away from him nor could they change his mind. He knew his family had problems, and he also knew music was our sanity. Therefore, he did everything he could to keep his dream alive. No matter what, he kept us focused on the vision.

Bobby's pill popping miraculously ended after the prescriptions were gone as did ours. By this time, Tony and I had unwittingly formed a debilitating habit. We found out just how debilitating as soon as we did not have access to pills. Determined to kick the habit, we went through the nightmare of withdrawal. We had no idea sickness would result. It was a hellish week of flu-like symptoms, and our spirits were down. Not to mention we had trouble sleeping. We did not feel like doing much of anything. We finally made it through the withdrawal after several days and vowed never to go cold-turkey way again. The withdrawal from the pills was physically and emotionally painful. No one could have prepared us for the aftereffects. Bobby was not as successful with kicking his addiction. He went on to find another substance to replace the pills—he started drinking cough syrup and was paying top dollar for it.

TOMMY AND DUCK AND LITTLE TOMMY

CHAPTER 21

MOTOWN 25

It was late January 1983, and our lives had still not slowed down. Tony Jones, a member of our management team, called to say he needed to see DeBarge in his office immediately. There were great things happening at Motown, and the chairman wanted us to be a part of the celebrations. Tony Jones was very excited when he called and made a point to state it was important for all of us to be present for the meeting. The meeting would include all three managers—Suzanne De Passé, Suzanne Coston, and Tony Jones. Whenever the three of them convened to meet with us, it was always something significant and of great importance.

We arrived at Motown, and Suzanne De Passé headed the meeting. I could tell from the excitement in her eyes she had some very good news to share. Hardly able to contain her excitement, Suzanne announced it was Motown's twenty-fifth anniversary. For this milestone, Motown had planned to do something on a grand scale and unlike anything ever been done before. Moreover, she was set to produce the show. She explained that a bevy of legendary Motown performers of yesterday and today would unite onstage to celebrate the silver anniversary of the greatest soul and pop sounds in music history. Our managers billed the show as being one of the most important concerts ever to be produced. We also learned that the show would be televised!

Suzanne dropped names of the performers, which included Michael Jackson along with the Jackson 5, Marvin Gaye, Smokey Robinson and the Miracles, Stevie Wonder, Diana Ross and the Supremes, the Temptations, the Four Tops, among a slew of others. They also planned to invite other artists in the music industry who were inspired by these legendary performers. We were very happy our managers were sharing their plans with us. However, I began to wonder why they needed to schedule a meeting with DeBarge when our names were not even mentioned. They could have simply told us their celebratory plans over the phone and called it a day. I did not want to seem disinterested. However, I was beginning to believe the meeting was a waste of time until Suzanne revealed where we would fit in. Mr. Gordy specifically wanted DeBarge to be a part of this historical and monumental event. It took a moment for her announcement to sink in. DeBarge would be sharing the stage and the limelight with some of the biggest names in the industry! We felt so honored, and it was not lost on us the privilege of sharing the stage with artists we had come to greatly admire. We were informed it would take a lot of preparation on our part to get ready for the big day. Mr. Gordy and management surmised it would lead to great exposure and be a great promotional arrangement for the group. My brothers and I looked at it as favor from GOD! I thought, *what a beautiful time to be with the company! We would be introduced to the world as the next legends twenty-five years from now.*

The program was due to be taped before a live studio audience at the Pasadena Civic Auditorium in Pasadena, California, on March 25, 1983. It would then be broadcast on NBC May 16, 1983. Our managers told us we were officially on the clock and would be given an itinerary stating the days and times we were to be available for rehearsal, wardrobe fitting, etc. We were told to expect a lot of changes, and we would be informed of those changes as time drew near.

Our days leading up to *Motown 25* were filled with endless rehearsals. We were informed there would be no lip-synching. We were expected to sing our songs live to tracks. Also, we no longer had the freedom to come up with our own choreography. I was glad Motown hired choreographers to teach us dance routines. It was time we learned to move together. Up until this point, everyone did their own thing onstage during performances. Marty was notorious for getting lost in the dance routines and stepping on the person's toes next to him. Not one of us were ever enthused to be dancing next to him. When we were not working on the fancy footwork the choreographer had arranged for us, we were glued to the first row of the auditorium watching as the stage designers built and positioned the sets.

A crucial part of live performances happens behind the scenes before a production is mounted and during its runs. Props were being made and set up for each segment of the respective artists' performance of their hit song. It was fascinating watching as the sets were rolled off to the left of the stage and another set appeared to the right of the stage. There were even props coming out of the ceiling. Then there were the dance routines that captured the nostalgia of the '60s and '70s. I was tickled pink watching the dancers capture the few good memories of my childhood. Although I was never a good dancer, I still enjoyed dancing—even if it was swaying from side to side.

Martha Reeves and Mary Wells would be featured as the First Ladies of Motown. They had somewhat aged. However, it did not matter because they were living legends and I respected them as such. Growing up, we were not allowed to listen to what the church referred to as 'devil music'. Still, I knew every single word to "My Guy" and "Heatwave." I had heard those songs at school or whenever we visited our cousins. As the ladies were rehearsing and singing their respective song, I sang right along with them. I enjoyed listening to Mary and Martha more than my brothers since they were too young to remember when these ladies ruled music. I went on and on talking about how thrilled I was to be in the presence of these legendary women. Even though they may not have taken to their music, I did not want my brothers to take for granted the privilege of soon performing on the same stage as these women. They had come before us and paved the way for DeBarge to be featured on the Motown roster.

A rumor was swirling that Marvin Gaye would soon be coming to the auditorium to rehearse his part in the program. Suzanne De Passé knew how fond we were of Mr. Gaye and promised she would introduce the group to him. Each day, my anticipation grew as I looked forward to finally meeting him. I let nothing stand in the way of me arriving to the auditorium early and leaving late. After all, meeting Marvin Gaye and Stevie Wonder was my ultimate dream, and I was determined not to miss this once-in-a-lifetime opportunity. I examined the schedule closely each day to see if Marvin and Stevie would be in the building. I was their number one fan. I loved and cherished them immensely. I listened to and studied their music faithfully—so much so it was as if I knew them personally. In my eyes, they were geniuses and jewels in the music industry. I admired their artistry. There were no better songwriters in my eyes than Marvin Gaye and Stevie Wonder. Their voices were mesmerizing, and their songwriting and producing abilities were unmatched. The messages in their songs were real and resonated with me. To me, their lyrics were always inspirational and represented love. The concept of love was something DeBarge believed in and represented very well. These musical pioneers would go on to inspire me, as well as my brothers, in our songwriting abilities. I already knew meeting them in person would be overwhelming. I would probably have to be brought back to life!

We were in the studio working on the dance steps to our song "Can't Stop." Suzanne De Passé told us the girls of High Inergy would be performing the song with us onstage. She informed us we would begin rehearsing with them soon. Looking down at her watch, she promised she would be right back and rushed out of the room. We had become accustomed to Suzanne popping in and out of meetings and rehearsals. She always seemed extremely busy. Therefore, we paid her no mind and went about our day rehearsing the dance routines. About a half hour or so later, Suzanne returned and asked us to stop rehearsing for a minute. She had a huge surprise waiting for us. My feet were hurting, and we were ready for a break anyway. We graciously obliged.

My brothers and I looked at one another trying to figure out why Suzanne was wide-eyed and giddy. Suddenly, the door swung open, and into the room walked Marvin Gaye! I was immediately put in a trance as my eyes became glued to the tall handsome brown-skinned man who gracefully sauntered into the room. *Ecstasy just entered the room!* I thought. His whole personae breathed pure perfection. My heart skipped a beat, and I went from being an artist to a big-time groupie! Much like the crowd reacted during our promotional tour in Saint Louis, I wanted to scream, run up to him, and grab a piece of him for safekeeping. I was amazed he looked exactly as he was pictured on the album cover of *What's Going On?* I was starstruck and found it hard to believe that standing right there in front of me was a legend we all had come to love and admire. Not a single day passed where at least one of us was not playing Marvin's music.

Mr. Gaye was a perfect gentleman and embraced our amazement. He made small talk, which finally put us at ease. "Ahhhhh, DeBarge," he stated with a singsong voice. He then reached out and shook each of my brother's hand. When he came to me, he gently held my hand and stated, "To the lady in the group: *Tu bi incroyable.* I still care!" No, he did not! Sweat began to pop off me, and my knees began to shake. I was trying hard to compose myself, and I begged GOD to please not let my legs give out. I really could not help myself. Here was this beautiful man standing in front of me holding my hand and speaking to me with the most incredible voice I had ever heard. I dared not look to the left or the right of me. I just knew my brothers were laughing at me making a spectacle of myself. Yes, I was overwhelmed and lost in this fairy-tale moment. I knew he was quoting from his song "'Til Tomorrow" and those French words meant "You are incredible." I was so upset with myself. Everything I had rehearsed to say to Marvin was gone. My mind drew a blank, and I was at a loss for words. The boys knew I was mesmerized. As captivated as they were by his presence, they tried to play it cool and seized the opportunity to tease me relentlessly. "Forgive my sister, Marvin. She is your number one fan," stated El. "In fact, it would be right to say we are all your number one fan."

Marvin took El's compliment graciously, and he lavished a few praises on us. Never in our wildest dream did we ever think that Marvin Gaye had listened to our music. However, to our surprise, he spoke very highly of our background vocals on "All This Love." He recognized his influence in the background parts and went on to commend us by calling our choice of the arrangement "tasteful." Once the ice had been broken, we all began to talk over one another to tell Marvin our favorite song by him. He had been a huge influence on our music, and now we were able to tell him face-to-face. Marvin simply smiled and politely bowed to our kind words. He went on to encourage us as well as welcome us to the industry. Marvin spent a good fifteen minutes with us, and I must say it was a blessed time.

All day long, thoughts of Marvin's warm reception continuously flooded my mind. The visual of this striking, tall, tan, and handsome man played over and over in my mind. I held on to the memory for dear life. One of my childhood dreams had finally come true. My Prince of Love Songs had held my hand and delicately quoted those famous words to his song I loved so tenderly, "I Still Care."

Each day brought new beginnings. We never knew from one day to the next who we were going to meet or what was going to unfold behind the scenes. Basically, we were quickly finding out that stars were humans too. Behind closed doors, they experienced life as ordinary people. There were fears, financial struggles, even butterfly stomachs before walking onstage. Among each other were disagreements, discomforts, their likes and disdain for one another. As we mixed and mingled with everyone, we had opportunities to laugh, joke, and even get in on some good gossiping sessions—there was plenty going around. For a while, my brothers and I had remained quite insular. We only spent time with each other and our family. Slowly, we had started associating ourselves with other stars. We did not have any trouble getting along with fellow artists and were beginning to fit right into celebrity circles.

Mr. Gordy did not grace us with his presence until preparation for the show was in its final stages. Each of the artists were learning their cue—when to come out and when to exit the stage. Richard Pryor was selected as the show's host. Initially, he was reading from a script Motown had prepared for him. As he learned and practiced the script, he began to incorporate his own genius personality. It was great witnessing how he was able to improvise and insert his jokes into the script. To me, he made the script better. I guess the powers that be felt the same way because he was not met with any resistance.

It was a special day once the chairman was in the building. Not long after his arrival, in walked Diana Ross. She strutted past everyone and took her place next to the chairman. My eyes were fixated on the mega superstar. I had heard so many rumors about her and the chairman. Most of the rumors centered on the chairman's love for her and how much he spoiled her at the expense of other artists. There was also a rumor about bad blood between the alleged lovebirds, which caused her to leave Motown on bad terms. I had also heard about the daughter they had together and how it was being kept a secret. This only intensified my curiosity about Ms. Ross. I wanted to see for myself if any chemistry flowed between her and the chairman. If what people said were true, it would be obvious and something they could no longer deny.

From the time Diana Ross stepped foot into the auditorium and made a beeline for Mr. Gordy, I was taking notes. My attention was fixated on the pair. I was intrigued and hoping to get a closer look to examine their relationship dynamic. I know their relationship was none of my business. However, my fascination with Ms. Ross and Mr. Gordy got the best of me, and I wanted to know everything about the legendary duo. I was hoping like crazy Mr. Gordy would introduce us to Ms. Ross. My wish finally came true. After we were done rehearsing our segment, Mr. Gordy called us over to where he was seated with the legendary diva.

It was not as exciting to finally meet Ms. Ross as it had been when I met Mr. Gaye earlier. However, it was interesting to see the diva who played Billie Holiday in *Lady Sings the Blues* up close and personal. She was a stunning beauty. She graciously agreed to be formally introduced to us after prompting from Mr. Gordy. Once introduced, she simply stated it was nice to meet us then turned her full attention back to Mr. Gordy. She was not shy about letting everyone know she commanded the chairman's full and complete attention. Next to where they were seated together sat a young girl in her early teens. She was introduced to us as Rhonda Ross—*Diana's daughter*. Based on the child's features, it was easy to recognize her as Mr. Gordy's daughter. My overall impression of Ms. Ross led me to conclude she was every bit the spoiled brat many had described.

Our day had been mentally and physically exhausting, and we were ready to eat dinner. Our managers granted us permission to leave the auditorium. However, after dinner, we were to return to the venue. We all wanted something different than the cold cuts and fast food we had been eating lately. We decided on a restaurant that served fish. After a quick dinner, we returned to the venue to put in our final rehearsal for the night. We were waiting on the side of the stage listening for our cue when El started to itch uncontrollably. He had broken out in hives all over his body. He was in a lot of distress, and his face turned beet red. Suddenly, he began experiencing shortness of breath. We all ran to find management. I was so afraid because I had never seen El have an allergic reaction. Mrs. De Passé called the ambulance, and he was rushed to the ER. Although we were worried to no end, the EMTs assured and reassured us he would be okay. They stated it must have been something he ate that caused the reaction. Management stayed with El, and the rest of the group was left to go on rehearsing without him. El did not return to finish rehearsal. After he was released from the hospital, Motown set him up in a hotel to rest. A doctor would come visit him early the next morning to see if he was well enough to rehearse the next day.

We had a couple of days off from rehearsing the show but still had to be fitted for wardrobe. It had been weeks since I had spent quality time with my husband and children. My days started early and ended late. I only came home to sleep then it was back on the job. Bobby was busy as well. He was out of town working on his solo project. The group Switch had finally broken up and were subsequently dropped from Motown. The remaining band members, minus Bobby and Tommy, went on to sign with Total Experience Records—home of the Gap Band. Bobby was still signed to Motown. With my busy rehearsal schedule, I was missing his calls. This day, I got to sleep in late. However, a limo was scheduled to pick me up midday to take the group for wardrobe fitting.

The phone was ringing off the hook and interrupted my sleep. When I answered the phone, it was Bobby on the other end. He was out of pills and very sick. Not having any pills was interfering with his ability to work. He needed me to get a prescription for the pills and mail them to him overnight. I had weaned myself off the pills and was feeling great. Preparing for the *Motown 25* performance kept me busy and my mind preoccupied. I barely had enough time for myself and my family so I sure did not have time to deal with Bobby and his dilemma. Bobby's addiction and demand of my time was too much for me to focus on. I was tired of being afraid of getting caught doing something illegal just to feed his addiction. I would not agree to mail drugs to him. What if I got caught? What about my husband and my girls? What about my career? What about my freedom? No! I would not do it no matter how much pressure Bobby was putting on me. I had to put my foot down and stop allowing Bobby to control and manipulate me. "I can't do it, Bobby," I firmly stated. "I am scared of getting caught."

Bobby did his best to convince me that everything would be all right. "Bunny, all you have to do is put it in a box, put an address on it, and send it thru overnight mail. I will call Larry (the drug dealer) ahead of time and tell him you're on your way." I could tell my brother was sick. I had been there myself so I could truly relate. Yet I had done everything it took to move past abusing the pills. I had gone through withdrawal and not being able to sleep. It had not been enough time between now and when I last used pills. Dealing with Bobby made it far too easy to just pick up the habit again. I weighed out everything and felt I had too much to lose. I wanted no parts of Bobby's constant scheming to score drugs. I kept telling him no, but Bobby would not listen nor would he take *no* for an answer. It was mentally and emotionally draining.

"There has to be another way," I pleaded with Bobby. "You can't continue to depend on me." I hung up the phone with an unhappy Bobby on the other end. I grew anxious because I knew my brother would not give up pressuring me to get him more pills. It would not be the last I would hear from him on this issue. I could tell from his tone he was desperate and determined to find a way to convince me to get the pills he needed. He called back, and I wanted to just let the phone ring. However, I knew Bobby would continue calling back-to-back until I answered. I decided to go ahead and answer the phone. As soon as I picked up the phone, Bobby started talking.

"Okay then—how about I send you a ticket to bring it to me? Then you can go right back home." He had it all planned out. There was no way I was going to agree to anything he proposed.

"Bobby, I cannot leave right now. The group is busy getting ready for the *Motown 25* show!" I was over it and did not want to deal with Bobby any longer. As I was about to hang up, a thought came to my mind. "Where is Andre, Bobby? Maybe he can do it." Andre Abney, our cousin, was still living in California, and he and Bobby were close. He would love to take a trip and visit with Bobby. Andre and Bobby did drugs together so perhaps he could help.

"Yeah, that's right." Bobby seemed relieved. "I forgot about Andre. Let me call him, and I will call you right back." Bobby immediately hung up the phone without saying good-bye. I was hoping Andre would be his ram in the bush. I never received a call back from Bobby, and it was okay with me. I knew Bobby was fine since later I heard from Andre. He called me all excited about taking a flight to see Bobby. It was a trip he did not mind taking at all. He was also happy he did not have to return to California right away. He was going to spend a couple of days with Bobby. Andre's call took a load off my mind. I knew my brother was desperately sick. He needed the pills to get him through the sessions. Meanwhile, we had wardrobe fittings, and the days were narrowing down. The time was drawing near, and *Motown 25* was only days away. Everyone was on pins and needles.

CHAPTER 22

THE FINAL FINALE

THE DAY OF THE SHOW was finally here. The auditorium was buzzing with excitement as the production crew finalized the details. As each star arrived, they were rushed into their dressing room to get ready for the show. There would be no more rehearsing. The show had been fine-tuned, and today was the final finale. It was a waiting game now, and my stomach was tied in knots. Makeup artists were in designated areas, and the artists were being called out according to their scheduled time to get their makeup applied. Wardrobe designers were assigned to different artists and were in their respective dressing rooms.

Everyone was dressed to impress for the five minutes they would grace the stage. We had practiced so hard for two months straight for what would amount to five minutes of stage time. Because of the significance of the event, it meant everything to do our best tonight. The two months we spent in rehearsal swallowed up every second of our lives. Since late January, we all breathed, ate, and slept the *Motown 25* performance. Tonight, though, it did not matter who did not like whom. If you wanted to have a great performance, you had to put aside your differences. We were on a mission to make the show a historic event. The *Who's Who* of the industry would be present. I am sure we all wished one another the best. My brothers and I came together and prayed not only for our performance but for everyone else's performance as well.

The makeup area was oddly quiet. Maybe everyone, like myself, was having butterfly stomach. The makeup artists applied our makeup with precision. They were busy wiping, patting, and smoothing. It seemed to calm down many of the artists except for me. For some strange reason, getting my makeup done was never a fun experience. I do not know if it was because someone I did not know was touching me. Perhaps because the makeup artist had to get uncomfortably close to apply the makeup. Whatever the reason, it was always a very uncomfortable experience. I kept telling myself to be still and remain calm. After all, this was simply the life of being a star. I had to look great for the cameras, and the cause of beauty often meant being uncomfortable. Still, I wanted to get the makeup session over with so I could get to myself and calm my nerves.

My brothers were antsy as well, which was no surprise. The DeBarge boys were born with ants in their pants. We were all told to stay in our dressing rooms. However, El, Marty, James, and Randy were constantly finding excuse after excuse to venture around backstage and cause mischief. They were all over the place. Normally, I would have been fussing at the boys to do as they were told and stay in their dressing room. Yet I felt the need to get out of the room as well. There were too many people in such a small space. I stepped out into the hallway to see if anything exciting was happening. I wanted to see if anyone else was overcome with nervous tension. As I began to walk the hallway, I ran into Nick Ashford and Valerie Simpson. I had briefly met them earlier during rehearsals and felt confident enough to strike up a conversation with the lovely couple. As we were making small talk, this phenomenal voice began echoing throughout the hallways. Sounding regal and angelic, the voice soared up and down the music scale with ease. The singer rhythmically and melodically sang *hehe's* and *haha's* at the top of their voice. The sound was exquisite and unlike anything I had ever heard before. It blew me away. Looking with amazement at Nick and Valerie, they did not seem fazed at all. "Who in the world is that with such a powerful voice?" I asked.

Valerie smiled and said, "Oh, it's Michael. It's a warm-up technique he uses when he is getting ready for a show."

"Michael Jackson?" I asked, not sure if I wanted to believe what she was saying. "Really?" I was amazed! "That is awesome!" I stated, still in disbelief. I was familiar with the vocal scale, but I had never heard anyone practice it quite like him. *He's here!* I thought. *He made it!* Everything surrounding Michael Jackson had been a great big mystery. During the entire two months of rehearsals, no one had laid an eye on a single member of the Jackson clan. Rumor had it that the Jacksons (Tito, Marlon, Jackie, Randy, and Jermaine) would be there, but Michael had refused to participate. Not only was there bad blood between Michael and Motown, but Michael also had now left his family's musical roots and stepped out on his own. His brothers were unsure if Michael wanted to reunite or simply focus on his own career. Negotiations had broken down between company executives and Michael. Michael was no longer willing to deal with anyone at Motown except the chairman. I did not concern myself with the behind-the-scene shenanigans. None of the ego tripping meant anything to me. It was now confirmed Michael Jackson was in the building. I had heard him with my own two ears. His unique voice stopped me dead in my tracks. Tonight, Michael was gearing up to showcase his new unique moaning and groaning, which would soon become a part of his signature sound.

The show was now in full swing. The anticipation of performing onstage for this historical event was overwhelming. Even though we had witnessed many of the performances during rehearsals, there were still segments of the show we had not seen. There was no way I planned to stay in our dressing room until it was our turn to perform. I was not going to wait until the show aired on television either to see the parts I missed. No way was I going to miss the Jackson 5 or Marvin Gaye's once-in-a-lifetime performance. I was going to see every magical moment as it unfolded onstage. So fully dressed and vowing to stay out of the way, my brothers and I were positioned on the side of the stage while watching the show.

Every segment of the show was magical, and the improvisations from the artists were on point. Watching the battle of the Temptations and the Four Tops was very much like the church services I had witnessed growing up. The performances made me appreciate my upbringing in the church when we sang with Uncle James. It might have been on a smaller scale. However, Uncle James taught us the art of stage presence during church musicals. Then there was Stevie Wonder who captivated me from the moment he opened his mouth and belted out his first note. I could not believe his voice sounded better live than on his recordings. I was in heaven as he sang a good ten minutes of his Motown hits. Marvin Gaye's performance touched my heart as well as my soul. I felt a twinge of sadness in my spirit as I watched him perform. At this moment, I did not fully understand the reasons why my heart was bleeding for him. All I knew was I felt a connection with him unlike I had ever felt listening to him before. I wanted to know more about his life and what was driving his melancholy. It was almost as if we were living with much of the same type of pain. We were battling the same demons, and I could relate to him.

We were so engrossed in watching the show we nearly forgot we were also set to perform. Our managers hurried us back to the dressing room where we freshened up our makeup and finished getting dressed. The time had finally arrived, and DeBarge was headed to the stage. Suddenly, everything shifted from excitement to panic. The spotlight was now on us. Oh my GOD! How would we measure up to these legendary performers? *GOD has not given me a spirit of fear!* I kept telling myself repeatedly. I looked around at my brothers. Without a single word being spoken, we could all feel one another's anxiety. Everyone had sweaty palms as we held one another's hands and stated in unison: "In Jesus's Name—let's do this."

The stage was set for DeBarge and High Inergy. The first song was "All This Love." We had to walk down steps to get to the front of the stage. The music began, and immediately my legs froze. All I could think about was not tripping over my own feet. We walked out with huge smiles on our faces. It was not until we reached the bottom of the steps that the pressure let up. I gained a little confidence as we began to sway from side to side in unison. We were onstage, and El was working his magic with the audience. I was so happy the song was faster than the original track. Before we knew it, we were running off the stage to the left. As we were exiting, High Inergy was running onstage belting out their single "Pretender." I was in a trance as we waited to go back onstage and join High Inergy and perform our song "Can't Stop." This is where all the rehearsing with the choreographer came in to play. I had gained a bit of confidence in my dancing abilities and was able to put a smile on my face and dance around the stage. The entire performance between the two groups lasted approximately five minutes. Once we sang the final words to "Can't Stop," the audience stood to their feet and applauded. We did it! I was now able to breathe and relax. The worst was over. We went back to the dressing room to take pictures and do press interviews. Now out of my trance, I was able to take in the moment. There was a lot of hard work put into our performance, and the audience's response made every moment worthwhile.

The Jacksons featuring Michael Jackson would be onstage soon enough, and I could hardly wait to watch them perform. It saddened me to know my favorite childhood group was no longer a group. They were still family just like my brothers and I, but now the group was no longer together. I could not imagine singing without my family by my side. The thought made me shiver. We had always done everything together, and our lives were so intertwined. What happened to them? I wondered. Why did Michael not want to perform with his family any longer? The Jacksons came out, and the audience went wild! They were out of their seats with their hands in the air singing right along with them. Michael's voice was flawless as he took us back to the days of our youth. Once they finished performing together, the brothers exited the stage, and Michael began to speak. He spoke on the old days at Motown and how much he appreciated everyone. Those days, he stated, brought him to where he is today. Then he stated, "Yes, those were the good old days, and they did us well. But time moves on, and this is the new." Suddenly, the track to "Billie Jean" began to play. People had heard this single, but no one had ever seen Michael perform the song. Sitting on the edge of their seats, the audience was hypnotized with his every move. When he did his now infamous moonwalk, the audience went wild! It was as if we were at a football game, and our favorite team had just scored a touchdown. Michael Jackson brought the house down! The entire auditorium was in a frenzy. Even those of us standing at the side of the stage was cheering him on. Michael Jackson set the world on fire with his performance and debuted his signature dance move—the moonwalk. Michael had the entire audience in awe, and there was no topping his performance! The little boy who grew up with Motown was on his own and making a statement to the world: *I'm a man now and I'm bad!* Several minutes passed as the audience and the artists stood there marveling over Michael's historic performance. The show was not yet over, and we still had the final finale.

Suddenly, the music to "Ain't No Mountain High Enough" belted through the speakers. It was now Ms. Ross's turn to captivate the audience. Michael's performance was so memorable I had forgotten all about Ms. Ross. I looked at the stage, but no Diana Ross. *This is different*, I thought. Where was Ms. Diana Ross? Everyone backstage began to whisper and ask, "Where is Ms. Diana?" It had become obvious that something was amiss. This was the ultimate *uh-oh moment*. The audience was looking around the auditorium, confused as well. Out of nowhere, Ms. Ross came running from the back of the building onto the stage. She was holding a microphone singing the song. It was shocking to the audience but even more shocking to the artists who knew the outline of the show. Why was Diana running from the back of the auditorium? Something was going on, and whispers had already begun to float backstage.

In rehearsal, she was supposed to already be onstage immediately after Michael's performance. She was to announce Cindy Birdsong and Mary Wells. The Supremes were to perform a song together. Diana rushed through introducing her former group members then quickly jumped to the final song: "Someday, We'll Be Together." The audience had no idea what was going on, but everyone who was a part of the program knew that something was not right. Ms. Ross was being the boss, and she was determined to do things her way. Nevertheless, it was time for all the artists to appear onstage. They were showing up from both sides of the stage. I was so tickled because this segment reminded me of our church home. Everyone began singing over each other. Artists were pushing each other out of the way trying to make their way to the front of the stage. Egos were clashing left and right. I was standing next to Valerie and Nick, and we had a ball laughing at everyone. It was the *final finale*, and boy, was it a free-for-all!

The show was finally over! There were many pictures taken and interviews given. We were invited to an after party, and the boys were all for it. I chose to go home. I was wiped out and needed sleep. However, there was one party that only El was invited to attend. It was a party for the "We Are the World" recording. Only a select few artists were invited to the coveted party. We did not find out about the invitation until the following day. I did not think much of it, but I certainly would have gone to the party had I been invited. Little did I know this was only the beginning of many more parties and events my brother El would be invited to that excluded the rest of the group.

CHAPTER 23

AFTER THE DANCE

Our second album, *All This Love*, went gold, and we did not miss a beat. Right after *Motown 25*, we were summoned back into the studio to begin working on our third album. Our release date was scheduled for some time in September 1983. We were elated when El was tapped to produce the album. This would give us more creative control than we had had on the previous albums. It also allowed us the freedom to do things the DeBarge way. El hired Barney Perkins as our recording engineer. We had become great friends with Barney after meeting him when he assisted other engineers on our previous albums. At the time, Barney was just learning studio work alongside each of us. Now, we all had the opportunity to put the skills we had learned to good use. He suggested we work at Kendun Studio in Burbank, California, and Westlake Audio in West Hollywood. We were individually and collectively on the grind with writing new material. It was an opportunity for us to showcase the DeBarge sound on each track. We would be able to critique our own music and determine if it made the final cut.

Bobby had finished his solo project. Both he and Larry Blackmon had produced the album. The final production was great, but Motown put a halt to its release. Bobby returned to California to take pictures for the album cover. However, it had become evident to Motown that he was still struggling with addiction. Unwilling to spend money on promoting the album, Motown dropped Bobby from the company.

Afterward, I watched as my brother's life spiraled downhill. He became severely depressed and no longer interested in the music business. Bobby's drug addiction further escalated. He had gone from abusing Tussionex pills to drinking a cough syrup named Citra Forte. Bobby never went back to smoking cocaine, nor did he touch heroin again. The cough syrup he was abusing was based with morphine. It had the same effect as heroin and was just as damaging. My brother enjoyed being sedated. This was truly his preference, which is why he used sedative medication as opposed to drugs that increased his energy level such as cocaine. Bobby believed the Citra Forte calmed him down and sedated the pain torturing him mentally. He had never dealt with the pain of our childhood. Then to add to the pain he was enduring with the lifestyle he had chosen made life for him nearly unbearable. Bobby talked to me often about his tortured soul—but not without being under the influence of the medication he was abusing. He was caught up in a vicious cycle. He was now hooked on the syrup and big-time. He would purchase bottles and bottles of syrup at one time. He started out taking just an ounce. By now, though, it had intensified to ounces at a time. I was truly afraid for my brother's life.

No longer with Motown, Bobby did not have the money to finance his addiction or lifestyle. He sometimes looked to family members to help him out. This was devastating to us as a family. We loved and respected Bobby so much. We looked up to him and relied on him in so many ways. It was devastating to come to the realization he was caught up in the tangled web of addiction with seemingly no way out. He was in such a fog of addiction, we could no longer rely on his expertise in the studio or to guide our songwriting abilities. However, Bobby was instrumental in helping us gain unfettered access to drugs. We were able to obtain drugs because Bobby needed drugs. Although it was sad to witness his descent, Bobby still had a very strong influence over his siblings. The more he used, the more we used. It started out as a very slow crawl downhill. Besides Bobby, the rest of us used recreationally in between working on the album. It was not an everyday occurrence, and neither of us were hooked—yet. However, every addict has a starting point. Even Bobby seemed in control of his drug use at one time.

My naïveté caused me to deny I was sinking deep into the abyss of addiction. It saddened me that Bobby had resorted to using drugs daily. I felt grateful to have had a grasp on my drug use and not use every day. I was bound and determined to keep a limit on how much I used and to keep my use strictly recreational.

One morning, Bobby came to my home distraught. He stated between tears that he was tired of being addicted to drugs. He begged me to help him. He wanted to go cold turkey but wanted to do it away from everyone else. Bobby and I had talked about him getting clean numerous times. There were times when I would locate a place for him to go for treatment. Once everything was set up, the hard work needed to get clean and sober would freak Bobby out. He would either flat out refuse to go, would disappear, or not follow through with treatment. I figured today was just another one of Bobby's feigned cries for help. I did not take him seriously. I felt he was playing on my kindness, looking for sympathy, or trying to get money out of me. Bobby stated he did not want anything except my help. He had enough drugs on him to last a few more days.

As the day drew on, Bobby finally convinced me he was serious about wanting help and he was tired of being on drugs. He had a plan and asked me to go to Detroit with him. To my surprise, he wanted to be with our father. He felt he needed Daddy's help but did not want to do it alone. I knew that a big source of Bobby's pain could be traced back to Daddy. The only thing with a stronger pull on Bobby than drugs was his desire to feel love from his father. For him to be willing to put trust in our father while in such a vulnerable state moved me immensely. Bobby wanted his daddy, and I was hoping I could fulfill his heart's desire. As much as I wanted to go to Detroit and support Bobby, I was unable to do so. My husband and my children needed me in California, and I was also busy with the new album project. I hoped Daddy would agree to help Bobby. I worried that if Daddy rejected Bobby, my brother would not survive. Daddy was the only thing standing between life and death for Bobby. I whispered a small prayer and called Daddy.

I informed Daddy of Bobby's dire situation and how bad his addiction had spiraled out of control. I told Daddy that Bobby spending time with him and getting help from him would go a long way in helping him get sober. Surprisingly, Daddy was receptive and very sympathetic to Bobby's present circumstances. He did not think twice. In fact, he welcomed him to come stay with him and said he would do all he could to help him get clean and sober. Bobby seemed relieved by the news. My brothers and I chipped in and planned for Bobby to go live with Daddy in Detroit. Everyone was in support of Bobby returning to Detroit and getting some much-needed help. It took a load off us mentally, and we could now begin to focus on completing the album. Worrying about Bobby day in and day out affected us inside the studio. We had an album to complete and a brother we wanted to save. Knowing Bobby had made plans to help himself meant everything to us. The best part was he had reached out to our father for support.

Bobby was a man of his word and went to Detroit to be with Daddy. We drove him to the airport and promised him we would check on him daily. I prayed he would put aside any differences with Daddy while in Detroit. He and Daddy's relationship was not the greatest. However, to go live with Daddy was originally Bobby's idea. He must have felt as if this was something he needed at this point in his life. Bobby was spiritually broken, and he wanted his father. Daddy was open to helping him, and my prayer was they both find restoration during this season. As DeBarge, we went on with our lives as Bobby was desperately trying to rebuild his own life. We had work to do and obligations to fulfill. Regardless of the circumstances, our lives could not stop because Bobby's life was in shambles. Besides, we all had to deal with our own vulnerabilities. Bobby was just way ahead of us in this game called life. He had experienced the highs and the lows—the blessings and the pitfalls. Little did we know, we all had a day of reckoning whereas we would be forced to confront our individual demons as well.

***

El met a girl on *Soul Train* who left him smitten. Her name was Roberta. At the time, she had just ended a relationship with the artist O'Bryan. It appears my brother was modeling his life after his idol Marvin Gaye. He heard about the tumultuous love story between Marvin and Janice. They had met on *Soul Train*, and she was a dancer on the iconic show. El, loving everything about Marvin, was obsessed with this story. What had once been a mere fantasy was now El's reality. Roberta had caught his eye and was now becoming the center of his existence. El would play "After the Dance" nonstop. He was head over heels in love with Roberta. He was living with me at the time he met Roberta. We were very close, and he often spoke of his relationship. After listening to certain details of their relationship, I became very concerned about my brother. El invested a lot of himself into the relationship. However, Roberta was not shy about sharing that she still had eyes for O'Bryan.

To me, it appeared as if El was her rebound lover. The fact that Roberta did not reciprocate affection toward El was torturing him. Of course, as big sis, I felt my little brother deserved someone who had eyes for only him. I would console his ego with wisdom and words of encouragement. I was also very frank with El. I felt that Roberta was playing a number on his heart. This did not sit well with El, and I quickly learned to only give my opinion when asked. The more I tried to help El see Roberta for who she was, the more he was determined to win her affections. Eventually, I only spoke when spoken to, but I was very much in my brother's corner. There were many times I would see my brother heartbroken and in distress. He and Roberta were always on again off again. I would then have to be there to help rebuild his confidence and speak life into his emptiness. It was exhausting witnessing the ups and downs of their relationship. Troubling as it was, I finally accepted it was his life and his mistakes to make. If he was satisfied with a one-sided relationship, then I would leave him to his own devices. Before this relationship, El and I rarely, if ever, had any disagreements. I was not going to allow Roberta to come between my relationship with my brother. It was a rough road, and I had to learn the hard way to keep my mouth closed.

Each of my brothers were now in serious relationships. Mark and Kim were expecting a baby. In fact, baby fever had hit the DeBarge family. Duckie was pregnant again. Randy just had a baby with a girl named Sibylene. However, they had broken up, and Randy had no idea where she was with the baby. He was left heartbroken and longing for Sibylene and his child. Amid his heartache, Randy quietly wed a girl named GiGi whom he had only known for a couple of months. The other boys were incensed. They felt that Randy had made a terrible mistake. I wondered what Randy was thinking. The boys felt that GiGi had been hanging around not really knowing which one of the brothers she wanted. She married Randy because he was the only one foolish enough to propose. This did not come as a surprise to me, and I totally understood how she was able to manipulate Randy into marriage. After all, Randy was the most sensitive and kindhearted out of the entire sibling group. We all had made it our mission to always protect him. It would be nothing (and came quite naturally) for each of us to stand up for him if we felt he was being taken advantage of in the slightest regard. Randy's heart was still with Sibylene, and he was not over her when he married GiGi. Nothing about his quickie marriage felt right to us. We did agree not to interfere with his marriage though. However, we let it be known to GiGi we would keep a very close eye on Randy.

James and Janet's relationship was solid and going strong. They were inseparable and very much in love. We counted it all joy because for once, James seemed genuinely happy. Not only was he happy to be in the group, but he was also courting the love of his life. The relationship had a positive impact on his creativity as well. For the album, James brought in three songs: "Need Somebody," "I Give Up on You," and "Be My Lady." Each song he brought in was completed from start to finish. His songs were the first music tracks to be taped.

Tommy was not faring well. Fortunately, he and Bobby were apart from each other for the time being. It was a welcome relief because whenever they were together, they ended up arguing and fighting. Being apart, they would be able to see how they were their own worst enemy. Tommy had fallen off the wagon yet again and was back to freebasing. We had become accustomed to not seeing him for days at a time, and apparently, so did Duckie. For whatever reason, Duckie was still clinging to her relationship with Tommy. She found strength in our sisterhood, and we continued spending time together. Duckie trusted me and knew I was fair and would not steer her wrong. If Tommy was in the wrong, I was not the least bit on his side despite him being my brother. I would not be shy in telling him the cold, hard facts. There were many days I felt Tommy was wrong and Duckie should just up and leave for her sake and the sake of their children. However, it was clear as day that Duckie was in it for the long haul. She was not going anywhere. Therefore, I continued to look out for her best interest as best as I could. Duckie had now become an important part of our family. I would often say she was the eleventh DeBarge.

Bobby remained in Detroit with Daddy for over a month. He was able to kick his drug habit and return to Los Angeles clean and sober. He shared with me it was an extremely difficult journey. However, our Father was there to assist him every step of the way. Daddy took him to his doctor who prescribed medication to soothe the pain Bobby was experiencing while detoxing. I must say Bobby looked great and he spoke highly of Daddy's support. I was happy Bobby was happy. He appeared to be back to his old self again. He was talking music again and could not wait to hear what we were putting down in the studio.

CHAPTER 24

TEAMWORK MAKES "A DREAM"

With DeBarge being granted full creative freedom over development of our upcoming album, the vibe in the studio was vastly different. We did not have management and Motown personnel breathing down our necks and monitoring our every move. I am not sure if this was a good or bad thing. Perhaps we needed the accountability we did not particularly like but had grown accustomed to at Motown. Now, it felt as if something was stirring around in the atmosphere interfering with us being on our best behavior. Not having personnel tapping our shoulders at every turn, you could see the difference in our work ethic.

We were happy not having to commute into Los Angeles to record. Kendun recording studio was in the Valley where we all lived. It was not only convenient, but it also felt like home. Another thing we were grateful for was El having full control over the album's development. To keep the momentum going, he booked us weeks at a time in the studio. We would be able to work nonstop if we chose. Putting James's songs to tape was a magical experience. It took us no time to complete them because James was always diligent with completing his songs from start to finish. All we had left to do was add in the strings, horns, and vocal parts on the songs he presented. El developed a production technique he first used on James's songs whereas he did the rhythm tracks first.

This made it much easier for us to record the lyrics and background vocals afterward. El ended up completing all our songs in this manner.

Mark brought in an idea to record a song he was working on called "Stay with Me." The hook to the song was great. He asked El and I to help finish the song. We ended up writing the verses and adding in the bridge. The memorable line *"Ahhh . . . you should be right here with me babe instead of going around this frantic town—stop messing around"* was all I needed from El to complete the story. I then took the lyrical impression Mark had created for the hook and finalized the lyrics. Musicians were then called in to lay the tracks. I did not have to be present for this part of the creative process. I decided to spend time with my husband and children.

I was still tasked with writing my own song. Writing for me was always a collaborative process mostly involving El and Bobby. I was intimidated by the process of writing a song myself. It was very stressful coming up with a concept for a song. I had melodies playing around in my head. It felt like melodies I had heard before. I wanted to come up with a fresh new sound. I was overwhelmed because many things were transpiring in my life. The constant drama was draining my inspiration. I remember thinking to myself, *why am I able to help everyone else with their songs? Yet when it came down to my own songs, I do not have a clue what to bring to the table?*

One day, Hall and Oates were doing an interview on a local television program. I always admired the duo and their music. I decided to take a break from brainstorming about the song and the melody. I sat attentively in front of the television watching and listening to them describe aspects of their creative processes. I found what they were sharing inspiring. What stuck out to me was when they stated, "Our songs come from just about anything. Sometimes from a dream or from a billboard we see on the highway." The phrase "a dream" jumped out at me. "I like that," I said to myself. A lightbulb immediately went off in my head. Finally, I had some necessary inspiration. I jumped up and grabbed a pen and piece of paper and began jotting down my thoughts. *Let's see: What is it we girls dream about? Maybe it is a special guy we wished was our own? Perhaps he belongs to someone else, and we fantasize about him belonging to us. Perhaps he is not aware we even care. I have been there many times myself.*

The inspiration started pouring forth from my heart onto the paper. A smile of satisfaction began spreading across my face. With each line I wrote, I felt a release in my spirit. My song was dressed up in my head: *"A dream . . . a simple fantasy that I wished was reality."* I decided this line would be my hook. Now I needed a melody. A bass line for the song began to develop in my mind. I grabbed my recorder and began to sing the notes. Listening to the bass line I had recorded enabled me to hear the melody for the verse and hook.

I was brimming with excitement and eager to showcase my masterpiece to El. I wanted to know what his thoughts were about the song so far. El had been busy around the clock with studio work. There were other songs he was working on that were in various stages of completion. It never dawned on me he may have been exhausted from all his hard work. However, I was antsy and wanted him to immediately cater to my creative needs. I was used to having his expertise at my disposal. He was now busy not only in the studio but also with his personal life. I was not planning to wait for his personal life to slow down for him to hear my song. I called him and quickly shared I had written a song. Before he could respond, I started playing the recording into the phone. I sensed that El's focus was elsewhere. He was short with me and said to drop the recording off to him and he would get back with me later.

Before I dropped off the recording to El, Randy came over for a visit. Soliciting his input, I shared a snippet of the song with him. I could not quite read his face to determine if he liked it or not. Although he eventually agreed he liked it, he felt as if he could not judge if it were good enough for the album. Randy simply stated, "Take the song to El." By the time I reached the studio, El was rushing out the door. He stated he would return to the studio later. We would be laying backgrounds to "Stay with Me." Since the song was a ballad, I had no choice except to be present. Our ballads were always done by El, Randy, and me. I stood there lost and feeling as though I was the only person enthused by my song. El and Randy had both burst my bubble. I brushed it off and hoped El would eventually get around to listening to it. I went on my merry way to mentally prepare for the studio session.

As I walked into the studio, I could not believe what was taking place. I questioned if we were there to record an album or have a grand ole time. *The boys cannot be serious*, I thought. Food had been ordered, and alcohol was pouring from every corner of the studio. The boys were lounging around on the couch with girls spilling out from every side. It was obvious this was a new group of girls. Looking at the beautiful yet scantily clad girls, I could not help but wonder if they were picked up off the street. After all, my brothers were friendly to a fault. They had no enemies and never met a stranger. "Is it break time?" I asked sarcastically. "Or are we *literally* having a party?" I looked around the room and saw marijuana joints being rolled and passed around. The boys began to introduce the girls in the room. They pretended as though the names had just slipped their minds. Each one of the girls ended up having to introduce themselves. Just as I assumed, they had just met these young ladies.

I sat back, relaxed, and watched my brothers in their element. Whenever ladies were present, it would be so much fun watching the boys become these smooth operators. The girls my brothers met always felt privileged to join them in the studio. I was pretty sure the ladies had put aside all plans they had made for the day to enjoy this golden opportunity. They were easily amused by the slightest jokes my brothers made (even if the jokes clearly were not funny), and they were starstruck. Looking around the room, I took a mental note of each brother in their element. There was "So Smooth" El, "Slick Talking" James, "Laid-Back" Randy, and "Energizer Bunny" Mark. It was par for the course to see El standing nonchalantly off to the side. It was a weird strategy he used to create an aura of mystery around him. He was never easy to read and wore his charm well along with a million-dollar smile. Women would always be drawn to his quiet allure like a moth to a flame. *Okay*, I thought. *These guys are not in work mode.* In fact, there was a friendly competition going on betwixt the brothers. I took a drag of a joint and sat back, observing the ensuing chaos. The ladies were giddy and could not keep their eyes and hands off the boys. They were desperate to rise to the top of the pecking order. *Choose me! Choose me!* was written all over their faces (and scantily clad outfits). It became evident that no matter how much the boys talked about getting to work, *play* was the only thing on the agenda. I decided to stick around a while longer, enjoy the freak show, then make my way back home to my sanity. The atmosphere was lively, and all types of people were coming and going. The boys were having a ball! Finally, I had had enough of the partying and people watching. I was buzzed and decided to leave. I said my good-byes then exited the studio.

As I was about to drive off, El pulled up alongside me. "Where are you going?" he asked.

"I'm going home, El. It's obvious we're not *working* tonight." I looked at El matter-of-factly.

El laughed. "Yeah, you're right. But I'll be here all night if you want to come back."

"I'm not coming back. I'm going to bed." El was blowing my high, and I was over the small talk.

"All right then. See you tomorrow," he stated. "By the way, Bunny, I listened to your song. It's great, sis! I can feel what you're trying to say. It's going to be a masterpiece! I really love the bass line!" He then pulled off.

My day was made. I no longer felt as if my day had been spent in vain. El said the magic words and lifted my spirit: *I listened to your song, and it's going to be a masterpiece!* I was finally able to rest. Knowing El loved my song and was going to make it happen meant the world to me. I went to sleep with the song on my mind and literally dreamed about the concept. The song, which would eventually become my signature song, was written in a dream. As Bobby often reminded us, "You know it's a hit when it writes itself."

My song was now in good hands. El was a phenomenal producer, and I was his number one fan. El, the consummate perfectionist, would not just settle for any typical chord for the song. After hearing the concept, he envisioned the direction he wanted to go with the song. He meticulously played around with each chord until he found the perfect one that spoke to him. I would sing the melody to him as he danced around with the chords on the piano. Of course, El did not need my help finding a chord. I just enjoyed being in the studio with him and witnessing his creative genius unfold. El critiqued each chord with precision then found a way to add something special to make it his own. I found each chord he played to be the perfect one. Not El, though. 'It's a dream and it must sound like one,' he kept reminding me. Bobby came to the studio and joined us. As El tinkered around with the chords, Bobby fell in love with the song. He was inspired and ended up writing the B-section of the song which carried me back to the hook at the end. *What a dynamic team and a perfect love song!* I was elated. The song became an instant classic. It was another *DeBarge song* that went on to make history!

CHAPTER 25

MAMA, HELP ME TO UNDERSTAND!

My relationship with my husband, Tony, was going well. Everything seemed to be running smooth for once in our lives. We were handling business and built a social life outside of immediate family. We enjoyed spending time with our new friends, Kevin and Michele. We had met the couple through Tommy and Duckie and became fast friends. We did everything together. Kevin was a very talented artist who ended up drawing logos for DeBarge. We were learning about each other's lives and spent nearly every day together. Either they were at our home or we were at their home. They also had a young daughter whom I grew fond of rather quickly.

Michele filled a sisterly void in my life. We spent a lot of time buying food and shopping for clothing and furniture. We dressed the girls alike, and Michele and I would sometimes buy matching outfits. Birthdays were always a family affair, and we celebrated each person's special day together when it became time. We frequented restaurants together. We even got high together.

One day, we had secured tickets to the Budweiser Festival. Afterward, we stopped in Los Angeles at one of Bobby's connections to purchase some cough syrup. We never tried cough syrup before, but not having access to pills was getting stressful. Bobby convinced us the syrup would give us the same high as the pills. Tony and I had introduced Kevin and Michele to pills, and they liked taking them as well. They agreed to try the syrup in absence of the pills. Bobby took us to his connection, and we were on our merry way. After experimenting with the syrup, we found the high to be the same as the pills. However, Michele and I ended up in the bathroom throwing up. Despite the side effects, we felt the high was cool. We agreed it was not something we needed to do every day and did not understand how Bobby tolerated it as well as he did. The syrup was very addictive so we decided not to indulge again for a while. It would be something we would play around with every now and then, we concluded. After all, our lives were too busy to be spent constantly nodding. Therefore, the syrup became our weekend high.

We arrived home after the festival. It was a perfect night, and I topped it off by listening to some soft jazz. I had spent an eventful day with my children and friends, and I was tired. I decided to turn in early. Kevin and Michele had to work the next day so they went home early. Soft jazz always relaxed me, and I wanted to carry the relaxation I was feeling into my bedroom. I let Tony know I was headed to bed and asked if he was coming. "I will be up later," he stated. It never bothered me whenever Tony stayed up late, and it was not unusual. Although I enjoyed sleeping with my husband, I also enjoyed spending time alone in our bed. I could stretch out my legs and get in some "me time." This night was no different—I was tired and wanted to stretch out my legs. Before I knew it, I was asleep.

I was in a deep sleep but had to get up and use the toilet. I tossed and turned for a minute before realizing Tony had not yet made it upstairs. I figured perhaps I had not been asleep as long. Therefore, I got up and headed toward the bathroom. I was going to head downstairs and check on Tony afterward. I always used my bathroom runs as a time to check in on my girls. Their bedroom was right before I reached the bathroom. I was half asleep, and the hallway was dark. I stopped outside the girls' room and reached in to feel for the light switch. Finally, my fingers felt the switch, and I turned on the light. I expected to find my girls curled up in their twin bunkbeds. This was not the case at all. I walked into a nightmare.

I do not think anyone can begin to imagine the pain from the knife that went straight through my heart. What I stumbled upon was beyond devastating. Kneeling between the girl's bunkbeds was my husband Tony. I shook my head because everything began to feel like a dream. What is he doing in my girls' room? This cannot be real, I kept saying repeatedly. Tony had a look of sheer panic and horror on his face. After realizing what was happening, I freaked out. It was as if someone had stuck a knife in my heart and twisted it. I placed my hand over my heart and began gasping for air. Tony sat on the floor paralyzed like a deer caught in headlights. He appeared to be in shock and unable to speak as I cursed his very existence. He was beside my daughter Damea's bed with his hands underneath her gown fondling her private area. My baby lay there pretending to be asleep, but I could see she was in obvious distress.

I do not think anyone can imagine the pain I felt and was reliving. My worst fears stared me in the face. I had a vision I was standing somewhere in pain and bleeding profusely. A womb had been opened, and I wanted vengeance. I began to grieve for the little girl who knew the pain and confusion my own daughter was now experiencing. At this moment, I had no time to focus on my own pain. I was angry, and it manifested itself as rage. Like a lioness protecting her cubs, I looked around for anything and everything in sight to do damage to this disgusting person. No longer paralyzed with fear, Tony jumped off the floor trying to protect himself from everything I was throwing at him—physically and verbally. I was not just fighting him, I was fighting Daddy, my uncle, and every other sexually perverted experience in my childhood. I was kicking, screaming, hitting, spitting, and cursing.

"What are you doing? Why did you do this? Why?" I wanted answers for what was happening to me and my baby. No way was this happening—not to my child! Not to my baby!

The look on Tony's face was wild and crazy. It was as if the cat had his tongue. He had nothing to say. He looked like a child who had been caught doing something he had no business doing. I began to grab my stomach and gag. The girls were now wide-awake sitting in their beds watching me have a nervous breakdown. Their little faces were frozen in fear as they watched their mother fight for their lives. Janae (now five years old) was probably wondering what was happening. However, Damea (only seven years old) knew exactly what was going on but was still frightened. The only father she had ever known had betrayed her trust and violated her in the worst way.

"I caught you this time, nigga!" I cried. "My sister was not lying! You are a pervert! Get out of my house! It is over! Get out now!"

Tony was trying his best to escape my wrath. Whatever I could get my hands on, I threw it at him. Then I heard Janae yell, "Mommy, stop!" Hearing her little voice stopped me in my tracks. I looked at my baby girl with tears streaming down my face. Suddenly, I began wondering if he had touched her too. I had to know so I asked Tony, "Did you touch her too? Why didn't you touch her?" I asked, pointing to Janae.

Then it dawned on me that Damea was not his biological child. "Oh, I see. It's because she is your daughter, and Damea is not! Well, Damea has a daddy, nigga—one you did not want her to know, you bastard!"

I thought about how Tony did not want Damea to know her biological father. In fact, he was adamant about her not knowing her father. He wanted her to only know him as the father. Against my better judgment, I allowed this to happen. After all, part of the way Tony captured my heart was taking on the responsibility of being Damea's father. What he was discovered doing to her was a crushing blow. Why was I going through this with my own child? Tony was aware of my past and everything I experienced as a child. I always had the feeling that my childhood was cursed. Now I was believing that my cursed childhood was following me and affecting my girls. I was devastated and trying to make sense of everything transpiring in my life. After finding my voice, I let Tony know Damea has a father—one whom he insisted she not get to know. Now here he was, the only father she had ever known, taking advantage of her innocence. I began to attack him all over again. Tony was trying desperately to make it to the door while ducking and dodging my blows. I wanted him out of my life, and I followed him downstairs to make sure he made his exit. Once he was out of the apartment complex, I was left to deal with the aftermath of his betrayal.

Despondent, disheartened, and defeated, I sat on the couch feeling abandoned, betrayed, and alone. I felt as though I had no one in this world. Not only was it late at night, but who could I confide in about this embarrassing situation? Suddenly, I thought about Mama and what she must have felt the moment she found out what had happened to me. I needed desperately to talk to her about my feelings. Mama, of all people, would be able to understand this gut-wrenching pain. I wanted to know why this curse was following me around. Every child when they are hurting wants their mother. I was no different but had to weigh it out. I was not sure if it was Mama I wanted to confide in. After all, there was a strain in our relationship. There were so many questions in my mind and so many uncertainties. My heart was crying out, saying, "Mama, help me to understand!" I battled for hours about whether to talk to Mama. I was not sure when I would be ready to share this deep, dark pain. One thing I was sure of was I needed to medicate and had nothing.

I finally lifted myself from the sofa and ran to the kitchen. I stood there staring at the phone until I gained the courage to dial my mother's number. The tears were pouring as I dialed each number. It was late, but I needed my mama.

"What is wrong? I feel it in my spirit," were the first words out of her mouth when she answered the phone. "What is it, Bunny?" she asked again.

After swallowing my pride and becoming vulnerable, I began speaking in a little girl's voice. "Peaches was right! He did touch her, Mama! He did and he's been touching and playing with Damea!" By this time, I was hysterical again. Of course, she wanted to know who and I told her, Tony. I tried to explain to her the details when suddenly I remembered my babies were upstairs alone. Through the whole ordeal, they had been quiet as a mouse even though they must have been hurting too. Mama wanted more details, but I needed to get to my girls. I did not even say good-bye. I just hung up the phone and tried to pull myself together before facing Damea and Janae. I felt so much guilt.

I heard their little feet scurrying around in their bedroom. However, when I reached their room, they pretended to be asleep. A part of me was glad they were asleep—or at least pretending to be asleep. I had no words to explain what had just happened. Janae was now in bed with Damea.

I sat on the edge of the bed and whispered, "Oh my GOD, Mommy is so sorry. I am so sorry." Now whimpering, they both sat up. I looked at Damea who had so much confusion etched on her face. Then I looked at Janae. Even though it was not her body he had violated, it might as well be as far as I was concerned. My girls were close and not just in age. They loved each other immensely.

Suddenly, I heard a knock at the door. I figured it must be Mama. She did not live far, and I knew she would come to check on us. I opened the door, and Bobby came in with Mama. I was glad to see them both. The first thing I asked Bobby was if he had some pills. We both walked away from Mama so he could slip them to me. Finally, my heart took a leap of joy. I had some pills and could at least numb the pain I was experiencing. I rushed to the kitchen for a drink of water and swallowed the pills immediately. Taking the pills relieved me and made me believe everything was going to be fine. I could now face Mama. I had many questions for her—ones she often found too painful to answer so I would just leave it alone.

The effects of the pills enabled me to relax and calm down. I felt my heart beat in a slower rhythm and thought I could sleep. I attempted to get in my bed, but it felt tainted. I assured Mama I was okay. I allowed her to take the children with her until the morning. After Mama and Bobby left, I went to lie down on the couch. *Men*, I thought. *Can any of them be trusted?* My mind revisited a conversation I had had with Uncle Bill. He had uttered these comforting words to me after finding out what Daddy had done to me. With tears in his eyes, holding me and rocking me gently, he stated in his soothing voice, "All men are not like that." These words coming from Uncle Bill gave me strength to believe in men again. If my Uncle Bill said it, then it must be true because GOD knows I trusted him with my life. There was no way Uncle Bill would tell me anything wrong. However, I was saddened to think maybe he was wrong in his beliefs because here I stood yet again with the exact same thing happening to my child.

My mind began to have flashbacks of the terrible experiences involving my father and an uncle (not Uncle Bill). I recall how easily they both took advantage of my innocence and childhood. Two men I trusted and loved dearly destroyed my faith in men. I wanted the abuse to stop, but I could not bear the burden of exposing them. If you truly loved and trusted someone, you cannot lay them bare is what my mind was led to believe. Plus, I was fearful other people would be upset with me for telling the truth. Each time my father, my uncle, or other people close to the family sexually abused me, I wondered if I brought the pain and suffering on myself. I could not help but be hard on myself, especially when it seemed like the abuse was coming from everywhere and not going to stop. Was I wearing a sign in big bold letters inviting the abuse? HELLO! I AM BUNNY DEBARGE! I HAVE BEEN MOLESTED! I ACCEPT IT AND YOU CAN DO IT TO ME AGAIN AND AGAIN AND AGAIN!

The experience of sexual abuse is always so devastating and shattering for the victim. I never wanted this for my daughters. Yet here I was having a shared experience with my Damea and experiencing the exact same feelings the first time I was violated. I started blaming myself. I became angry with every part of myself and surmised that perhaps it was all my fault. Maybe the way I carried myself gave men permission to hurt me. Was I really inviting such actions? Maybe men were reading into my life, and I was giving off the wrong impressions. Did I need to dress differently? Walk differently? Talk differently? I was a ball of confusion at this point in my life. The beliefs I held about myself, my mama, my daddy, and life in general had been mentally buried for years but were bubbling to the surface. It appears my life was becoming a series of unfortunate events. I had no idea how to stop the onslaught.

Emotional wound after emotional wound reopened, and the pain became unbearable. My little girl was being touched by someone we both trusted—the man she knew as Daddy. Is the pain I am feeling the same pain Mama felt all those years ago? Just as I entrusted Tony to be a father to Damea, Mama also entrusted my daddy to be a father to me as well. Fathers are not supposed to molest their children! I had no idea how Mama felt because we never talked about the sexual abuse. The memories of the day my mother found out that Daddy had molested and raped me and the tears she shed were painful reminders of how Daddy destroyed the lives of two women he was supposed to love unconditionally. I felt Mama believed me, and she was sorry for what happened to me. The little girl inside me still wanted to talk to her about this painful chapter in my life. But was it necessary at this point? After all, I was dealing with craziness in my own life. I was desperately trying to figure out how not to make the same mistakes in my daughter's lives as my mother had made in mine. Should I just leave it alone?

The one thing still haunting me was Mama never asking for details. However, I felt as though details were something I needed to know concerning my child. I intended to speak to my daughter and get to the bottom of this tragic matter. I knew I had to handle her with kid gloves, but I was too emotional at the time it happened. Was this the only time? I could only hope. I racked my brains trying to figure out where to start talking to an innocent seven-year-old child about such a devastating experience. It was eating at me and tearing me apart. My little girl was violated by someone she looked to as her daddy.

CHAPTER 26

STOLEN INNOCENCE

I WAS TAUGHT THAT GOD knew us before the foundation of the world and He is the Author of our life's book. Our book was written from beginning (when we first come into the world) to ending (when we leave this world). He is aware of everything happening to us as we meander through life. He does not cause things to happen, but He does allow them to happen—at least this is what I was taught. Satan peeks into the book of our lives and realizes our destiny. It is his job to prevent our destiny from unfolding. He begins chipping away at our spiritual foundation at an early age. Oftentimes, Satan works through those tasked with protecting us. The innocent ones suffer. As we maneuver through life, we are warned not to tell anyone about our dirty little secrets. At other times, we are made to believe speaking up is wrong. No matter how many times I told my daughters they could come to me if anyone hurt them, a heartbreaking secret was kept from me.

Damea, much like myself, was an innocent victim. She was a victim of stolen innocence. In this respect, I could relate to this shared experience. However, it was difficult to help her process what had taken place because I never processed my own hurt and pain. How could I help my daughter? I walked amid my pain as someone who was busy, confused, and broken. Now I was being forced to pull this thing called motherhood together for the sake of my child. I could only help her with the tools I possessed at the time.

I reached out to Tony's mother and told her what occurred. I began by sharing his violation of Peaches to his latest violation of Damea. She was shocked and sympathized with me. She talked to me woman to woman—something my mother, unfortunately, was unable to do. She validated my feelings toward Tony even though he was her son. I confided in her and let her know I wanted him to leave and did not want the marriage any longer. She understood. As I cried, she began to pray for GOD to guide me through this valley experience. It was a welcome relief as she did not side with Tony. What could she say when he was obviously in the wrong? In talking with her, she mentioned that Tony's father had molested his own stepdaughter. Years later, the young lady finally found her voice and told her mother. Maybe these behaviors were hereditary, I thought to myself. His mother wanted me to send Tony home before he did any more damage. "Only GOD can fix this," she stated with reassurance.

I went to talk to Damea. In talking to her, I found out the sordid details. Thankfully, he had not gone as far as my daddy had gone with me. However, this did not make me feel any better. She disclosed that he had molested her more than once. Had I not caught him in the act, the sexual abuse would have continued and eventually progressed. I tried my best to make my child feel comfortable speaking to me. Much like myself, Damea had a difficult time finding the words to describe how she felt. She was hurt and confused by it all. More than anything, she was a seven-year-old innocent child. I let her know that her inability to articulate her feelings were okay. To be quite honest, I was still very much confused even after so many years had passed. She loved Tony as her father—he was the only father she had ever known. It sickened me to think about his role in her life as a father figure. When Tony first came into our lives, he completely took over. He put his foot down and insisted on Damea no longer seeing her real father because he wanted to become her father. I allowed all this to happen because I felt his intentions were pure. As a mother and protector, I reassured my child it would never happen again.

Looking back over the entire ordeal, I began to understand why my childhood was being played out through my children. The very thing I could not understand about my mother I was repeating. In my mind, I lost all reasons to criticize Mama because I ended up taking my husband back despite his betrayal. Perhaps the reason for my decision was I began to view my situation differently. I was never a victim of domestic abuse like Mama. Daddy violently abused her for years in addition to how horribly he treated his own children. Tony never abused me or our children physically or mentally. For all intents and purposes, he was a good husband and father who worked hard and took good care of his family. Amid my confusion, I felt somewhat relieved he had not gone as far with my daughter as my father had gone with me. However, the pain was still the same. Wrong is wrong. Sadly, I was a product of my dysfunctional upbringing.

We pattern ourselves after whatever it is we witness and experience growing up. Sometimes we do this subconsciously. We do not realize we are recreating our childhood experiences—good, bad, or indifferent—until it is too late. I certainly had no intentions of repeating my mother's failures and mistakes. When I first became pregnant, I made all kinds of grand plans for Damea. The first plan was to protect her at all costs. However, here I was repeating the same mistake I was unwilling or unable to forgive Mama for making. What scared me the most was that the choices I made concerning this egregious act came so naturally. My ease of forgiveness had much to do with how my family handled the transgression. Without hesitation, my family forgave Tony as if they understood his actions in some way. After all, Mama forgave Daddy, and we all lived as if nothing ever happened. Forgive and forget was truly par for the course. We covered Daddy's wrongdoing for years. This was very much a part of how our family functioned. Even though we were aware of and impacted by his transgressions, we allowed him to walk freely in forgiveness and forgetfulness. We never axed him out of our lives though as adults we were still suffering the effects of his abusive nature. For everything Daddy had done, he was still very present in our lives. Therefore, this notion of forgiveness had been with us from the very beginning.

Growing up in a religious family, we were taught that GOD required us to forgive. It would take me years to figure out that my knowledge of forgiveness was completely distorted. I assumed the boys should have been furious at Tony for what he had done to their little niece. I did not understand their attitude at all. They forgave him and moved on. It was perplexing to say the least. Tommy even stated he understood what happened between Tony and Damea. Maybe I should have accepted if my brother could easily understand another man's sickening acts toward a child; perhaps he was simply identifying more than forgiving. I did not see or understand this distortion at the time. Damea had been violated, and it seemed as though a simple handshake absolved Tony of all wrongdoing. The way this scenario played out with my brothers haunted me for years to come. I had no one to understand my frustration. I knew about GOD, but at this point, I needed a human being to hear my heart. All I had to comfort me through this confusing time were pills. My dependence on them began to increase exponentially. They became a constant companion.

In the beginning, I used the pills to relax. As past trauma constantly invaded my mind, I began dropping pills to numb the emotional pain. When I did not have any pills, I simply drowned in sorrow and misery. I had so many questions for my brothers. How could I expect them to understand why my husband had molested my child? What could make them understand my heart? I did not want to say it, but the answer stared me straight in the face. Unless familiar with committing this kind of violation themselves, there was no way they could identify with Tony's behavior. Not having a male perspective broke my heart, but it was okay. I was able to cope because I had my pills.

Allowing Tony back into my life certainly changed our relationship dynamic. It was never the same ever again. I had lost all respect for him. Continuing to stay married to him had nothing to do with love. It was sobering to accept I knew nothing about the true concept of love. I had been going through the motions and playing the part. I no longer considered Tony to be Damea's father. It was time for me to come clean to Damea. For once, I would be honest about her biological father—Kevin Murphy.

Kevin Murphy was a childhood boyfriend whom Damea only knew as her uncle. When I finally informed my daughter that Kevin was her dad, she blossomed and became a better child. For some odd reason, I thought Damea knowing her real father would take away the pain I was experiencing. But it was yet another cover-up. In the short-term, it seemed like all was well. Farther down the road, the pain behind Damea knowing her father would resurface. For now, I found a remedy, and it was much easier to simply numb the pain. I guess Tony felt the same way. He was abusing pills to numb what we were going through as a family. He kept me sheltered through this rough time. I was not involved in scoring the pills—Tony took care of this job. I was not out in the streets seeking a high and was grateful. However, it was no secret we were both hooked. In my mind, I had it all together since I was able to still work. Unfortunately, I had become a functioning addict.

CHAPTER 27

MY SWEET LITTLE DAMEA

When I first met Tony, I had no idea what was truly happening in his life. Neither did Tony. He did not know anything about his real father until he was an adult. We really do not know what we are getting ourselves into when we meet and connect with people. When deciding to intertwine our lives with others through marriage, it seems as though we marry the sins of the mother and father. Tony appeared to be a well-adjusted person when we first met. He was the son of a preacher and knew about the Lord. His life certainly seemed to be more structured and disciplined than mine. He had a good head on his shoulders and always took care of business. Tony was also a homebody who loved spending time with his family. He worked hard and did whatever it took to provide for his family.

With one despicable act, our entire world was turned upside down. I did not know my next move. Tony was not my lover anymore, nor did I honor him as Damea's father. He no longer had a say in Damea getting to know her real father as far as I was concerned. I was going to tell her the truth without his knowledge. When he violated her innocence, he lost the right to dictate to her as a father.

One day, Damea and I were out shopping. This felt like the perfect time to reveal to her that "Uncle Kevin" was indeed her father. I was always one to play games with my girls by telling them wild stories and convincing them they were true. It was our silly mother-daughter moments. I knew Damea was going to think I was playing one of our games so I had to come at her from a different angle. We were walking around the store as I picked up a few items for the apartment. It was just the two of us since Janae had stayed behind at Mama's. "You know, Damea," I began. "Before Mommy met Daddy, she had a boyfriend. In fact, Daddy came and took her from him, and she was no longer his girlfriend."

Damea looked at me, ready to play one of her "for real" games. "For real?" she stated, not really believing me. "No, you did not, Mommy." This is where convincing her had to start. Damea would not let her little mind imagine Mommy being with anyone except her daddy—Tony. Even though I promised not to allow Kevin in Damea's life, from time to time, I did go behind Tony's back and allow Kevin to visit. She was not told he was her father. She only knew him as her uncle. Kevin respected my decision and went along with not telling Damea until we both felt it was the right time in her life. This day felt like the right time. My child needed to know the truth. I wanted her to know that her real father loved her very much and would never cause her harm.

Damea and I continued walking around the store talking. I wanted her to become comfortable with the truth. I let her know that Mommy had a boyfriend and we were in love. We went to high school together and had planned to get married. Damea was now looking at me with a more serious face. She wanted to know if I was really going to marry my boyfriend.

"Yes, Damea," I stated. "Want to know what else? We had a little baby girl together." Now my child is really into the story.

"You had a little girl together? What little girl, Mommy? Where is she?" I could tell Damea wanted answers so it was time to spill the beans. I let her know she was the little baby girl. She took the news surprisingly well though I know she preferred I come up with an actual baby girl instead. I explained that Tony was her stepfather and Kevin was her real father. I reminded her that Kevin was the "uncle" I took her to see sometimes and he would buy her gifts and they would take pictures together. She remembered him. I went on to tell her how Tony and I met and how Tony wanted her to be his daughter. Tony figured if she knew him and Kevin, she might become confused. Therefore, Tony became her daddy. I admitted to my daughter I was wrong for letting this go down. However, it was time she knew her real father loved her dearly. I then apologized for being so shortsighted.

"Where is he, Mommy?" she asked.

"In Grand Rapids, Michigan! I have his phone number. Would you like to talk to him?"

"Yes!" she shouted. "Is Daddy going to be mad?" This was just like Damea to always think about the feelings of others before her own. It sickened me to know my child was thinking about Tony's feelings despite him stealing her innocence.

"Don't you worry about him," I reassured her. "Mommy will take care of everything. We do not have to hide the truth any longer, okay?"

"Can I tell Janae?" She wanted her little sister to know. She was beaming with excitement.

"Not yet, Damea," I stated. "Let Mommy tell her, okay? Just like I told you, I want to tell her too. Now let's call your daddy Kevin."

We finished shopping and walked out of the store to a payphone. I called Kevin collect. I prayed he would answer. I had not talked to Kevin about anything going on—not even about telling Damea he was her father. This would be a surprise. Kevin answered the phone and accepted the call. I put Damea on the phone and told her to say, "Hi, Daddy!" Can we say the rest is history?

Kevin was moved to tears. He was indeed surprised and stated that this call had made his day. Of course, Kevin wanted to know what brought this on. I did not want to talk about what was happening inside my home. I just reassured him everything was fine, and she needed to know the truth. From this moment on, I watched my daughter blossom. She became a different child because she had a true sense of self. I saw her begin to smile more and realized she was okay. I had my sweet little Damea back. It was not long before I told Tony what I had done. He cried, but it did not matter to me at all. Damea deserved the truth. Besides, it was his sickness that messed up their relationship.

CHAPTER 28

FROM MY HUSBAND TO MY PARTNER IN CRIME

My sex life with my husband was a complete and utter mess. I was no longer sexually attracted to him. I would participate only to uphold my wifely duties. I used every excuse in the book not to even sleep in the same bed as him. It was easier to simply sleep on the couch in the living room. Before everything happened with Damea, I was struggling to enjoy sex and would never initiate with Tony. Sex always left me feeling nasty, much like when Daddy would rape and molest me. With Tony's true nature exposed, I had nothing left to give. Having him back in the home only increased my drug use. The drugs only served to keep our relationship, which was hanging by a thread, together. Drugs also helped me accept Tony back into my life. Once he returned, he did not keep as tight a rein on my drug use. I guess he felt that allowing me to freely use would appease me and keep him in my life longer. This unbridled access was a disaster in the making. Tony was the only person who could tell me no, and I would listen and take heed. Now I managed how often and how much I used.

To be quite honest, our marriage should have been over a long time ago. GOD knew what he was doing because the marriage sheltered me from a lot. We were both on drugs, but Tony closely monitored my use and knew when to say enough. He also purchased the drugs to keep me out of harm's way. He had control over the bank account and therefore made the drug transactions. For a while, only he had access to the drug dealer. At the time, I did not see the convenient setup. In hindsight, this was Tony's method of control and the only bargaining tool he had to keep the relationship going. It may not have been his intention, but it was happening. I was just living in the moment and not focused on the big picture. Tony was tolerating my escalating drug use because he felt he had to in order to remain with me.

Tony had to have known our marriage was over the moment he was caught molesting my daughter. Afterward, he lost control in the relationship and just kept the drugs coming. We both were covering pain. I was covering lifelong hurt, and he was covering the fact I no longer loved him. He lost my heart that he never truly had in the first place. Tony lived on the dysfunction of my heart, which knew absolutely nothing about love. He learned how to turn my shortcomings in life against me. I was covering pain coming at me from every angle. Tony was afraid to face where he would be in my life had it not been for the drugs. Sadly, I was married to my drug pusher. Despite the sad reality, we kept our lives functional. The bills were paid, the children were well cared for, and I continued to work without drugs hindering my obligations to Motown. No one was able to tell we were out of control.

Bobby was now back in Los Angeles after working on his album. He was so strung out on drugs he had to leave Los Angeles in order to finish the album. He voiced wanting to get some help but seemed too far gone. He began having trouble finding the cough syrup. Tony and I knew his struggle to find the syrup firsthand. We also started having trouble getting the syrup for ourselves. All three of us (Bobby, Tony, and me) were searching high and low, only to come up empty. When we did manage to find it by some small miracle, the price had gone up by the ounce from $10 an ounce to $20 an ounce. We had a cousin Tim, my aunt Margie's son, whom Bobby and I would get the syrup from time to time. He was using also and had found a place where we could cop some. We decided to visit Tim. It was our last resort after exhausting all our connections. Tim was happy to see us. He had recently married a girl named Marie. Of course, the first thing out of their mouths were to inquire about James and Janet. He and Marie had read magazines and was excited to hear firsthand information about the couple. We talked about the new it couple for a few minutes then told him why we had paid him a visit. He let us know he would not be able to help us find any syrup but had another remedy.

Tim had heard about a concoction of pills. "It's called fours and doors," he said. "Tylenol 4 and a pill called Doriden. You take them together and *wham!* It will substitute for the syrup. I promise you will like it, and it will do the job. You will not get sick, Bobby, I promise. It is even cheaper, and I know a person who has the pills right now," Tim promised. We all agreed because we needed a quick fix. By now, Tony and I were exhibiting signs we had formed a bad habit ourselves. Bobby was no longer the only one among us struggling with a drug habit. We were too blind to admit how fast our habit had progressed.

Tim took us to a dealer named Larry then introduced each of us so he would not have to be bothered every time we needed pills. After purchasing them, we handed Tim some then left. Tony and I started out using a set that were two Tylenol 4s and one Doriden. By the time we reached home, we were feeling the effects. Of course, Bobby had taken much more. His habit was too far gone, and he required more pills to achieve the same high. We all agreed we liked the high. After we arrived home, we called Kevin and Michele, and they were on their way over. We let them know there were enough pills for them too. The girls still needed to be picked up from school. Michele and I ended up staying behind while Tony and Kevin went to get the girls.

Michele and I sat and talked about our lives growing up. We had a lot in common since we were both biracial. However, she had a much different childhood than mine. Michele had a white mother and a black father. She was also very supportive of her husband and his career. She wholeheartedly believed he was a great artist even though he did not really buy it. Michele was always pushing him to achieve something greater with his gift. Michele is very talkative and enjoyed having conversations. The pills did little to turn her from being a chatterbox. Quite the contrary, they caused her to become even more talkative. I could talk your ear off, but Michele had me beat. Her continuous babbling always got her into trouble—especially with Tony who always complained she was getting on his nerves.

Kevin and I was always protecting Michele from Tony. Kevin and Michele were really my friends. Tony could not have cared less if he never saw them again. In fact, Tony never hit it off with anyone. He had a nasty temperament, and it sucked at times. I would step in whenever his nastiness ballooned out of control. There were times he would strike out at family members. It did not matter if it was his side of the family or mine, he would just be ugly for no reason. Tony's nasty persona toward my family was tolerated because of our marriage. The boys put up with him because he was my husband. However, there were times when their personalities clashed. I was tired of making excuses for his bad behavior and was not sticking up for him as much. After he violated my daughter, I really did not have his back. If he came to blows with someone because of his offensive nature, I did not get in the middle. At this point, I was barely tolerating him myself. However, Tony did remain helpful to me in everything I had to do regarding my career. I did not love him at all but felt obligated to have him in my life. He was there filling in for everything I could not and did not do as a mother. He was an excellent homemaker. While I was out working, he did everything to ensure the children's needs were met.

CHAPTER 29

JAMES AND JANET

LIFE WAS CHANGING FOR THE members of DeBarge. Everyone seemed to take life one day at a time. We were trying very hard to get the album completed and submitted to the record company. Out of nowhere, James's whirlwind romance heated up a million degrees and blindsided the group. In between cutting the album, James decided to return to Grand Rapids. He took Janet with him, and they ended up getting married. It was done in secret, and no one had any idea it was going to take place. They told no one of their plans to elope. James was adamant about Uncle Bill marrying them. Therefore, he called him up, and they were married in the church's office. Mama did not know about their secret wedding until it was over, said, and done. Surprisingly, she kept their secret closely guarded.

I am not sure when the Jackson family found out. Hopefully, it was not in the same way I found out. I went to the store to purchase some cigarettes. The newsstand area was unusually busy with people grabbing and reading various magazines. I could make out very little what they were saying. It sounded as if they were saying James DeBarge and Janet Jackson had eloped. I pushed through the crowd. Lo and behold, the couple was on the front page of the magazine: JAMES DEBARGE MARRIES JANET JACKSON! They were pictured together smiling and holding hands. I grabbed a copy of the magazine then went to the counter to pay. I was shocked along with the rest of the world. My brother, only nineteen years old, was now married to Janet Jackson. *They are too young! They have no idea what they are doing*, I thought. I knew they were an item. They had attended *Motown 25* together. However, I never thought their relationship was serious enough for them to elope.

Everywhere DeBarge went, the DeBarge-Jackson marriage was the topic of discussion. In every interview conducted, we were questioned about details of their marriage. We grew sick of it very fast. To us, Janet was like any other girl, and the media should get over the fact that she is a Jackson. Stars are people too. I guess it was a hard-learned lesson firsthand how fans see stars. Fans will not just let it be and move on. After all, James's marriage to Janet ended up a huge mistake. They were too young and from two vastly different worlds. Unfortunately, James had to contend with Janet's family not being particularly fond of them eloping. This placed a tremendous amount of pressure on my brother's shoulders. He did become very close to Janet's mother, Mrs. Katherine Jackson. Janet was a quiet and busy girl at the time. She was filming for the show *Fame* while James was busy completing DeBarge's third album. It was a wait and see approach about how well the couple could withstand pressure from the media as well the Jackson family.

CHAPTER 30

DEBARGE IS FALLING APART

DeBarge was working hard getting their songs together for the third album. El agreed to produce us again. We all worked with El on tracks for the new album. By this time, Bobby had lost his contract with Motown. He was never able to finish his solo project due to his ongoing drug addiction. Everything seemed to be going downhill for him. Since Bobby was no longer under contract, he had no income and lost his home. I was quite worried about him. He was in obvious turmoil and unhappy with life in general. His every waking moment seemed to be spent calling me on the phone. It did not matter what time my brother called, I got up for him. I was afraid he was having a nervous breakdown. The boys were just as concerned and began spending more time with him.

Bobby was going through other personal issues in his life. He had just ended a relationship with his live-in boyfriend after catching him in bed with someone else. The relationship being over was devastating and driving Bobby mad. It was all he talked about at every opportunity. He told me all the time how much he loved him and how much he wanted him back. Bobby was distraught over losing this guy as though he was crying over the loss of a woman. Personally, I did not understand his strong feelings for the same sex and did not wish to hear him lament over losing a man. However, he was my brother, and I loved him (still do). So I decided to see him through this rough patch.

I had never witnessed Bobby be intimate with his male lovers before. However, my other brothers had knowledge of his interactions with males and would report to me about it. Bobby never acted feminine; he was very masculine in every sense of the word. In fact, he was not very fond of males he considered a "sissy"—a man who wanted to be a woman. He was very vocal in his distaste for feminine-acting males. Bobby dated men you would never believe were gay. I found the guys he was with very attractive and masculine—basically guys I would consider dating if I did not know any better. Bobby would often share his preference with me by stating he wanted the guy to be a "virgin." He wanted to be the one who introduced the guy to his first homosexual experience. He would discuss with me how there were a lot of "closet cases" out there and people not being honest with themselves. Bobby told me I would be very shocked if he ever spilled the beans.

Bobby had a reputation of being the master of first-time givers. He had the uncanny ability to charm and turn out males who vowed never to have sex with another man. I was taught from a biblical perspective it was wrong for a man to lie with another man. As a result, I would often voice to Bobby that sleeping with men was wrong. He would simply state he was born this way and in turn I would say, "Not so, Bobby." I believed in my heart he was introduced to this lifestyle by entertaining thoughts of homosexuality. More than this, I believed his sexuality had a lot to do with his poor relationship with our father.

Lately, every time I saw Bobby he was high and nodding. He was no longer hiding his drug addiction, his sexuality, or any aspect of his life. He was behaving overly dramatic and acting out every moment of his life. Every little thing meant so much to him, and Bobby was draining my life. I received calls all hours of the night from him crying and complaining yet never listening. I could never get a word in to offer him any level of comfort. He also had very little money left. Therefore, he was getting money for pills the best way he could mostly from family members. The boys (Randy, Mark, and James) were there for Bobby in his time of need. We were all helping to support his habit. Little did I realize that the boys, minus El, were using the pills themselves.

Life was spinning out of control in the DeBarge camp. James was now leaving Janet stranded at the set of *Fame*. She would call around looking for him. He began staying out late at night, even staying gone for a few nights, just to get high with his brothers. I received numerous calls from Janet worried about James. El was worried about everyone. After all, he was the only one among us not getting high. During this time, he felt as though he could not depend on anyone except me since I was better able to hide my addiction and continue functioning. "What are we going to do about this?" El would often ask, very discouraged. "We need to be writing songs, Bunny. They are messing up, I cannot find them half the time, and Janet is always calling looking for James." El voiced his frustrations with the state of the group time and time again. He seemed to believe James was getting high at the Jacksons' compound now. According to El, the Jackson family were all wondering what was going on with James.

El was also growing weary of Bobby's addiction impacting the group. One day he stated, "I know everyone is worried about Bobby—I am too. But we have an album to complete." He was very emotional and had a worried look on his face. Indeed, he had a lot on his plate besides the album. To make matters worse, he was having major relationship issues with Roberta. Rumors swirled she had begun talking to the singer O'Bryan again. Not only was this a concern for my brother, she was now pregnant. El wanted to believe she was pregnant with his baby. However, he could no longer ignore the rumors about Roberta.

El went on to share with me a rumor that Janet was allegedly pregnant as well—and for the second time. I began to wonder if perhaps Janet's alleged pregnancy was the reason the couple eloped. Word inside the family was that Janet allegedly miscarried during her first pregnancy. Now we were hearing she was allegedly pregnant again. Janet knew of James's escalating drug use. She was worried about him but never talked to me about how she was affected. During this time, I do not imagine she was confiding in anyone—including the Jackson family. I am sure they had moments where they talked to her about how she was affected by the situation. Of course, I was never privy to what they may have said to possibly influence her to leave the marriage. One thing I do know, she was sticking by James and trying to keep his addiction hidden from her family. Eventually, James and Janet moved out of the Jackson family compound into their own apartment.

CHAPTER 31

JAMES AND BOBBY

EACH OF THE DEBARGE SIBLINGS had their own unique relationship with Bobby. Bobby and I were very close in age and had a lot of shared experiences—granted they were very difficult experiences. Still, we were joined at the hip and fiercely loved and protected each other no matter the cost. Bobby and Tommy started out as typical brothers who were always at each other's throats. This eventually morphed into a love-hate relationship they carried throughout their brotherhood and career. Regardless of how much they fought, being a member of Switch cemented their shared legacy. Now Randy was the brother who was always protected by everyone. We all made a pact early on to protect him at all costs. Mark/Marty marched to the beat of his own drum and was annoying to everyone. Bobby was most annoyed with everything concerning Mark—especially his singing voice and him not taking music seriously. Everything was a joke to Mark except his obsession with healthy eating habits. He was both a health freak and a neat freak. A few years before he died, Bobby and Mark became extremely close. Bobby and El shared a close bond despite their age difference. They shared a similar musical style. While honing his musical gifts, El spent a considerable amount of time learning from and creating with Bobby. There was a pretty big age gap between Bobby, Chico, and the twins, Peaches and Dakey. However, Bobby and Chico had a pretty solid big brother–little brother relationship. Chico has always been very spiritually gifted and loves to pray to this very day. While Bobby struggled with his spirituality, he never held this against Chico. Peaches and Dakey rounded out the DeBarge clan yet still held a special place in Bobby's heart. One relationship was a particularly sore spot for Bobby—his relationship with James.

James Curtis DeBarge was the seventh DeBarge child and came onto the scene in our childhood when life at home was much different. He was too young to know the daddy and mama the five oldest knew. James only knew of a kind, gentle father whom he adored and followed around the house. Whenever Daddy moved, James was right on his heels. James only knew a father who sang songs to him and told him stories and funny jokes. He only knew of a father whom he could talk openly to and share his innermost feelings. James only knew of a father he never feared. He only knew of a father he loved so dearly and who loved him dearly in return. James had no knowledge of the deep level of abuse the first five of his siblings endured at the hands of his beloved father. He was not privy to the struggles we bore growing up in the DeBarge household with a vicious father and passive mother. What little he did know was because we told him and perhaps not in the most productive manner. He did not have the full scope since we only shared bits and pieces.

James was a precious and spoiled little boy by Daddy and the older boys. However, not everyone felt the same way about James. In fact, Bobby resented this show of affection, and it was eating him alive. In his hatred, Bobby grew blind to how much he meant to his little brother. After all, Bobby was Big Bro, and James simply adored him and admired him immensely. He cared deeply what Bobby thought of him and wanted Big Bro's approval. More than anything, James wanted to feel loved by Bobby. Unfortunately, he caught the brunt of Bobby's rage beginning at an early age.

James had no idea why Bobby treated him differently and harshly. However, James and Daddy's relationship sickened Bobby to his core, and he turned his anger and frustration toward his little brother. James never understood why. It broke my heart to see my little brother so confused by Bobby showing the rest of us love and affection and only showing him rage and contempt. We knew enough about Bobby to know it was neither fun nor advisable to be on the receiving end of his wrath. Fortunately, or unfortunately for James, he was not there to witness or live through the abuse Bobby suffered from Daddy. *Why does my brother hate me so?* James often asked. *Why am I the only one he picks on?* he would lament. When Daddy still lived in the house with us, he was able to protect James from Bobby. When Daddy finally left, James was left to fend for himself and contend with the boogeyman living inside of Bobby. By James not knowing what was driving Bobby's intense hatred, he suffered prolonged abuse from his big brother.

I can only lend validation to the terrible childhood James experienced being tortured at the hands of Bobby. Sadly, Bobby tortured James as Daddy had tortured him. Bobby had become the boogeyman and made James's childhood unbearable. He did to James whatever Daddy had done to him. Through everything, James longed for Bobby to love and protect him unconditionally. Basically, James deserved no less from Bobby what was given to the rest of us. For everything Bobby had gone through, he was still capable of being a loving, protective, and civil big brother. He was this way toward all his siblings except James. The same way neither of us had to beg for his love, protection, and civility, James should not have had to either. With Daddy gone, James wanted and needed his big brother more than ever before. Sadly, when James saw his beloved big brother in trouble, he went down a treacherous path to relate. Perhaps James had concluded in his mind if you cannot beat them, you might as well join them. So he joined Bobby's hellish nightmare, almost as if to say, "Let me suffer with you, Big Bro." James wanted to relate to Bobby in the worst way without knowing the true depths of Bobby's despair and what had really taken place between him and Daddy.

James was in a one-sided battle for Bobby's approval and love. He wanted a relationship with Bobby who wanted nothing to do with him. As a grown married man, James knew very little about what had happened to make Bobby turn this way. He was just now beginning to find out some of the details of the abuse we had suffered from Daddy. One day, I received a call from James who was distraught and demanding answers about what Daddy had done to the five of us. "Is this true, Bunny? Did Daddy do this?" he asked. After sharing some of the details (because at the time, the abuse was still very difficult to discuss), he began to apologize profusely, "I am sorry, Bunny! I'm sorry Daddy did those things to you!"

Not knowing the extent of the abuse hurt James terribly. It also began to affect his relationship with Daddy—a daddy he once held in high regard. I am sure he talked to his wife about his feelings, and Janet did her best to be understanding of what her husband was going through. My heart went out to Janet and James—they were so young, and their marriage was suffering tremendously. They married way too young and both had experienced abusive childhoods. To add insult to injury, Bobby did nothing to make life any easier for James. Hurt people hurt people as the saying goes. I believe James and Janet would have functioned better as friends more so than lovers. This was in part because they lacked the tools to love themselves apart from each other.

I was not quite sure about Janet's level of understanding of love. I knew for a fact that James knew absolutely nothing about love, and he was not alone. Not a single DeBarge knew how to love themselves let alone drag another individual into our mangled lives. Here we stood, sick children thrown into a world we were emotionally unprepared to navigate. We knew nothing about being responsible men and women. All we knew was pain and how to self-medicate.

We were truly lost along life's path. From time to time, we managed to find our way. Perhaps GOD was on our side after all I believed. Through the fog that made our lives difficult to navigate at times, I do believe we were being kept. We were being kept by our maternal grandmother and grandfather's faithful prayers stored up before some of us were ever conceived. Those prayers were then passed down to our mother, her sisters, and her brothers. All in all, we had sense enough to hold on to this revelation: we were the kept ones. GOD's Grace, His Favor, and His Mercy were very real. We held it close since it spoke of our heritage and legacy. Therefore, all was not bad in our lives. We had the wonderful Word of GOD keeping us while we were in our valley experience.

CHAPTER 32

THE BOYS

As the eldest DeBarge, I always felt a sense of responsibility to each of my younger siblings. For all intents and purposes, they were more my children than my siblings. When they hurt, I hurt. When they cried, I cried. When they needed a shoulder to lean on, I did my best to lend them support. I had always protected them, cared for them, and fed them. I did everything a mother was supposed to do to for her children. Imagine the pain of learning just how bad they were messing up.

The boys (Randy, Mark, and James) were beginning to crack under pressure and royally screw up. I became very concerned for them both personally and professionally. We still had songs to complete for the album. Days would go by, and no one would hear from them. Everyone was so focused and worried about Bobby. Yet no one had enough sense to take a long hard look at the mess they were creating in their own lives.

Bobby always seemed to be the one most in trouble mainly because he never felt the need to hide any of his misgivings. He was a diva, and what you see is what you get. By this time, he was overcome by his drug addiction, and I was so afraid we would lose any moment. One day, he decided to finally seek help. He enrolled in a methadone clinic and complied with the program for a while. With Bobby starting to get his act together, the rest of us should have been able to regroup and focus on DeBarge. However, the boys (Mark, Randy, and James) had gotten a taste of the pills and began indulging. It was not as bad as when Bobby was still using. But it was still just as concerning. They seemed to enjoy the effects of the pills a little too much for my liking. The boys made excuses as to why they had to get the pills and always pointed the finger at Bobby. I reminded them Bobby no longer needed the pills because he was going to the methadone clinic for treatment. Therefore, they should now be able to focus on completing the album. They did stop for the time being, and DeBarge was able to regroup and focus on our purpose—create beautiful music. Looking back, I was concerned about everyone else except me. I had a drug problem but so far had convinced myself I was handling it properly. I was not getting high on the job. Also, when it came time to perform, I always showed up sober and in the right frame of mind. Sadly, I fooled myself into believing I was not an addict. In hindsight, I was a functioning addict. Who would worry about me while I worried about everyone else?

Bobby grew tired of the rigors of the methadone clinic program. He saw it as another way to feed his addiction. He expressed wanting to be completely free of drugs once and for all. Therefore, he decided to return home to Detroit again and stay with Daddy and go cold turkey. I was relieved he made such a hard decision. It certainly took a load off my shoulders. In fact, it was a load off everyone's shoulders. Bobby was with Daddy and out of our hair. He was finally okay, and DeBarge could put every ounce of energy into completing our album.

DeBarge was alone in the studio and able to do anything we pleased. We could bring whoever into the studio and not have to answer to management. I would bring Tony and the girls with me, and sometimes Kevin and Michele would tag along. We would stay in the studio all day and night. We were having so much fun. I would put the girls in another area of the studio so they would be able to sleep throughout the night. The boys were having a ball. They brought random girls in and out of the studio and disappeared with them and did their thing. When they assumed El did not need them in the studio, the boys would really act up and start back getting high. El would become very frustrated when he was not able to find them. He did not need them there for anything except to offer moral support. The boys were used to spending every waking moment together. Since Randy, Mark, and James were behaving badly, they began hiding from El and excluding him. Toward the end of the project, Bobby returned home to Los Angeles and helped El put finishing touches on the album. He was clean, sober, and such a pleasure to work with in the studio. Alas, it was not long before Bobby was back on the lam doing drugs.

El faced tremendous pressure from Motown to complete the album. We still needed to finish James's and Mark's vocals. We had trouble locating them, and once we did, they would be so high they could not perform or record. Ignoring their own failures due to drugs and a hard-partying lifestyle, they began taking out their frustrations on El. They acted as if El thought he was the better brother. He was bullied and insulted by Mark and James as being a know-it-all. It was true Motown was giving El all the attention, and it had started way before the boys started acting out. They felt it was unfair that Motown was not giving them the same opportunities as El. It caused division and infighting among the boys. They rebelled against El and overlooked how their own actions contributed to their disillusionment. At the end of the day, El was not using drugs, and he was in the studio day and night working overtime to get the album completed.

El had hard decisions to make, and he knew his brothers would not approve. However, he desperately wanted their songs included on the album. He came to talk to me about his dilemma. "Bunny, I cannot get them to sing the songs right," he stated. "They sound high, and Marty is giving me a hard way to go on his vocals. He is deliberately not doing anything I tell him to do. The company is on me to finish by next week, and I cannot get them here on time or in their right mind. All the songs are done except for James's lead vocal on 'I Give Up on You' and Marty's vocal on 'Stay with Me.' I do not want to sing their songs, Bunny! You know what that will do. They are already talking bad about me, but I do not have a choice. It's either I sing the vocals or the songs are not going to make the album." By this time, El was very emotional. I know he wanted to believe his brothers would come through, but reality stared him right in the face. I knew this was a very hard decision for El to make. Regardless who sang the lead, it was still going to be something his brothers would take personally. He had to decide what to do and soon.

"Sing it," I said. "Sing the songs, El. At least they will get their songs on the album. I am behind you, bro. You must bring this project home. Do what you have to do, and they will get over it," I promised my little brother.

I could tell El was deeply conflicted about how his brothers might feel. He loved and cared for them very much. He knew that his position and the favor he enjoyed at Motown was a sore spot for the boys. James and Mark were especially vocal. Each felt talentwise that they could do just as well as El if Motown gave them the same opportunities. Randy did not feel the same as James and Mark. However, Randy would always be the one to root for the underdog. If Randy saw you sad or crying, he would take your side, no questions asked, even if he knew you were in the wrong. It was his way of offering his brothers love and support. Not really meaning to, he ended up giving James and Mark moral support at the expense of El. Division started among the brothers, and El was under a lot of pressure from all angles.

"El, I will talk to them and explain your position. Just go ahead and do what you must," I reassured him. I am sure El also talked with Bobby and he reassured him too. El went into the studio and finished the lead vocals on both songs and brought them home. He sang the songs in the way he wanted Mark and James to sing them. The album was finally finished, and El was left to deal with the fallout from his brothers. Alas, the company was satisfied, and this was the only thing that mattered in the end.

Mark's and James's strong reactions were expected. They lamented about El's decisions and expressed being very hurt. They came to my house high and pouring out their heart. *How could El do such a thing? He is just being selfish.* They felt El just wanted to sing all the songs. They accused El of not working with them in the same way he worked with me on my songs. Again, they brought up how unfair El and Motown were treating them. It was one accusation after the other. *Motown likes El better! Motown is treating El better! Motown this . . . Motown that!* It was emotionally exhausting listening to Mark and James go on and on about everyone except themselves. As big sis, I was the listening ear and keeping the boys from killing each other. Mark's and James' finger-pointing at El was nothing new except this time it was too much and getting in the way of the group's progress. It was time for me to have a heart-to-heart with Mark and James.

I began to explain to Mark and James the pressure El was under with the company and that he had come to me to discuss his concerns. "He did not want to do your songs," I let them both know. "He cared how you felt and did not want you to feel this way. He is not being unfair. El had a decision to make, and if he did not deliver, Motown was going to pull your songs off the album. He tried to get you all to do your own songs. What did you expect him to do when he only had a week to get the songs completed? No one could find you. When he did find you guys, you gave him a hard way to go," I stated honestly. Mark and James began to deny their part in the whole ordeal. "That's not true, Bunny," they both stated in unison.

"That is only what he is telling you," Mark stated, not sounding very convincing.

"El just wants to sing all the songs—believe me," James stated, very accusatory. I sat and listened to them, but I guess they could sense I was not buying their story. Like always, they accused me of taking up for El at their expense.

Each of my brothers knew me to be a fair and reasonable person. Unlike Randy who based his decisions solely off who shed the most tears, I would sit back and listen to both sides before drawing any conclusions. For Mark and James to insinuate I was unfairly taking sides upset me a great deal. I did not play favorites with any of my siblings and loved them just as much as I loved El. Had I felt El was mistreating them in any way, I would not have stood for it. I took up for them equally when it came down to it. They were special in their own unique way. Watching them fight and bicker with one another was breaking my heart. We were family, and I was all for us loving, understanding, and just getting along with one another. Now there was trouble in paradise, and the boys were at each other's throats.

Motown was pleased with the finished album. Management was hearing bits and pieces about the infighting among the brothers. Then there were rumors about James and Janet's situation falling apart. The wild parties, the different women, and the drug binges had all come up on the company's radar. Our manager, Tony Jones, wanted to talk to us individually and as a group. Management wanted to get to the bottom of the rumors and innuendos to keep the group's image intact. The solution was to find ways to keep the group members busy to keep the boys out of trouble. We ended up recording a Mountain Dew commercial, going on several interviews in addition to performing on *Solid Gold*, *Soul Train*, and *American Bandstand*. We were brought into the studio to sing on Smokey Robinson's upcoming album. It was a song written by Stevie Wonder. DeBarge was quite busy to say the least. As if this was not enough, Motown decided it was time for us to go on our first tour. We learned we would be the opening act for Luther Vandross! Right before the tour began, we completed a song on the soundtrack for the movie, *D.C. Cab*. The song was called "Single Hearts" and was performed by El and me. At least for now, the tension in the group had subsided.

CHAPTER 33

THE BUSYBODY TOUR

Keeping busy before the tour was time well spent. We were able to refocus and enjoy our accomplishments thus far. Now it was time to get ready for the tour. Management hired a choreographer to teach us dance steps, and we ended up writing out our own show. DeBarge hired studio musicians to help perfect our live sound and rehearsed with them every day. We used the group Ozone, which was also a band signed to Motown Records. We became very close to the people in the band and did our best to prepare for life on the road.

As the tour date drew near, I became concerned about my own drug habit as well as for Tony. It dawned on me I could not go on the road in my present condition. Therefore, Tony and I started weaning ourselves off the pills. As our use began to taper off, we were finally able to focus on the task at hand. Kevin and Michele were trying to kick their habit too. After Tony and I were down to taking one or two dosages of pills a day, we were ready to quit altogether. We ended up taking a four-day trip to Phoenix, Arizona. We did not want to be around any influences or have easy access to the pills.

Once Tony and I reached Phoenix, we were physically sick and had problems sleeping. We were so tempted to use again but decided to go through the withdrawal. Tony could have easily decided not to go through with our plans to withdraw from the pills. However, I had no choice. There was no way I could have withstood the rigors of the road being addicted to pills. The boys (Mark, James, and Randy) had also formed a pill habit. I do not think their use had progressed as bad as Tony and mine. Tony and I had begun taking the pills daily just to function as normal human beings. The boys did use regularly but would allow days to lapse between each use. They took the pills to get high (recreational use) whereas Tony and I took the pills to function (a sign we had indeed become addicted).

Up until we went to Phoenix, Tony and I were able to hide our escalating addiction to the pills. When we returned from Phoenix, we were off the pills for now. I looked forward to going on the road. It was our saving grace as well as the boys. Everyone needed to get away from their influences. When it came time to leave, I found myself craving the pills again. I was not able to sleep, and my body felt very weak. We were traveling from one place to the next, and I was tired. I figured it was due to not having my vitamins. I would make the shows but not be able to sleep at night. The grind of the tour was killing me, and it was barely off the ground. The boys were also struggling without the pills. Our tour manager, Bobby Reed, realized we looked physically drained. Therefore, he called in a doctor to prescribe us vitamins. The doctor prescribed us vitamins and gave us all B-12 shots that worked liked a charm. Even though my sleep was taking its time to get regulated, I began to feel much better as the days passed.

We performed during the week and on the weekends. There were radio interviews between the performances, and we were under security at each stop. Our first night on tour was frightening. We were scared to death, and our performance was quite stiff. However, as we continued to tour, our performance became sharper. Our steps were more in sync, and we grew more confident as the crowd anxiously cheered us on. There were good shows and not so good ones. A few of the shows were very special because everything seemed to go perfect.

The boys had fans in every city. The girls were screaming, crying, and begging to be their own personal lady. As for me, I was not very popular with the girls. In fact, I had many enemies due to the proximity to my brothers. This made no sense. After all, I was merely the big sister! There was a part in the performance where we all separated and worked different sides of the stage to engage with the audience. I dreaded this part of the show and would never get the warm reception the boys received. The girls would say, "Move! We do not want to see you! We want to see Mark, El, Randy, or James!" I took their disdain with a lot of class and tried to understand I was in a space they wished they occupied. Plus, I was used to dealing with jealousy directed at me as we were growing up. The jealousy and envy had made high school unbearable. Now here I was onstage with my brothers who were heartthrobs. For as many females who threw themselves at my brothers, I also experienced overzealous male fans. However, male fans are different. I would receive a sea of roses and cards in my dressing room. I was given a special honor when we toured in New York. While in Washington, DC, fans lined up to come onto the stage and give me roses. The adoration from fans was very much appreciated. I wondered how we would be received once we toured in our hometown.

We were slated to tour in Detroit and Lansing, Michigan, as well as Chicago, Illinois. I had my special fans who made themselves known with smiles and signs. Our Lansing, Michigan, show was special because all the Grand Rapids fans came to see us perform. In many ways, it was a performance I will never forget. We upped our stage game and did our very best performance for family and the home team—at least we felt this way. DeBarge was halfway through the tour when friction between the brothers started again.

El was getting a lot more recognition everywhere we performed—much more than the other brothers. It was to be expected since he was the one up front and leading most of the songs. He was invited to parties the rest of us knew nothing about. He was also taken to various places without the rest of the group members. It felt awkward as if management was deliberately trying to separate El from the rest of us. The special treatment El received caused him to behave differently. He became curt and short-tempered during rehearsals and would go off about the smallest issue. The other boys noticed it first. He did not want to hang out with them and always made the excuse he had other things planned. They would complain to me about it. At first, I ignored them until I noticed a difference in his attitude—especially during the show in Lansing.

The show in Lansing was beautiful, and we thought it went well. Each of us were onstage giving our all. At the end of performing "Time Will Reveal," we noticed that once El hit the high note, he dropped to his knees in James Brown fashion. He had begun doing this at the start of the tour. However, lately, he was staying in this position longer and longer. He was acting overly dramatic while the rest of us would be standing onstage looking confused. El was making a spectacle of himself. All we wanted was for him to get up so we could gracefully exit the stage. However, the night of the Lansing show, El stayed in this position and would not get up. He seemed to disregard the fact we were just standing there waiting for him to come to his senses. We thought it was a bit too much. *Okay . . . we get it!* I kept saying over and over in my head. It seemed as if El knelt for hours while we stood onstage waiting for our set to formally end. Finally, he stood up and walked around the stage looking up and pointing toward the ceiling acting as dramatic as ever. He was clearly in full-fledged diva mode. Out of nowhere, he goes back into the high note then dropped down to the floor with the James Brown theatrics *again!* I was outdone! As a group, we decided for now not to speak on whatever was going on with El. The show was over, and for the most part, our set went very well. Hopefully, El would behave better at the next show.

After the set was over, we prepared to host a meet and greet with the radio stations, magazines, our fans, and loved ones. Before going out, we were all together in the dressing rooms changing out of our stage attire. We were so proud of our performance and began giving ourselves compliments. Suddenly, El blurted out, "I don't know why you all are so pleased about the show. You were flat and sounded like shit!" At first, we all stood dumbfounded. We were taken aback by his attitude and felt he had no reason to be so rude. I wanted to understand where his attitude was coming from because this was unlike El. *Perhaps he is just joking around*, was my first thought. However, in observing his face, it was obvious he was serious. I knew the direction this was heading and decided to step in before everything went up in flames.

We had performed our hearts out, and El was wrong in his assessment and being unfair to the group.

"Wait a minute, El! How dare you come down on everyone like this? You are not perfect and sang flat notes! Plus, you crack too, nigga!" I was over it. As if it was not enough him acting like the second coming of James Brown onstage, now he insulted the group. I was not having any of it!

El was upset by my words. Usually, I was on his side because he made excellent points. However, El was wrong in this instance and was coming down on the group hard for no reason. I felt he was acting a little too bigheaded because some of his die-hard fans were feeding his overblown ego. Nevertheless, group dynamics aside, we were family first, and I did not like what was happening to us as siblings. "I'm calling Mr. Gordy! He will hear about this!" he screamed as loud as he could. Now I could see clear as day what was going on with El. Obviously, Motown was in El's ear and was beginning to separate our brother from the rest of the group. I yelled at the top of my voice, "Mr. Gordy is not Jesus, El! He is a man like everybody else! Forget Mr. Gordy!"

Everyone was beginning to wear their heart on their sleeves. We were sensitive to what was going on within the group and was hurt as a result. What hurt even more was the feeling as though El was putting the opinions of others before family. People on the outside influencing how we felt about each other had never happened before this moment. Though we had our ups and downs, we were a very close-knit family and had never allowed anyone or anything to come between our relationships with one another. There were signs of division going on behind our backs, but we decided to turn a blind eye to it for now. We chalked up El's outburst as a family argument and carried on as though everything was still intact. There were many more cities on the tour, and we desperately needed to get along for it to be a success.

It dawned on me one morning that I had missed my menstrual cycle for a second month straight. Initially, I figured stopping the pills had made my cycle irregular. However, smells began bothering me, and I was sleeping all the time. I then began experiencing morning sickness and having wild cravings. It was obvious I was pregnant. I was not ready for another child and was unsure of the father. No one except me knew this secret. I had engaged in a one-time affair, which was a huge source of personal regret. However, it was possible this young man could very well be the father of my child. When I saw my sister-in-law Kathy at our show in Pittsburgh, I shared with her that I might be pregnant. She looked at me and stated, "Yep, you look like you are pregnant." Kathy was convinced she had an eye for these things and could spot a pregnant woman a mile away. I responded, "I feel like it. Kathy, I do not want this baby. I do not want any more kids. Plus, it's only going to be a girl. It would be different if I knew what it was going to be. I have my two girls, and they are enough." I was just venting to Kathy, not knowing my words would come back to haunt me.

"Oh, go on and have the baby! If it is a girl, I will take it," Kathy stated. I looked at Kathy, and she had a serious look on her face. I figured she was just joking around so I played along. "I am going to hold you to it. If it is a girl, it is yours."

"All right, sis," she stated. "I cannot have any more kids, and I want a baby." It did not take long afterward for Tony to figure out I was pregnant. By now, I had constant morning sickness. Every morning, I found myself complaining because the rigors of the tour was overwhelming me mentally and physically. I finally went to management and told them I may be pregnant and needed to see a doctor. They arranged for me to have an appointment right away. I took the pregnancy test, and just as suspected, I was three months pregnant. I wanted to go home so I went back to management and let them know it would be too hard for me to continue the tour. They understood and had no problem with me leaving the tour early. We only had six more weeks to go, and the boys agreed to carry the rest of the tour. I was grateful and gave a two weeks' notice. Tony left immediately so he could get the girls from my aunt's house. Now it was just me and my brothers left on tour.

The boys became overly protective once they learned I was pregnant. They took turns staying the night in my hotel room. My last night on the tour was in New York City. Luther Vandross and his crew threw me a surprise going-home party. Because I was pregnant, they gifted me with everything for the baby. Luther even gave me a huge teddy bear. During the tour, I had grown very close to many of the people in Luther's crew, and they were sad to see me leave. I had a lot of fun on the tour, and I learned a lot. Luther told me my baby would be a dancer and a singer. I told him I received the words he spoke, and I felt the exact same way. After all, I was doing a lot of dancing and singing the past few months on the tour. It was bittersweet leaving my brothers behind. Yet I was tired of the road, hotels, and eating at restaurants. Most of all, I missed home and my children. Further, I could no longer tolerate the long bus rides. There was no two bits about it; I just needed to go home and allow the boys to carry on without me. I knew they would be fine. I kissed them all good-bye and rode to the airport in a limo headed back to my life with my family.

CHAPTER 34

BABY FEVER!

I NEVER SHARED WITH ANYONE my concern about the child's father. I kept this secret to myself. On the plane home from the tour, I prayed over and over that Tony would be the father. It had nothing to do with me loving my husband. Rather, I did not want to add any more drama to my life. Tony and the girls met me at the airport, and I was so grateful to see my girls. I immediately shared with Damea and Janae I was having another baby, and they were thrilled. Janae had been my baby for eight years, and Damea was now eleven years old. Both were growing up so fast. They took the news very well, and this allowed me to start feeling less anxious about the pregnancy.

Kevin, Michele, and Renee (their daughter) came by to welcome me home from the tour later in the day. Tony was in a good mood and prepared a good old-fashioned soul food dinner. For once, it felt good to be home. The boys kept in touch with me every night while on tour. They let me know how the remainder of the tour was going and how they were getting along. There were not many dates left on the tour so they would be returning home soon. Bobby and Tommy were also glad I was back home. Unfortunately, Tommy was still walking on the wild side smoking cocaine, and Bobby had started abusing pills again. Mama moved back to Grand Rapids, and Tommy and Duckie were considering moving with her as well. Duckie had gotten used to having Mama around and expressed sadness about her being gone.

Tony was also abusing pills again. This made it very hard for me not to indulge. I was not using every day. However, every once in a while I would take one. Kevin and Michele's addiction to pills had gotten worse while we were on the road. I was worried about them. Being away from the environment and not using as often helped me see just how bad off I must have been at the time. I was pregnant now and could not afford to use the pills every day. I was afraid my child would be born drug exposed, and this was something I did not want or need. It was hard living around drugs day in and day out. After all, I was being tempted since the drug use was going on in my home. Concern for my baby was the only reason I was not back to using every day.

The boys returned safely from the tour and to the daily grind of their lives. They were not very happy with what was happening on the home front. Each of them was having problems with their mates. The girls seemed to have all gone astray at some point while the boys were away on tour. Since returning home, the boys tried to get their love life back under control. They were devastated, hurt, and not understanding what was happening to their relationships. My brothers came to me crying and complaining about how their lives were falling apart. I decided to take this opportunity to be up front and honest. I let them know they had a whole lot of nerve to act as though their mates were being unfair. "Come on, boys!" I stated. "It's not as if you were angels while on tour. All of you were playing around, and I know for a fact there was a different girl in each city. Why is it so bad if the woman does it?" I asked them bluntly.

The boys could not accept the shoe being on the other foot. I know temptation was tough for the boys while on tour. The women made it very difficult for them to remain faithful. They were plentiful and available in every city. The women sported their finest outfit, displayed their greatest asset, and presented their best when it came to the art of seduction. One thing I learned while on tour (as well as growing up with very good-looking brothers), women can truly make a spectacle of themselves when it comes to a man. We are blessed with the ability to easily tempt a man. Once we see something we want, we go all out to seduce it.

The boys have always been surrounded by beautiful women, and each of these women carried an apple. They were temptresses. However, I always questioned why it was acceptable for my brothers to be wild and promiscuous yet completely unacceptable for the woman. For my brothers, their dog ways were counted as a rite of passage and was understood simply because they were men. I always questioned this double standard. In my mind, women have the same feelings as men. I let them know that as women, we are equally as hurt knowing our man had been with other women. We cannot stomach knowing another woman has been with the man we love. I wanted my brothers to understand the female perspective and to stop all their whining. They could have easily taken their mates on tour with them and remained faithful.

I did not know if anything I spoke to them eased their pain, but I wanted to give them an honest female perspective. I ended up writing a song entitled, "A Woman in Love" after having a heart-to-heart with brothers. I fell in love with the lyrics because they were deeply personal and came directly from my conversation with my heartbroken brothers: *Do you need a girl who won't let go tomorrow? One who is on your side? Is there through thick and thin? Do you need a girl who won't drown in her sorrows? One who is by your side who wants to see you win? A woman in love, will give all her love. But if there is just one thing she needs to know, if she is there with pride—Will your love come home by her side; Will she be shown that her man is in love, too?* I dedicated the song to my brothers, wanting them to know a woman wants and needs her man to be true as well. I looked at my brothers. Here were little boys trying to become men. Then it dawned on me: *Are not all men little boys?* Seeing them distraught made me realize men cannot bear the same level of pain they put women through.

With the boys back home, DeBarge was now on vacation from everything concerning the group. It did not take long before their dysfunctional lives had them in search of drugs again. They were all getting high again except for El. Randy and GiGi had separated, and she was seeking a divorce. The boys never approved of the marriage from the start and ended up setting a trap whereas GiGi expressed interest in being with them. Of course, this broke Randy's heart, but it also opened his eyes to the reality of his wife.

James and Janet were having major relationship issues too. Once James started getting high again, Janet could no longer shoulder the burden of his addiction. They separated, and Janet wanted a divorce. Unfortunately, Janet had a hard time sorting out her feelings for James. She still loved him and was weak for him. She found herself putting up with James calling her and crying over the phone. As a woman, I am sure she found this very overwhelming. She was trying to move on, and James was pulling her back into his emotional turmoil. Janet decided to move out of the country to Japan without informing James. He did not know how long she would be gone—he only knew his wife was far away, and he was unable to make contact. Sadly, his drug use began to increase as a result. We were getting calls from the mall informing us he was there and unconscious. When we got to him, we found him knocked out with his face flat in his food. He was miserable and staying high to numb his emotional pain.

Mark and Kim were also on the rocks. Their relationship had always been stormy. They were on one minute and off the next. Mark was tripping right along with James and Randy. The boys were now hanging close and getting high together. I referred to them as the Three Stooges. They convinced themselves they had to hang together in order to have each other's back.

El was on a lonely island going through his ups and downs with Roberta. His saving grace at the time was he was not getting high. Roberta had finally given birth to little El, and my brother was left wondering if he was the father. He suspected Roberta of being unfaithful. Roberta got a kick out of telling him she had been unfaithful just to hurt him. She figured he had been out on tour footloose and fancy-free, and there was no way he could have been faithful.

As for me, other than worrying about the father of my unborn child, my life was going smooth. No one knew my secret except me. I was not going to say anything unless necessary. However, all I could do now was pray for the best outcome.

CHAPTER 35

KEVIN AND MICHELE

KEVIN AND MICHELE WERE NOW a huge part of my family, and we loved them dearly. They knew everyone in the family and loved us just the same. They were there to witness everything unfolding in our family. They hurt and cried with our family. They shared in our joy, our GOD, knew about our lives and our testimony. We prayed together, fellowshipped together at church, spent time in the studio, went to shows, and got high together. Yes, they were family in more ways than one.

Kevin ended up receiving a promotion at his job. Both he and Michele were very proud of his recent accomplishments. Not only did he get a new position, but his salary increased as well. Kevin was now able to buy the new Toyota truck he had been eyeing. Tony, the girls, and I made plans to ride to the beach with Kevin and Michele in his new truck. Out of nowhere, Tony changed his mind about us going to the beach. Kevin stated he would pick up some pills on his way from the beach and come over to our apartment later. Time passed, and before we knew it, it was evening. I mentioned to Tony it felt strange not hearing from Kevin and Michele since earlier in the day. As Tony and I were talking, the phone rang. I ran to the living room to answer hoping it was either one of them calling. "Hello," I stated. "Michele, where are you guys? It is late. Is everything okay?"

Michele stated in a low, even tone, "I am okay. Kevin is going to be all right. We lost Renee." Her voice was flat, and I was trying to understand what exactly she meant by *lost*. Initially, I thought maybe they had lost Renee at the beach. Perhaps someone had kidnapped Renee. If something bad had happened, why was Michele so calm? Without really understanding where Michele was coming from, I became emotional. "Michele, what are you talking about? Where is Renee?" I do not know if I was in denial about what I heard Michele say, but I was not readily accepting anything she said.

Renee was just shy of turning six years old and was as cute as they come. She was a very precocious little girl who was wise beyond her years. Renee and I had become very close, and she was just as much my baby as she was Michele and Kevin's. My baby girl, Janae, was initially jealous of me giving Renee any ounce of attention. Janae was the youngest between herself and Damea. She did not want to share her mommy nor lose her spot as the youngest. Renee loved me as much as she loved her own mother. She was so excited about me having a baby and would often lie on my stomach to talk to the baby and feel it move.

"Is it my baby too?" she would ask. I would answer, "Yes, it is. The baby belongs to us all."

Now, my heart was beating a mile a minute imagining something might have happened to Renee. "Where is Renee, Michele?" I cried. By now, everyone in the apartment overheard my phone conversation. They were curious and gathered around the phone. "We lost her, Bunny," she stated. "Renee is dead."

Her words hit me like a ton of bricks. "No, Michele!" I was in complete disbelief. "Please stop saying that! She's not dead! We will go and find her." I looked around to see my girls standing there with tears in their eyes. Tony, seeing how upset I was, asked for the phone. However, I had to know what happened to my sweet little Renee. "What happened, Michele? Where is Kevin?" I asked. Michele remained calm and let me know she was at the hospital in Los Angeles. They had had an accident in the truck. Renee wanted to ride in the back of the truck bed. At first, Kevin said no, but she kept asking. They finally agreed to let her ride in the back on the way home from the beach. While on the freeway, Kevin missed the exit. He was trying to get over at the last minute, and a car came out of nowhere. Kevin hit the curb at the exit, and the truck tipped over. Michele was not sure what happened next. However, when she came to, Renee was a little distance from the back of the truck. She was unconscious and had a broken jaw, and her mouth was twisted. Michele stated she ran to pick Renee up. As she went to cradle her head, she noticed her skull was cracked open.

"She died instantly, Bunny. She felt no pain," Michele was still very calm. I became hysterical. I was crying and could not get ahold of myself. Tony took the phone from me and began talking to Michele. The girls looked at me knowing something bad must have happened to Renee, but they had no idea just how devastating. They stood there crying, and I had to tell them the truth: "She is dead," I stated tearfully. "Renee is dead."

Damea and Janae were heartbroken and kept asking me what happened. I needed to get myself together to help my children process this tragedy. Renee was like their sister, and they were used to seeing her every day. Now, an important part of their childhood was gone forever. It felt as if I had lost my own child. Michele was handling the tragedy much better than me. I did not understand her calmness except perhaps she may have just been in shock. I needed to see Michele and make sure she was okay. Tony managed to get the name of the hospital. After taking the children to Tommy and Duckie, Tony and I headed to the hospital.

After arriving at the hospital, we noticed Kevin in the hospital bed and police everywhere. Kevin and Michele were high, and we had no idea what would happen next. Kevin's blood was drawn and indicated he had been intoxicated while driving. I overheard one of the police officers say to Kevin in a mean cold tone, "You killed your daughter." Kevin began crying. He was obviously in a lot of physical pain. However, for the officer to be insensitive toward him only made matters worse. Michele was on the phone with his parents back in New York. She still seemed to be handling the tragedy well. I knew she would eventually break down. Perhaps she had too much going on to mourn. Realistically, she did not need to cry because I was doing all the crying for her family. I was trying to process never being able to see my beautiful little Renee again.

The police allowed Kevin to be released from the hospital with a couple of tickets for the time being. He would have to appear later in court. He and Michele stayed the night at our apartment. Kevin's parents arrived in California the following day. It was a devastating time in our lives, and we all were in so much pain and turmoil. We ended up sedating ourselves to cope with the pain of losing Renee so tragically.

There was a memorial service for Renee. There was no viewing of her body. Kevin and Michele made the decision to cremate her remains and throw the ashes out to sea. From time to time, I would become overwhelmed with fear and anxiety for my own family. Had Tony not changed his mind about us going to the beach with Kevin and Michele, my children would have been in the back of the truck. I was thankful to the Lord for sparing their lives. I praised Him and thanked Him for not allowing the outcome to be any worse.

After a week of mourning, Kevin and Michele began to come back around. Life appeared to be back to normal. They ended up spending many nights at our apartment because they could not bear the emptiness of their apartment since Renee had died. They began looking for another apartment, and we allowed them to live with us until they found one. Kevin and Michele were deeply hurt. I knew after they lost their baby, there would be no getting off drugs anytime soon. They needed the pills for survival—at least this is what they believed.

CHAPTER 36

RHYTHM OF THE NIGHT

Berry Gordy was producing a movie called *The Last Dragon*, and he wanted DeBarge to play a part in the movie. We were to go into the studio and record a song entitled "Rhythm of the Night." An up and coming songwriter named Diane Warren wrote the song for the group. Motown was pleased with the song because it sounded like Lionel Richie's chart topper "All Night Long." Motown felt it would be a great song to follow Mr. Richie's explosive hit. We also learned *Rhythm of the Night* would be the title of our next album. With the rhythm tracks laid beforehand, the only part left to complete were the vocals.

Recording the song was a piece of cake, and we completed it fully in one day. We had perfected our sound and camaraderie as a group so there was not much to work on going into the studio. The biggest challenge came afterward when we had to film our first ever music video. According to the movie script, DeBarge was a big-name music group whose new single would be introduced by the character Laura Charles played by Vanity. We would start off driving a car then end up dancing in the streets. However, I was seven months pregnant, and Motown did not want to show off my stomach. Therefore, the producer of the video had a body double portray me in the video. They never showed the young lady's face. Shooting the video was hard work, and it went on for days until it was completed. The group worked well together in the studio and on the video set. However, I could not help but see noticeable signs of stress in my little brother El.

Roberta, El's wife, had begun coming to all our meetings and taking notes. She began invoking her unsolicited opinions and acting as if she was part of the group's decision-making process. She even auditioned for the part in the video as my body double. I refused to allow this to happen because to be quite honest, I did not like Roberta one bit. The feeling was mutual because she also did not care for me either. I believed she was not for my brother, and I wanted her out of his life. She was trouble from the very beginning. She only seemed to hang on, hoping it would take her somewhere in life. Roberta had unfulfilled dreams of becoming a star. She counted on the proximity to my brother for her fantasies to become a reality. However, truth be told, Roberta had no discernible talent to even become a star. Unfortunately, El was in love with her and willing to do anything to please his wife. My relationship with El was suffering, and I am sure my dislike of his wife was a sore spot. I was hardly seeing my brother anymore. We had always been very close, and he was even living with me when he first met Roberta. El knew I did not care for this girl so he was staying away. The only time I would see him was when she did something to hurt him. He would then confide in me and share everything bothering him about the relationship. Perhaps El did not realize he was fostering my deep sense of hatred for Roberta even though he was still very much in love.

After finishing both the album and the movie, DeBarge began looking forward to our next move. Kevin and Michele visited the set as we filmed the video. They kept an eye on my girls as they ran around the set. Kevin and Michele eventually found an apartment near us in the Valley. Michele was excited about her new place and decided to throw me a baby shower. She planned it as close to my due date as possible. Mama came to California for the occasion. She and Duckie helped Michele get the shower together. It was getting close to the time for me to have the baby, and I was so excited. This would be my *rich baby* since she had everything a baby would need and more. Mama bought her a baby bed. I had not seen it yet, and it was supposed to be a big surprise.

I decorated the baby's room with some pretty wallpaper. For once in my life, I had every reason to smile.

The baby shower was a wonderful affair. There were so many people who came out to celebrate. I never had a baby shower before and was surprised by the show of love and support. I still did not know the sex of the baby at the time but was hopeful for a baby boy. Therefore, everyone who came brought items that could be useful for either a boy or a girl. I decided to buy outfits once I knew the child's sex. However, not long after the shower, I went into labor. Tony's mother had made it to California just in the nick of time. She arrived in Los Angeles two days before I went into labor. It was her turn to be with me for the child's birth. After all, my mother had been there when I gave birth to both Damea and Janae.

My contractions started around midnight. It did not take long before they were five minutes apart. We needed to head to the hospital. Once we arrived, the baby was ready to be delivered. The baby came quickly so there was no time to numb the pain. It would not be until later when I learned that the birth was natural. Around 4:00 AM, I gave birth to a bouncing baby girl. I was not disappointed because my baby was a girl, I just really hoped for a little boy. The delivery was exhausting, and I needed to sleep. I began drifting off to sleep when the nurses asked me if I was ready to see my baby. "Oh yes!" I stated. "Let me see my baby."

I looked over toward my baby girl and noticed yellow and brown stuff all over her little body. This was strange since I already had two children, and they never had anything like this on their bodies. I began to panic. "What is that on her?" I asked, barely able to gather my thoughts. One of the nurses answered, "Oh, it's nothing to worry about, Mom. She just decided to have a little bowel movement on her way here." I was shocked. "Oh my GOD!" I stated. "Is she going to be like this all her life—full of shit?" The nurse laughed. "Let's hope not." She then whisked my baby girl away for a bath. I immediately fell into a deep sleep.

When morning came around, I woke up refreshed and ready to hold my baby. I could hear the nurses in the hallway dropping off babies for their morning feeding routine. I waited patiently for a nurse to bring my baby. I kept looking out into the hallway and was getting very impatient. I noticed that the nurses kept passing by my door, but there was no baby. Finally, the hallway grew quiet, and I rose from my bed and walked to the door. There were nurses in the hallway but no babies. My patience had worn thin so I headed back to my bed and pushed the button for the nurse's station. A nurse came into the room, concerned, and asked if anything was wrong. She then began to poke around at my belly as though I was in pain.

"Where is my baby?" I asked point-blank. "Is everything okay?"

"Oh, she is fine, Mrs. Jordan," she reassured me. "The doctor just wants her under a light right now. We detected a little jaundice on her skin. There is nothing to worry about as this is normal sometimes after birth. You will have your baby this afternoon after the doctor has seen her again. It is nothing for you to worry about, Mrs. Jordan. You just get some rest. Your baby will be here before you know it."

Though the nurse was nice enough, her words did nothing to make me any less anxious. I was wide awake and wanted to see my baby. "Can I at least walk down to see my baby?" I pleaded. Seeing concern all over my face, the nurse agreed to take me to my baby girl. She helped me out of bed and led me to the nursery. I looked through the window for the sign that read "Baby Girl Jordan." Then I saw a nurse in the nursery rolling a baby closer to the window so I could get a better look. When I finally laid eyes on my baby girl, she was so pretty, and I wanted to grab her and hold her close. I was trying to see if she looked like me or her father, but it was hard to tell. I wanted to count her tiny little fingers and toes. I wanted to feel her ears and rub her hair. I wanted so badly to snuggle with my baby. I stood at the window for a while until I started feeling weak. The nurse stated I needed to get more rest, so I went back to my room to lie down and rest until the next feeding.

I fell asleep, and when I awoke, my baby girl was there to greet me. After I fed her, I took off all her clothing and looked her up and down to make sure she was healthy. I looked at her ears and could tell she had one ear like Tony and the other ear like mine. One ear had a double fold of skin over it. It was just like Tony's when he was born. Janae had the same fold of skin on her ear, but it was just a single fold. I was able to finally breathe a sigh of relief because there was no doubt in my mind that Tony was the father.

Later in the day during visiting hours, family and friends came to welcome our newest addition. The first thing my mother-in-law noticed was the baby had an ear like Tony when he was a baby. "That is exactly how Anthony's ears looked when he was born. After I brought him home, I took a bobby pin and pinned them back." Everyone laughed. We did not know whether she was serious or not. The girls instantly fell in love with their little sister and grew antsy about her coming home. Michele and Kevin loved her too, and I know seeing her made them think of Renee. I named my daughter Tonee Marie Jordan. Had she been a boy, I would have chosen the name Anthony. Alas, she was a girl so I did my best to name her after Tony. It was close enough, I felt.

I was ready to head home. Lucky for me, the hospital did not keep new moms long. It had been eight years since I last had a baby. Everything seemed much different now. Tony came and picked me up from the hospital. He also brought the outfit Tonee would be wearing home. After arriving at home, the girls and my mother-in-law were super helpful. I was able to rest while they took care of the baby. The girls were now old enough to hold the baby while being supervised. Later in the day, my sister-in-law Kathy called. She let me know she was on her way to California for a visit. I had no idea what her plans were at the time. I was expecting a quick visit from her to see the new baby. Kathy and I were very close, and I was glad she was coming to California. It did not dawn on me at the time she had other plans during her visit. She was coming to California to take Tonee away.

Tony drove to the airport to pick up Kathy. The rest of us waited patiently for her arrival. We were so excited about her visit. I had gotten out of bed and was sitting with the children in the front room. My mother-in-law was holding Tonee when Kathy came rushing into the apartment with a baby seat swinging from her arm. As I got up to hug her, I took the seat and stated, "Oh, I already have one, sis." I did not wish to seem ungrateful and did not want her to think I was acting funny about taking another baby seat. I went ahead and accepted the baby seat then handed it to one of the girls to put up.

"Hold up!" Kathy stated abruptly. "Bring that back here. This is going with me. Keep the one you got—I bought this one for *my baby*." She then walked over to my mother-in-law and picked up Tonee. "Look at my baby girl," she stated while fawning over Tonee. "Auntie has bought all kinds of things for you." She sat down and started opening her suitcase.

"We don't have long to stay," she started saying. "We are only here for the weekend. I have to get us back home soon." My sister-in-law was smiling from ear to ear as she continued making plans for my child. She looked at me still smiling.

Suddenly, a previous conversation between us began to play over and over in my head. "Kathy," I slowly began. "You are serious—aren't you?"

Kathy looked at me and stated, "You're right. I am serious." She opened her suitcase, and it was filled with baby clothing. Kathy had traveled with multiple outfits because she could not decide which outfit Tonee would wear.

"Kathy, just stop it," I stated, smiling, trying to play it off. "Now you know I am not letting you take my baby out of here." I was hoping Kathy would take the hint and realize Tonee was my child and would be staying with me.

Kathy looked at me and did not bat an eye. "You said if she was a girl I could have her. I am here to collect my baby. I knew you were having a girl all along." I did not like the direction this was headed. It was obvious Kathy was on a mission, and I had to stop her before this got further out of hand. I walked over and took a seat beside her on the couch. "Kathy, you cannot have my baby," I deliberately stated.

Kathy seemed to tune me out. She began gently rocking and kissing Tonee. "Isn't she a girl?" she asked, not taking her eyes off Tonee. "You, missy, did not want the baby if it was another girl. I told you I would come and get her. Now give me my baby."

Okay, things had obviously gone too far. I started laughing but could see she was dead serious. "Oh, Kathy, now you know I was just saying any old thing. There's no way I am going to carry a child for nine months then give it away." I hoped Kathy understood, and I did feel bad for her wasting a trip to California.

Kathy ignored me and continued bonding with my baby. "Oh well, *you* said it. I'm just here to make sure you follow through with what *you* said." It was obvious my sister-in-law was not willing to give up so easily. She could not have any more children and desperately wanted a little girl. She had bought Tonee everything a child would need and more. I made an off-the-cuff remark, which she ended up taking to heart.

It took a bit of compromise. However, before she left, I promised Kathy she could be the godmother along with being the auntie. She seemed to be okay with this plan. However, she made it clear she was not coming to California for the christening. We would have to do the christening close to where she lived. We promised her we would come visit her during the Christmas season. Kathy stated she would make plans to have Tonee christened at her father's church. Kathy took her role as godmother and auntie very seriously. I felt relieved and allowed her to make certain plans for Tonee if she understood she was not going to take my baby.

Kathy had always been a great sister-in-law, and I loved her as a sister. She was very funny and always made me laugh. She had always been there for me, and I could tell her my deepest secrets. Most of all, I knew she loved me dearly. I cannot remember us ever having an argument or disagreement. Moreover, Kathy was a wonderful auntie to the girls. It was fair to say she was their favorite auntie on their father's side of the family. She had spent a lot of quality time with them as they were growing up. I knew at the end of the day she meant well and was not trying to take Tonee out of malicious intent. Therefore, we chalked this incident up to miscommunication.

After my in-laws left, Tony and I made plans to spend Christmas back home with family. For the time being, our home life was getting back on track. I was getting my routine together so I could balance having a new baby with my career. Kevin and Michele's lives had finally gotten back to normal. Michele enjoyed coming over and helping me care for the new baby. I knew how badly she needed the ray of hope Tonee brought into her life. For once, I could stop and smell the roses.

CHAPTER 37

MICHELE

It had only been a few months since we lost Renee. Although we could clearly discern Kevin's pain, Michele was still masking her pain—at least when she was in our presence. I loved Michele dearly. She had become a sister to me and an aunt to my children. We were there for each other in good times and challenging times. To secure our sisterhood, we took a blood vow. We used a pin to prick our fingers to draw blood. We then took our blood and joined ourselves together as blood sisters. We promised to always remain sisters and to be in each other's lives no matter what happened. Michele, now my blood sister, had lost her only child, and I had not yet seen where it was affecting her at all. She just walked around as if Renee were on vacation and would be returning any moment. To cope, she spent as much time with my children as she could, and the girls loved their "Auntie Chele."

It was Halloween, and Michele was busy getting my girls ready to go trick-or-treating. She purchased them both Halloween costumes. She had come over earlier to take them to pick out their favorite costume. Michele seemed more excited about trick-or-treating than the children. Tony, being a humdrum person, resented her enthusiasm. He began grumbling and making off-the-cuff remarks. This caused Kevin to become agitated, and he started in on Michele. I immediately knew why Kevin was reacting this way toward Michele. Tony was the one out of order, yet Kevin did not feel the need to tell him he was wrong.

To keep down the conflict between him and Tony, Kevin misdirected his anger toward Michele and lashed out. Not liking the direction this was heading, I jumped in to defend my sister. "Leave her alone and let her be. She is not doing anything wrong. She is just being herself and does not need this right now."

I could see Michele was close to her breaking point. She was not her normal free-spirited self but did the best she could under the circumstances. She got the girls dressed, put a little makeup on her face, and off they went on their venture. Michele was a lot of fun so I knew the girls would have a nice time. I did not go with them since I was busy with my newborn. Additionally, Michele and I were a little high already. We planned on using the rest of the pills when the girls returned and were tucked into bed.

I was busy caring for Tonee, and before long, it was dark outside. I could hear children in the complex yelling, "Trick or treat!" Suddenly, over all the little voices I could hear my clan. They were so excited. Michele came in, telling me all about their adventure. I was listening intently while Tony, once again, began making snarky comments. He was also rushing the children off to bed. Michele tried her best to ignore him, but I could clearly see her feelings were hurt. "Okay, girls, you do not want to get in trouble. Go get ready for bed. Your mom and I will put the candy up for you." Damea and Janae were saddened but headed toward their room to get ready for bed.

Michele then turned to me and asked if she could take a shower. I looked at her and could tell she was tired. The girls must have worn her out. "Go ahead," I stated. "You can use the shower in my bedroom." I sensed that something was not right with her so I followed her and sat on my bed as she showered. "Are you all right?" I asked as she closed the shower door.

"I am fine," she stated in a quiet voice. She was not convincing at all.

When I heard Michele turn on the water, I got up and closed my bedroom door then lay back down on the bed. On my nightstand was a picture of Renee taken not long before she died. As I was looking at her image, I heard a loud yell. "Renee, it's time to come home now, baby! Mommy misses you!" Michele then let out a bloodcurdling scream I will never forget. I ran into the bathroom, and she was still in the shower bent over holding her stomach. She was crying from deep within her soul, travailing in the spirit and wailing out a mother's cry. Her pain touched my heart. As a mother, I felt her loss within my own womb. Without giving it a second thought, I climbed into the shower still wearing my clothes and held her tight. We both cried. I began to ask GOD to send a comforting spirit.

"It's all right," I reassured my sister. "It is time you cried, Michele. Just go ahead and cry." I held her in my arms as we both stood in the shower with the water still running and cried. We cried until there were no more tears left to cry.

Kevin and Tony never heard Michele crying, and I was grateful. Tony would have been insensitive for sure, and Kevin would have gone right along with his insensitive shenanigans. However, this was a mother's cry for the child she had carried in her womb. I do not think they would have understood. It was not for them to understand. As mothers, we understood the pain of losing Renee. Michele openly grieving over the loss of her child was much needed and well overdue. She had been in denial for a while and was refusing to let Renee go. Tonight, Michele let go of Renee and gave her child back to GOD. She finally accepted Renee was not on vacation. She finally accepted Renee was also not at her in-laws. She finally accepted Renee was never coming back home. This night, Michele and I grew even closer as sisters. It was a tender moment neither of us would ever forget. Michele could now move forward and have other children if she so desired. For the remainder of the night, we sat and talked about the beautiful little girl named Renee who had now become our guardian angel.

CHAPTER 38

HOLIDAYS WITH THE DEBARGES

THE CHRISTMAS SEASON WAS FINALLY upon us, and my little Tonee was now three months old. As promised, we would head home for Christmas. We would first fly into Grand Rapids, Michigan, and rent a car. Afterward, we would drive down to Steubenville, Ohio, where little Tonee Marie Jordan would be christened. I was very excited about going home. I had not been back in a while and thought it would be nice to see snow at Christmas for a change. Tommy and Duckie had moved back and were now living with Mama. I had bought something for everyone and was excited to shower my family with gifts. Mark, Randy, and James also flew home for Christmas around the same time as me. El would fly home later.

Once we exited the plane, family and friends were there to greet us. It felt as if it was a homecoming convention for DeBarge. We never expected to see so many people, but here they were, happy to see us. There was so much excitement going on, and everyone wanted their chance to hang around us. We were the stars of the show, and everyone was clamoring for our attention. Everyone seemingly had cameras and were snapping one picture after the next. A caravan of people followed us to Mama's house and piled inside. We were absolutely delighted about the love and attention we were receiving from loved ones. Everyone showed so much love since they had not seen us for a while. There were so many outlandish questions asked. Family and friends had been hearing about us on the radio and watching us on TV. While we were in town, they wanted an up-close-and-personal glimpse into our lives. Mama cooked every kind of food imaginable, and people brought food from everywhere. The house was truly filled with the Christmas spirit as we sat around singing Christmas tunes. It was a beautiful and joyous occasion for all. People continued pouring into the house throughout the day. For as many people who left, the same number showed up to sing our praises. They were genuinely proud of our success and fame.

I kept a very busy schedule while in Grand Rapids by visiting my cousins and best friend. I was delivering gift after gift because I wanted to make sure everyone was happy. Whomever I visited would not want me to leave. They opened their home and offered my husband, children, and myself a place to stay. I did my best to stay with everyone who offered. It was truly a blessing for them to even want me in their company. We received such a warm welcome even though it was extremely exhausting and took a lot out of me physically and emotionally. We made plans to leave Grand Rapids on Christmas Eve for Steubenville, Ohio. I was hoping to get some much-needed rest once we arrived in Ohio. Kathy was there eagerly awaiting our arrival and to spend time with Tonee. She was also preparing for the christening. All she needed me to do was show up with the baby. I also had gifts for everyone in Steubenville.

When we arrived in Steubenville, Tony's side of the family was there waiting with open arms. They were also glad to see us. Honey (my mother-in-law) had cooked a huge dinner. Tony and I stayed at my in-laws our first night in Ohio. Afterward, we piled up at Kathy's house where we would be more comfortable being ourselves. Before our visit, we decided to limit the number of pills we would be taking. Therefore, we only brought a small amount and were running out fast. We had to be conscientious of our intake because we did not want to become sick before arriving back in California.

Kathy had the day all planned out for the christening of little Tonee. She had bought the most beautiful dress for her to wear. We agreed to stay in Steubenville a few more days after Christmas then travel back to Grand Rapids and drop off the rental. Once we were back in Grand Rapids and had rested up, it was time to return to Los Angeles. We were extremely tired but could not deny we had such a beautiful time back home. To top it off, it was also a wonderful snowy Christmas!

As soon as we arrived in Los Angeles, the sunshine was there to greet us. As much as I enjoyed Michigan, it was good to be home in California again. Tony drove straight to Larry's house and picked up some pills. We barely made it back to LA from Michigan and Ohio before we ran out of pills. Unfortunately, we were now sick and needed to get to Larry quick. Upon our arrival to Larry's house, we met James, Randy, and Mark who were there for their supply as well.

Bobby was still in Michigan trying to kick his drug addiction. Mama was trying to help him get into a rehab program. Things were not looking any better for Tommy. He was on the wild and living recklessly. Tony and I ended up buying Christmas for his children. Duckie was grateful because she had no idea how they were going to get Christmas. I called her ahead of time and told her not to worry and I would help her out with Christmas for the children. She was grateful her children would wake up to toys and gifts on Christmas Day. My heart went out to Duckie. Despite everything going on, she truly was a good mother and a good person in gen. She was going through so much with Tommy. Yet I never saw her cry nor did I ever hear her complain. Her favorite words when it came to him were, "Tommy will be all right." Duckie had faith the day would come when she and Tommy would be all right. For now, she was living with Mama, and everyone was pitching in and helping financially with her and the children.

Duckie was also getting involved in church, and this seemed to bring her much joy. Even with everyone assisting, I could not help but think Duckie wanted to make her own way in this world. She wanted to be independent and not rely solely on family. After Switch broke up, Tommy was left with virtually nothing. He found himself left out in the cold. His drug use was already bad but had gone from bad to worse with the snap of a finger. When the group disbanded, he just seemed to have given up and no longer cared who knew about his junkie lifestyle. Tommy would openly share every single detail of his personal life. His business was everyone's business. All he needed was a listening ear, and he would go on and on spilling intimate details. Bobby, who was very guarded and private, was ashamed of Tommy's loose lips. If Bobby went somewhere and was told Tommy had been there, he would simply turn around and leave. Bobby did not like how Tommy conducted himself around people when he was high. He also did not like people's mistreatment of Tommy either. Whenever Tommy was on a drug binge, people would treat him poorly. Yet Tommy would still hang around those same people as if they cared about him. This would infuriate Bobby who often referred to Tommy as a fool.

Tommy was well known in the streets of Grand Rapids. There was not a person in Grand Rapids who did not know my brother. By default, this also meant everyone knew his personal business. Tommy had no shame in his game. Once he was high, he displayed no boundaries and would say anything that came to mind. The sad part was his words did not necessarily have to be truth. He just wanted a listening ear so he could run his mouth. We would tease Tommy about many of the things coming out of his mouth. When confronted, he would oftentimes say, "Y'all think it's just me. It's Duck too." His favorite comeback line especially when downplaying his actions was, "My baby needs milk, and my baby needs diapers." Sometimes this comeback line would not make sense in the context of the conversation. A person could be confronting him about discussing his sex life with his wife, and he would say, "My baby needs milk, and my baby needs diapers." Overall, Tommy was an anything-goes, happy-go-lucky type of fella. He was unapologetic, and for the most part, everybody loved him. Tommy did not have much during this time. However, whenever he did have it, he freely shared with everyone—family, friend, or foe. He did not have a stingy bone in his body. As far as Tommy was concerned, no matter what was going on in his life, he had Duckie. She was there for him and his biggest cheerleader. Moreover, she truly was the love of his life. Tommy was also grateful to have his children. Duckie was on cloud nine again because she was soon to give birth to her and Tommy's third child.

CHAPTER 39

FEELING LEFT OUT

It was springtime, and love was in the air. Motown was discussing us going abroad for a promotional tour. We all needed passports and soon. The promotional tour would start within the next few months. Motown was busy securing passports for us to travel outside of the country. This was not the only thing going on in our lives. I was hearing rumors about El and Roberta getting married. I did not pay the rumors any mind. After all, El was my brother and would certainly come to me if the rumors were true. We had seen each other often lately, and he never mentioned anything about getting married. I did know he and Roberta were headed back to Grand Rapids for a visit. For whatever reason he and Roberta had decided to pay a visit to Grand Rapids, I figured marriage would be too important not to mention.

El and Roberta eventually arrived in Grand Rapids for what I gathered was a minivacation away from the hustle and bustle of Los Angeles. I thought nothing of their visit until I received a phone call from Mama. Mama wanted me to know that El was planning a wedding. He had surprised everyone and let them know of his impending nuptials. His visit to Grand Rapids was not to get away but to plan a wedding. He was adamant about the wedding taking place in Grand Rapids and wanted Uncle Bill to officiate the ceremony. The wedding was also a surprise to the bride-to-be. Roberta had no idea El was planning their wedding. Everyone involved had to move quickly with planning the ceremony. Wedding invitations were printed and sent out to people everywhere. Guess what? I was not invited. I did not receive an invitation by mail nor a phone call inviting me to the ceremony.

Once Roberta and El arrived in Grand Rapids, he surprised her by taking her to buy a wedding dress. Her mother did not have to do anything for the wedding except show up. El paid all the expenses for the wedding. He even sent for her mother and other family members. He flew them all to Grand Rapids to take part in the wedding. What a great day for Grand Rapids to witness the star, El DeBarge, being joined in holy matrimony. What a sad day for me not to be able to witness my brother tie the knot. I did not even receive a phone call. The rejection hurt deep.

Everyone talked about how El went out of his way and spared no expense for the wedding. He did whatever it took to make the wedding day a success. Knowing my brother and the great romantic person he was, I knew he would go all out. Sadly, his wedding day marked the beginning of his own personal hell. To say Roberta was very difficult to please would be an understatement. Nothing El did could satisfy his bride, and they were constantly arguing. In fact, it was reported the couple argued all the way up the aisle. This did not surprise me at all. I was sad El had to endure Roberta's wrath. I wanted to be there for moral support if nothing else. I tried to convince myself I was okay not being invited. A small voice wanted me to believe that had I been invited, I would not have shown up anyway. Deep down inside, I knew it was a lie to make myself feel better because I was truly hurt. El and I were close. No matter what I felt about Roberta, I would have made it a point to be at his wedding.

The day of the wedding, I found myself very emotional. I never shared with anyone the tears I shed. A part of me still believed El was going to call and invite me to the wedding. He was my brother, and he had to know I was hurting. Sitting in LA knowing my brother was getting married, I tried to imagine what was going through his mind. I hated Roberta for him, and he knew it. In fact, she knew of my hatred toward her because I was never afraid to voice it. When I really looked back on the entire situation, El caused me dislike Roberta. There was nothing personally against her other than her callous treatment of my brother. Girls like her came a dime a dozen. What was funny was that I probably would not have had a problem with her had El not shared details of their tumultuous relationship. But he was my brother and confided in me. He shared with me what they were going through, always telling me specific things she would do to undermine the relationship. Knowing intimate details about their relationship caused me to form an opinion. Of course, I was going to take my brother's side. El painted her in my mind, and I thought it was unfair he still loved her while fostering my hatred of her simultaneously. Now the dichotomy in how he felt versus how I felt had somehow put a wedge between our sibling relationship. I was sad and grieving. Through it all, I loved my brother. El was always very special to me. His place in my heart was irreplaceable, and I found it to be a slap in the face for him not to invite me to his wedding.

The moment Roberta came into his life, El changed. He was no longer the brother I once knew so well. I missed the brother I knew to be warm, kind, and considerate. We did many things together so it was unlike him not to invite me to his wedding. He was very much a part of my life—not only as a little brother and group member. Rather, El and I shared a spiritual bond as well. I thought of the Bible and how in the days of Moses, his sister Miriam did not approve of the woman he was marrying. I felt Moses and Miriam were very much like El and me. In fact, El would often refer to me as Miriam, and I would refer to him as Moses. We both looked at it as our purpose. I missed our spiritual talks and working together in the business. I missed how we were as brother and sister. I felt the relationship with Roberta had taken my brother away from me, and I was angry about it.

Roberta made El do crazy things to satisfy her demanding attitude. She wanted to be a star, and he wanted to act as if he could make her one. Deep down in his heart, he knew Roberta lacked star quality. Nevertheless, I had to understand in El's mind that she was a star. She was something different in my mind. I remember telling El she was a witch from hell, and she only came into his life to break him. Further, she was an emissary of the devil who came to destroy him. I told him this often. Perhaps this was why he did not invite me to the wedding. Maybe he felt I would not be nice to Roberta. I was driving myself mad trying to come up with different scenarios. Whatever the reason, I was still in California, a wedding was happening in Grand Rapids, and my feelings were hurt. A part of me felt my brother was in big trouble.

People continued calling me the day of the wedding and the next day. I had to make up excuse after excuse as to why I did not attend my brother's wedding. Then there were those who were close enough to know what was really happening behind the scenes. I was hearing all about the wedding secondhand and having a hard time dealing with it. I could not believe El would just leave me out. It was not as if we were arguing or on bad terms per se. Maybe he thought I would "speak now" and not be able to "hold my peace" since I knew how stressful the relationship was for him.

I witnessed the hell Roberta put him through. He confided in me when things between them became too unbearable. I knew from the very start their relationship was a mistake. Roberta did not reciprocate my brother's love and affection. I then thought about the son they shared together. El had no more fears of little El not being his son, and he wanted to be a good father. He wanted to have a good relationship with his son. I finally had to stop the pity party and find peace amid the storm. Life goes on. All I could do was pray he could get through this time in his life. As I prayed, I asked GOD to give me peace, which surpasses all understanding. I would not worry about it anymore. It was over, and at the end of the day, it was his life and his mistake to make. I had my own life worries and was growing weary worrying about everyone else. I could not deal with myself for dealing with my brothers. I had always put everyone else, especially my siblings, before me, and it was time for things to change.

CHAPTER 40

HEADED ABROAD

A MEETING WAS SCHEDULED AT Motown in Tony Jones's office, and all three managers were to be present: Suzanne De Passé, Tony Jones, and Suzanne Coston. We would be discussing the trip to London. I arrived at the scheduled time, only to find El and Roberta seated in the office along with Tony Jones. The other group members had not yet arrived. I had not seen El and Roberta since they returned from Grand Rapids. I was surprised El even brought Roberta to the meeting. I get they were a married couple now. However, it did not mean she was married to the group. I held my composure. I figured there was nothing wrong with her being there for the moment. After all, the other group members had not yet arrived. I walked over to where they were seated and stated very nicely, "Well hello, newlyweds. Congratulations." I would normally follow my compliment with a hug. However, I was not feeling them and felt my acknowledgment was enough. They both sat there looking silly. Finally, they stated in unison, "Thank you." I then took my seat but was fuming inside. Tony Jones knew it and was making small talk to break the tension. I was doing good hiding my disgust of the couple. Tony Jones just kept talking, asking questions, going over who had IDs, etc. I knew Tony was trying to keep the tension in check. I answered his questions to the best of my ability. Suddenly, there was a ruckus going on in the secretary's office outside Tony Jones's door. The rest of the gang had arrived!

Tony Jones got on his phone and let Suzanne De Passé and Suzanne Coston know we were ready to start the meeting. After their arrival, I expected Roberta to get up and leave. However, she pulled out a pen and pad and began jotting down notes. Roberta stayed throughout the entire meeting. It was sickening to me. I felt she was out of place and should not be in our meeting. However, she was there because she was El's wife and apparently his secretary. We discussed the "Rhythm of the Night" video and how the movie, *The Last Dragon*, was coming along. They saw it to be something big for DeBarge and thought the video was coming along just fine. They were now editing the footage for the movie. They went on to explain how our popularity was exploding overseas. There was a demand for us over there, and they felt it was a good time for DeBarge to make their presence known abroad. We had done our promotional tour in the States, and it was successful. They were now setting up the promotional tour abroad. All we needed was for everyone's passports to arrive. Since it was such short notice, they had to find someone who could get it done right away. They did some under-the-table magic to make it happen. We then had to see doctors to get physicals and shots. There were two weeks left before we were set to leave. After everything was discussed, the meeting adjourned.

Before leaving the office, Tony Jones stated, "By the way, Mrs. Bunny, I have a present for you. It is something I know you will love." He then handed me a book. "It's Marvin Gaye's life story," he stated. "I know you are a big fan of his."

I was ecstatic. The title of the book was *Divided Soul: The Life of Marvin Gaye*, and David Ritz was the author. I was thrilled. It was a wonderful gift, and it took my mind off Roberta for a moment. Since Tony Jones and I were the only ones left in the office, I was able to openly voice my opinion about her being in the meeting. I had to say what was on my mind to someone because it was eating me up inside. After listening to me, Tony Jones reassured me the group was on to bigger and better things. He did not want me to let little things like Roberta bother me. Then Tony stated, "I knew you were upset, which is why I gave you the book today. I was saving it to give to you on the plane. It is such a long flight, and you will need something to read." I could not thank Tony enough. He did pick the right time. I was a little down, and the book made my day. I ran out of the office wanting to get home so I could start reading about the man whom I admired so much. I loved his music, and so did my brothers. The title of the book captivated me and spoke so much to how I was feeling. I had to know what tormented such a gifted singer. I started reading the book as soon as I got home and found it hard to put down.

My husband Tony would not be going on the road with me this time. Therefore, the children would be staying with him. My baby, Tonee, was now eight months old and actively trying to walk. I missed her already even though we had not yet left. However, this was my job and how I provided for my family. Tony went and got me enough pills to where I would not get sick while away. I had them stored in a pill bottle with my name on it and was able to hide them in my suitcase. Our passports finally arrived along with shot records. We were finally on our way to Europe.

The flight was the longest flight we had ever taken. We flew to New York first and then went through customs. This took a while so I pulled out my book on Marvin Gaye and started reading it again. It kept my interest the entire time. Finally, we were seated on the plane and on our way to London. We all sat together in first class. It was a lovely experience with lots of leg room. We also had access to the bar. I did not drink but took some pills as I sat there reading. I was in heaven as I vicariously walked through Marvin Gaye's life story. It was so exciting learning about his idiosyncrasies. I kept sharing everything I learned and discovered about him with my brothers.

The trip became a family affair. We decided to put everything behind us and pull together as one. We vowed to not let anything come between us as a family and as a group while in Europe. Tony Jones, Skip Starky, along with Bobby Reed accompanied us. Security would meet us once we arrived in London. It took eleven hours to travel from New York to London. It did not bother me since I had my pills and book to help me break the monotony. The Motown staff in London greeted us at the airport replete with limos and all the bells and whistles. Before our day started, we had to go through customs, which took a while. Finally, we were off to the hotel to rest.

London was beautiful, but much different than the States. There was also a major time difference. It was something we needed to adjust to quickly. During the nighttime, we were not sleepy because technically it was our daytime. Therefore, we stayed up reminiscing, marveling how far we had come in life and about all the fun we did manage to have as children despite everything that took place. When we were not acting silly, I was into my book. I had started reading it aloud to my brothers. We all saw Marvin as someone we could very much relate to. It was no wonder his music touched our hearts. We now understood why the book was entitled *Divided Soul*.

While on our weekend break, security accompanied us on a shopping trip. El bought me a little statue of a bunny with the bottom reading "My Bunny Kin." I was very surprised about his kind gesture. It was a special moment between us and represented our closeness. Since the fallout from the wedding, there was distance between us. We did not talk about the wedding or what was bothering us about each other. We just told each other how much we loved each other and held each other for a moment. Meanwhile, I was reading my book at every opportunity. Now I was having to read aloud to El who had become enthralled in the saga of Marvin's life. He loved how the story was unfolding and would come to me whenever I was reading. He would instruct me to read it aloud to him. El and I were huge fans of Marvin, so I obliged. It was interesting to read about the struggles Marvin had gone through. It let us know we were not alone, and there was someone else out there with a shared experience.

The weekend was over, and it was time to work. By this time, I was missing my family deeply. I did not have a chance to talk to them yet. Tony Jones had promised we could call home later in the day. It would be after our media appearances. I mentally prepared myself for the day ahead and topped it off by taking my pills. I only used enough to not get sick. I was mindful that Tony, my husband, had only given me enough to last the duration of the trip. We had many more days ahead of us, and I had to take the right amount or I would be in deep trouble. I did not want to go through withdrawal so I was being extra careful not to go over the amount by even one pill. The boys (Randy, Mark, and James) were showing signs of getting sick. However, they seemed to be dealing with it as best as they could under the circumstances. I was not able to share any of my pills with them because my husband ensured I had enough for me only. I did not talk with them before we left the States so I was not able to ensure they had enough to last the duration of the promotional tour. In fact, I was still under the impression they did not have a habit as big as mine or they may have decided to go cold turkey in London. The thought of not using the pills during this time in my life was a bit scary. The pills kept me "well" so I only took enough to not get sick. My brothers must have known I had a supply of pills somewhere. They knew about my habit and was wondering why I was not getting sick. However, I played it cool and did not show signs of being high. I behaved normal and did not take more pills than were needed. I did not want them to start badgering me for my supply.

The first official day of the promotional tour was grueling, but we made it through. We did radio stations and some TV appearances before turning in for the night. Tony Jones made sure we talked with our families back home before we went to bed. The next day, I did not use any pills since I felt okay and had decided to wait until later to take them. We went on about our day and visited more radio stations, made in-store appearances, and did more TV appearances. After eating, we went back to our apartment. I was feeling sick and went to my room to get my pills, only to find they were not where I had placed them. I panicked. I took everything out of my suitcases and meticulously went through each piece of my belongings. I was becoming overwhelmed and felt someone had to have gone through my suitcase and took the pills. I knew where I put my pills and could not find them anywhere.

At this point, I was getting very agitated so I went into the living room where the boys had congregated. I asked point-blank, "Which one of you have my pills?" They all looked at me as if I were crazy, and not one of them admitted to anything. I became furious. "Come on now! Do not play with me! You all know I need my pills! I know where I put them, and they are not there now!" They all claimed not to have any idea I even had pills and they had dared not enter my room. I knew they were lying, and one of them, if not all of them, knew what happened to my pills. Yet none one of them were forthcoming, and this made me even angrier. Mark made a statement that led me to suspect he was the culprit. Whoever did this did not have the decency to take some and leave some. Rather, the culprit or culprits took them all.

"Okay," I threatened. "I better not see one of you nod—not one time. If I must stay up all night and watch you, I will." I made it a point to let Marty know I was on to him without saying his name. Randy and James were amused and found it hilarious when I sat up all night watching Marty. I made sure he did not close his eyes—not even for a minute. Marty seemed oblivious to everything, but Randy and James knew what was going on and had fun at his expense.

The next morning, Randy (bless his heart) went to the dentist hoping to get some pain pills to help me get through. Randy knew I was getting sick. He got up early and acted as if he had a bad toothache and needed some pain pills. He did manage to get a prescription, and it helped a little. However, I ended up all the way in London sick and having to withdraw cold turkey. I was not looking forward to the cranky days and sleepless nights. We did a week's worth of promotional work in London then were off to Luxembourg. Going to Luxembourg was amazing because I was at the point in the book where Marvin Gaye was in Luxembourg as well. I imagined I was there with him.

Luxembourg was beautiful. However, I felt a sense of imprisonment during my stay. I learned it was a privilege to be from "the land of the free." I also learned we had die-hard fans in Europe. From reading his book, Marvin stated that fans in the States are borrowed and you are only as big as your last hit. On the contrary, Europeans are fans forever. Marvin talked about how much he enjoyed his stay in Europe. He felt the need to leave the States, and Europe brought him a sense of freedom. However, I felt a lack of freedom especially since we could not go anywhere by ourselves. Security was with us each time we stepped outside of our living quarters. We were hopping in and out of limos for the most part whenever we did leave the apartment. I needed air to breathe. The city was beautiful, and I wanted to experience it up close and personal. I wanted to take a walk solo around the city.

Even during our day off, security tagged along with us on our walk around Luxembourg. It was such a beautiful day for walking, and we were in such happy moods. We began singing and took a trip down memory lane by singing songs off Marvin Gaye's iconic album *What's Going On*. We broke out into the different harmony parts and felt we were doing Marvin justice with our impromptu concert. We continued singing and harmonizing until lunchtime. We came upon a cute little café where we could all sit outside and eat. After lunch, we went back to our hotel and prepared for the next day's itinerary.

Our next stop was Germany. Germany was quite the experience, especially the language barrier. We found the language difficult to decipher—even when they spoke English. People would say to us "Have a nice day," and it sounded as if they said a curse word. By the time we reached Germany, we were missing home and exhausted from working. Touring Europe proved to be much different than touring back home. We were so far away from home and longing for our loved ones. It had now been six weeks since we left for the promotional tour. Apparently, something was up, and El called a family meeting. There would be no manager present during the meeting.

According to El, the money Motown was spending on the promotional tour was money DeBarge had earned. El began to break everything down to where we could understand. All the money being spent on the European promotional tour was money we all had to pay back before we could recoup anything from album sales. Any amount of money spent was money owed to the company. Management never shared that the group had control over what was spent, where we spent it, how we spent it, and with whom we spent it on. El was now bringing everything to light.

"We don't even know how much we have spent already," he informed us. "We have not kept up with a single receipt. They can say whatever they want to say." El went on to educate us about what was happening. "They hire whoever they want. However, why can't we just hire our own people instead? Let's go home. They have not been right with us," he stated. We took a vote, and it was unanimous—we all voted to go home.

We went to Tony Jones, and El talked on our behalf. "We are ready to go home now," he boldly stated. "We want off this tour. There are some things we are not pleased with, and we need to sit down with the company and talk when we get back to the States." Tony Jones then told us he needs to call Mr. Gordy and tell him our thoughts and plans. We went back to our hotel and waited for his call. We thought Mr. Jones would get back to us right away. However, time went by, and we heard nothing. We then decided to call his room and received no answer. We called the other rooms, and there was no answer as well. This was a cause for concern. It appears they were deliberately trying to ignore us, and we were pissed. Tony Jones was supposed to call Mr. Gordy then get back with us. We began to doubt he had even called Mr. Gordy. Did he think we were a joke?

"They are out there doing whatever they want to do," El stated emphatically. "They're probably out spending more of our money and with no receipts. Let's go home. We have our own airline tickets, and we can book our own flights out of here."

We tried in vain all night long to get in touch with management and still received no answer. We followed El's lead and called the airline and booked flights for the next morning. El called Tony and finally managed to get him on the phone. He informed Tony we would be leaving on a flight in a few hours. I guess Tony realized the seriousness of the situation and put in a call to Mr. Gordy. We were not privy to their conversation. However, one thing was fact—we would be heading home with or without anyone's approval. The next morning, we woke up determined to leave the hotel before management could put a halt to our plans to return home. The boys even got into a rumble with the road manager, Bobby Reed. Even with all the commotion, we were determined not to miss our plane.

After boarding the plane, El went in on Tony Jones. He demanded a receipt for every dime he spent on the group only. Tony acted as if he did not understand El's demands. This only served to piss El off even more. We stood behind our brother and knew he was looking out for the group's best interest. It was a long ride home. I became lost in my thoughts. It was the only way I could survive the flight. Time seemed to drag on. There was nothing to preoccupy my time since I had finished the book and had no pills. Before leaving Europe, I had called my husband and told him what was unfolding and to expect me home soon. He knew to have some pills ready once I arrived at the airport. The boys asked my husband to have them some pills ready too.

We finally touched ground in Los Angeles. Of course, it took forever to get through customs. It appears customs was deliberately going through our luggage with a fine-toothed comb. My husband Tony was there to greet us, and we now had access to pills. It felt good to be home. We all went our separate ways to be with our loved ones. As El was leaving, he let us know he would get to the bottom of everything with Motown and our management.

I missed my children so much—more than I had ever missed them before. Tonee was now walking, and I was tickled pink watching her taking tiny, little steps. Six weeks had gone by, and I had missed so much at home. I was glad we left when we did. Had we decided against leaving, our stay in Europe would have been much longer. I had so much to share with them and a lot of catching up to do. I realized if I ever visited Europe again, I would take my family on a vacation. I would not go for work again. Although where we visited was beautiful and stunning, we were constantly surrounded by security and could not enjoy the scenery. Plus, it was too far away from my children, and I was lonely for them.

CHAPTER 41

EL TAKES THE LEAD

ONCE WE ARRIVED BACK IN the States from Europe, El began negotiations right away with Motown. He brought forth our grievances to the company. He demanded the company negotiate new contracts and had his newly hired lawyer draft a more equitable partnership. El advised us all to hire our own lawyers independent of the company. We got right on it and did as we were told. With El handling the business side of the group, everything appeared to be on the up and up this time around. DeBarge even hired a manager to specifically take care of all business matters concerning the group. His name was Fred Moultrie. In addition to becoming our new business manager, Fred Moultrie also took the lead and began managing the group. This was a welcome relief. No longer did we have to deal with Tony Jones and his crappy games. Mr. Moultrie promised transparency and to keep us in the loop as to whatever was going on. It was indeed a brand-new day with the company. We were all excited about getting new contracts. However, with the new contracts came division within the group.

The new contracts increased our salaries considerably. Even though we were earning more, each person was put on a different pay scale. Unlike the first contract we signed, which split the earnings equally, this time around, things were different. Each lawyer was tasked with negotiating the worth of their client to Motown and Fred Moultrie. Basically, everything boiled down to each person being compensated according to their individual value to the company. Therefore, it was a no-brainer when El ended up with the most lucrative contract. After all, he was more in demand by the company than the rest of the group members including myself. After El, I would become the second-highest earner in the group. Of course, I did not earn as much as El, but I was satisfied with the financial terms of my new contract. Randy, Mark, and James were placed on the same pay scale. Their earnings were the same and lower than both El and me. The three of them were furious. Oddly enough, they were not so much furious about El's contract as they were about mine. They did not understand why my earnings were higher and voiced how I should be making the same pay as the three of them. Tony Jones stepped in and tried in vain to explain the salary disparities. According to Motown, I was more valuable to the company as a songwriter as well as an artist and producer based on my work on previous albums. I had written more songs than the three of them and had the catalog as proof. It was not about anyone being a better writer. Rather, I just had more songs, which made me more in demand hence the higher salary.

Even after everything was explained ad nauseam, my brothers were still dissatisfied. I now had a target on my back and became a source of contention in the group. I explained everything to my brothers repeatedly, but our relationship had become very contentious. They acted as though they finally understood the financial decisions made when in my presence. However, behind my back, I was considered a "dirty dog," yet there was still no bad blood between them and El. The upheaval my new contract caused had gotten so bad I had to mentally tune out their harsh and threatening criticisms. I began to no longer care what they said or thought. At first, their words were getting under my skin. As the oldest and because I loved them dearly, I wanted them to understand why everything happened the way it did. They did not care to understand. It was just easier to disparage me by talking about the terms of *my* contract to everyone in our circle. The verbal hostility was nonstop until it got to Bobby's ear. Once Bobby intervened, things simmered down for a moment.

Bobby had just returned to Los Angeles and was living with his friend Dennis Warrick. After learning what was taking place between the boys and me, he helped get the situation under control. He talked to the boys and let them know the situation was over and done. Unlike myself, Bobby did not have any level of patience with his brothers. He spoke to them in a way only their big brother could. "It is what it is! Business is business, and bullshit is bullshit! Get over it and stop being such babies about it!"

Like magic, the boys begrudgingly went on with their lives. After all, there was no real reason for them to complain in the first place. Their talk with Bobby stopped them from voicing it aloud. I am sure in the back of their minds they were still seething and felt some type of way. Before Bobby was able to shut down their pity party, they were vocal about feeling as though they were treated unfairly by Motown, El, and me. They worked themselves into an emotional frenzy by believing El and I had let them down and were selfishly thinking about only ourselves. Their spirits were broken as they moped around griping and declaring only El and I were important to Motown. They called it "The El and Bunny Show." In their minds, if Motown depended on El and me, why should they be there pretending to be in harmony with us? It became apparent the division among us was becoming a very real thing.

With my new salary and business manager, I was able to finally purchase a house. I also went out and purchased a brand-new Buick LeSabre. DeBarge was moving up in the world, and my hard work was finally paying off. I began searching for a house high and low. It had to be in the Valley since I loved it here. It did not matter if the temperature was ten to fifteen degrees hotter. I had become a San Fernando Valley girl. We hired a realtor, and Fred gave him a price range. It did not take long before I found my dream home in Van Nuys. It was a four-bedroom home with a pool and a lemon tree. It was entirely fenced in, and I liked this feature as it shut out nosy neighbors. Inside the home were two fireplaces. One side of the fireplace faced the living room and was marble. The other side faced the den. Inside the den area was also a bar. I immediately fell in love with the home. We saw several houses, but this was the one. I could not believe we had our own swimming pool and Jacuzzi. I told the realtor this was the house I wanted, and he got with Fred to finish the deal. It took approximately two months before everything would be finalized. Finally, we were moving into our dream home. Kevin and Michele were there to help us move in. After settling into our new home, I decided to throw a pool party and invite my family. They were all excited. Bobby even helped me with the cooking. My brother had always been an excellent cook. The pool party was fun, and I received some housewarming gifts in the process.

Tony and I were living a happy family life and making big plans to furnish our home. We were getting along again. I thought maybe we were going to make it after all. Kevin and Michele were not getting along, and she voiced her frustrations to me. She was tired of the drugs, and her relationship with Kevin was going nowhere. She wanted both to get help for their addiction and threatened to leave him if he did not do something soon. I felt bad for Kevin and Michele. I loved them both dearly and did not want to be put in a position where I felt I had to choose between them. Kevin was just as much my friend as Michele. I knew if Michele ever left him, it would shatter his life. He had already gone through the pain of losing his daughter. I knew he needed his wife now more than ever.

We were all doing pills big-time now. Tony and I were doing pills just as much as Kevin and Michele. We indulged daily. I understood Michele when she talked about wanting to leave the drugs alone. However, as far as I was concerned, my life was not at a standstill. Perhaps I believed I was better than Michele. How blind of me. Sure, I was moving up in the world. I had a new contract, a new home, a new car, and my children were alive and well. On the contrary, Kevin and Michele's life was stagnant. We were both in the same boat when it came to the drug use though. When it came to the other aspects of our lives, we were in different spaces. I honestly did not know what to tell her at the time. I ended up just telling her everything was going to be all right. I told her Kevin loved her, and they both really needed each other right now.

"Stick with him, Michele," I told her. "I do not think he can make it without you right now. I do not think you can make it without him either. You guys need to make a baby. A baby will calm things down and make life better."

Michele responded by stating, "I think it's over, Bunny—I really do. I gave Kevin a month to make a choice to better our lives. I told him if he does not at least try, I am gone." I could hear in her voice she was serious. I had to talk to Kevin about his relationship to see how he was feeling. Maybe I could say something to help. One thing I knew for sure, we all needed to take a long hard look at how the drugs may have been impacting our lives.

Like Michele, I was sick of the drugs too. By now, my drug issues had gone too far and for too long. I could not remember the last time Tony and I even thought about quitting. Every time we got to the point of wanting to quit, something would happen in our lives to thrust us back into the throes of addiction. It was no longer fun. I finally began to consider my children and wondered if they may be affected by our problem. By now, I was not even hiding it. My girls were older now and could see my pain. They knew I was self-medicating. They had no idea I had a drug problem. Our home replete with drugs was a normal way of life. No one was telling them at the time their mother was on drugs and something was wrong. They wanted for nothing and had a roof over their heads. I showered them with every material thing they wanted. I was involved in their school functions, and they were doing well academically. When I thought about how my children viewed our life, they truly did not know any other way.

Then there was Mama. My mother knew about my problem. Despite everything, she was my mother and very involved in her adult children's lives. Sometimes her presence would be encouraging. At other times, her presence would be overbearing and domineering. It had gotten to a point in my addiction where I was sick and tired of hurting. Not so much from the drugs but from the burden of my childhood. During these moments, I would reach out to my mother. I would call her often in tears about what was bothering me. Memories were haunting me day and night. It became hard to shake the flashbacks. I would call her "Mommy" as if I were a little girl, and she would respond by saying I was acting like an immature little girl. I just wanted to talk about my childhood and how it was affecting me as an adult.

Mama had no patience with me. She was not interested in listening to any words coming from my mouth. She was impatient and dismissive. Her attitude toward me would hurt my feelings and make me feel ashamed for not being strong enough. Mama would always equate my feelings to being high and out of my mind. She accused me of only feeling this way when I was high. In her opinion, this was the only time I wanted to talk about my childhood. This bothered me a great deal because the pain I felt was real. She was my mother and should have been a listening ear. Her indifference made matters worse. Mama was using my lifestyle to diminish my hurt and say it was not real. In her opinion, I was only bringing up my childhood because I was high.

"Let bygones be bygones," she would often state. "It is water under the bridge," she would state at other times. Mama wanted to believe had I not been high, I would not bring up the past. However, when I reached out to her, I was never drunk out of my mind, talking crazy, or hallucinating. I was talking about what had happened to me. I was trying to figure out why my life was such a contradiction. I had everything I could ever dream of—a singing career, a husband, my children, a new home, a new car, and GOD. What was I covering up and why was I feeling so ashamed?

I was hiding and did not need to hide. What I needed was to talk about my feelings right then and there and process the hurt. I also needed Mama to listen to my heart. Yes, I would be under the influence of pills, and perhaps this did give me the courage to discuss the past. Because I had not dealt with the pain in my childhood, it was where I was stuck in life. To be quite candid, I was high most of the time. For Mama to use my lack of sobriety as a reason to be dismissive was unfair. I did not remember the last time I was sober. The hurting child in me looked to Mama to be Christlike. I wanted her to meet me where I was—sober or not. This was not asking a lot considering all the decisions I was forced to make during my childhood to appease her and Daddy.

Even though I was abusing pills, it had nothing to do with what had happened to me as a child. The pills only numbed my feelings and made hearing Mama's rejection a bit more tolerable. I was desperately reaching out to my mother, and she was callously tuning me out. Perhaps I should have been reaching out to GOD instead. Only He was willing to meet me in my mess. Like any heartbroken child, I wanted my mama to save me. Alas, the secret to my salvation was hidden deep within my soul and buried under the weight of an abusive and neglectful childhood.

Mama refused to see me as a genuine person. She exploited my drug problem in a way to define me as simply talking out of my head. This bothered me considerably. Mama knew the truth of my painful childhood, and she was not being real about what I had gone through. I was not talking out of my head. I could not stand when she said this to me. It only made me want to medicate even more. She used the excuse that I never wanted to talk about anything when I was sober. What did she mean by saying I did not want to talk about my childhood when I was sober? To me, talking about my pain when I was sober was not an option. When I was sober, I would be so glad about our relationship I dared not mess it up by talking about anything that made her uncomfortable. I enjoyed having a mother to spend time with, laugh with, and enjoy my life. We had tender moments, and I cherished them deeply. However, the hurt and pain was still very present just waiting to resurface at the right time.

I would be hanging with my mother faking it and pretending I was okay. I would be enjoying her as much as resenting her for what happened to me. I did not understand why she would always not be the same toward me. The times she knew I was not using the pills, she would be a loving mama toward me and treat me with civility. She would want me around, and I felt a part of her life. Only thing, I was not revealing to her my true feelings. It was difficult to deal with Mama because I did not want her to take her love away. However, I wanted to talk with her, get everything out in the open, and really begin to enjoy her in my life. I was tired of being high and wanted to be able to deal with my life. I also wanted to be heard and wanted Mama to listen to me about everything eating at my soul. But Mama's love for me appeared conditional. Not only was Mama not listening to me, but Tony was avoiding me as well. He had begun to not take me seriously either whenever I confided in him regarding my childhood. He took it as though I did not know what I wanted out of life because I was high. Why were my feelings being dismissed by two very important people in my life?

Michele was right all along—we all needed to look at our lives. We had already lost Renee, and this should have made us all step back and reexamine our lives. Alas, we were all out of control including the boys. Our lives had become like the domino effect. One thing after the other was happening to each of us. As soon as one person was over one hurdle, another stumbled.

My brothers' lives were filled with pain they could not quite deal with as well. We had no example of how a stable, healthy home life looked. We had no idea how to be mothers or fathers. We were going through life like a fish out of water. No one taught us how to take care of business. Our childhood was a complete mess. I never even remembered doing homework. The importance of education was not stressed at all in our home. We never prepared for or planned for our futures. There were never talks about where we should go and what we should do. Our home life was abnormal. All we saw was Daddy fighting Mama. We stayed glued to one another and did our best to help one another get through one difficult moment at a time. Now there was division among us, and we did not know how to handle it. All we ever had was one another, and now we were hurting one another. We did not know why, but it only made us self-medicate even more.

CHAPTER 42

EL'S BURDEN

WE WERE TO BE IN the studio and begin working on our next album. There was so much division and infighting among the group. El was still the only one in the group not getting high, and he barely had any dealings with us. He was carrying on without our input. There were times El would be in the studio, and we would have no clue. There was a lot of pressure on him to create another successful album. He had to fight with Motown alone while the rest of us did our best to stay mentally sane.

Although we were hurting, we loved one another very much. We all had a part to play in one another's lives and a special place in one another's hearts. People on the outside saw our love for one another and would marvel at our show of affection. Our love would draw people to us. They wanted to be around us just to feel our love. Now the love we had for one another, where we could lift one another up without ever speaking a word, had become our downfall.

El loved us dearly. He had spiritual insight into each of his sibling's lives. El must have seen our downward spiral and was doing everything in his power to save the group. Motown was riding his back and in his ear. He must have felt a tremendous burden to save the ship. I know my brother loved us and would not intentionally do anything to harm the family. However, Satan was now roaming free in our lives, and El had some tough decisions to make. Because of this, the time was ripe for Motown to plant ideas of going solo in El's ear. Rather than the rest of us taking heed and refocusing on the group, we became preoccupied with hurting one another. Our expectations for one another was high but also breaking us down.

The boys were tripping and bad. They did not understand what was going on with El and why he had become so distant. Once again, they went on and on about how El was Motown's star and they were being dragged along. Neither of them were being cooperative with El. They no longer cared, and their actions spoke louder than words. They became a nightmare in the studio. What they were doing to El was unfair. My heart went out to him, and I was on his side. Sadly, he did not know this because he had stopped talking to me. I could only trust he was doing what he felt was best for DeBarge. I understood the pressure he was under with the company as well as his family. I was depending on him to come through for our next album project. I figured if he needed help he would send for me. Therefore, I trusted him to make all the right decisions.

As I began to reconcile my personal and professional relationship with El, a call came from Grand Rapids, and it was Mama. "Your brothers Tommy and Chico were in a terrible car accident!" she stated, frantic. "Chico is fine. However, pray for Tommy. He might lose his hand."

"Oh, Mama! What happened?" I cried.

"They were on their way back from Detroit, and they got as far as Lansing when the car went out of control. They are blessed—they could have been dead, Bunny. They totaled the car. I pray Tommy does not lose his hand, but at least GOD spared his life. He goes into surgery tomorrow morning. Therefore, get with your brothers if you can find them. You guys need to have a family prayer."

I promised Mama I would gather the family together and pray. Immediately after hanging up, I was on the phone with my brothers. El already knew about the car accident and was also getting in touch with his brothers. They all came to my house, and we prayed for Tommy. I also prayed for Duckie. She had recently given birth to a baby girl whom they named Marina. The last time I talked to Duckie, she was so excited about her brand-new baby girl. I thanked GOD for sparing Tommy's life. Despite Tommy living on the edge, I knew he was not ready to die. In fact, none of us wanted to die trapped in our present state. Therefore, I prayed to GOD to keep a hedge of protection around us and cover us with the Blood of Jesus. I asked GOD to love us until we were able to love ourselves. I cried out to GOD to help us. I felt His Presence right there in my bedroom. I asked Him to forgive us and to see us through this dark moment. I knew GOD was real, and I knew He was the Way, the Truth, and the Light.

"Do not let us die like this!" I cried out. "Please, Lord! I do not want to be lost the rest of my life!"

GOD was truly in my home the hour I prayed for my family and cried out to Him. We were all miserable, and only He could help us through. I stayed on my knees for a while just to continue feeling His Presence. As I stayed on my knees, He strengthened me. I did not want His Presence to leave. Having Him close felt better than the high I had earlier. I wanted to stand in the gap and pray for all my brothers' continued salvation. I was worried about each of them.

Tommy's operation was successful, and we were grateful the doctors were able to save his hand. He had to undergo physical therapy. Eventually, he regained the use of his hand. I knew Tommy was concerned he would never be able to play the bass again. Learning to reuse his hand was something he had to work hard at each day. Thankfully, GOD saved his hand. Everyone was worried, but he made it through.

DeBarge's next big engagement was the Apollo Theater in Harlem, New York. Motown was hosting, and DeBarge would be part of the show. The engagement was a celebration in remembrance of older recording artists. It was a happy time for DeBarge. We had something to look forward to, which gave us the motivation to get clean. Also, the thought of losing our brother Tommy caused us to reevaluate our lives. We were desperately trying to do the right thing.

Life seemed to be going well back home between Tommy and Duckie. They received a substantial settlement from the insurance company as a result of Tommy's accident. They bought a car and was looking to buy a house. Duckie was very excited. Finally, she could live out some of her dreams of being a homemaker. I was happy for them. Perhaps now they could focus on their lives. Bobby was also planning to return to Grand Rapids to get sober. I was happy for Bobby as well. Tommy would have no problem with Bobby staying with him if needed. Tommy was always willing to share his last. But knowing Bobby, he would not dare stay with Tommy for too long. Bobby always needed his own place. Each DeBarge was trying to pick up the pieces and carry on with their tortured lives. We had an upcoming show in New York at the Apollo Theater. Motown asked El to sing Jackie Wilson's song "Lonely Teardrops" as a solo. He was delighted. The powers that be were slowly but surely moving El away from DeBarge. Although we were cleaning up our act, it no longer seemed to matter.

CHAPTER 43

HOW DID THIS HAPPEN?

WE HAD NOT SEEN MUCH of Kevin and Michele lately. Unfortunately, they were still having relationship issues. Michele ended up leaving Kevin after all. He had been staying at our home after their breakup. Once he found out where Michele was staying, off he went. Apparently, Michele was somewhere up north. It had been two weeks since we heard anything from Kevin. I just prayed they were safe.

Tony and I were busy getting our home together. We had bought a new couch and a new washer and dryer. I was excited about putting my personal touch on our home with plants and little knickknacks. There were swap meets being held everywhere. I always managed to find beautiful inexpensive items. I was really missing Michele since swap meets were something we did together. Today, Tony was not going with us. He wanted to stay home and watch the game on TV. I took my girls along instead. It turned out to be a girls' day out. On my way out the door, Kevin pulled up. I was surprised to see him. He was alone, and I wanted to know what was going on with him and Michele. "Where is Michele, Kevin?" I asked.

Kevin looked a little down in his spirits. "She's still up there," he stated.

I could tell Kevin was high. His voice had dropped, and he was scratching. "Are you all right?" I asked.

Kevin tried his best to put on a happy face, but I could tell he was faking it. "Yeah, I am fine. I left her where she wanted to be. I don't have time for it. It's my birthday, and I have not been high in two weeks off the pills. It is going on three weeks now, and I want to celebrate. All I have been doing is what she wanted to do. All her friends up there do coke. I needed a downer," he stated.

I was sad to hear they were up north indulging in coke. "Well, is Michele all right?" I asked. "Is she coming back or what, Kevin?" I was pushing him to talk but could tell he was brushing me off.

"Michele found a job there," he answered.

Kevin was really struggling with losing Michele. I tried my best to make him feel okay about her recent accomplishment. "That's good, Kevin. Are you planning to move there too?" I asked.

Kevin just held his head down. "I don't believe I am," he sadly stated. "I do not want to move there. If we are to be together, Michele must do what I say. I am the man. I am not following her." Kevin still had his job and was taking a leave of absence to work through his life issues. He wanted Michele to come back to him. However, he was not willing to compromise. I just listened to him rant and rave. "I am going to write her a long letter and tell her just how I feel," he stated. Kevin then walked toward the front door of the house. "Is Tony here?" he asked.

"Yes," I stated. "He is watching the game. Go on in." I wondered how many pills he had taken. If he has been off for as long as he said he was, I hoped he did not start back where he left off. He looked to be high, and I was concerned. I put the children in the car and went to speak with Kevin. I went into the den where I thought he would be sitting with Tony watching the game. He was not there. I asked for Kevin. Tony pointed toward the guest room. It appears Tony probably did not even look up when Kevin came into the house. "Did you even talk to him?" I asked.

Tony did not take his eyes off the game. "Yeah, he said a few things to me. Why?" Tony asked, annoyed.

"He looks really high, Tony." I was concerned for Kevin and hoped Tony would come out of the game for at least one second. Instead, he looked at me as if to ask what is the big deal? I rolled my eyes then started toward the guest room. Kevin was sitting on the bed with pencil and paper in his hand. He had nodded out. When I whispered his name, Kevin jumped out of his drug-induced stupor.

"Hey, Bunny," he stated, looking at me bewildered. "I am writing Michele a letter."

"Okay. But I need to know if you are okay, Kevin. I don't think you should have taken as many pills since you have been off them for a while. You do not start back taking the same amount. You need to start out taking less. Your tolerance for the pills has gone down. I just do not want anything to happen to you," I stated.

Kevin could see I was concerned. He knew I cared about him in the same way he cared about me. We were the best of friends. Kevin looked at me and smiled. "I will be fine. Thanks for caring, Bunny. That is so sweet of you. I am going to finish this letter and wait for Michele to call me. I'll go watch some of the game with Tony in a few."

I then told Kevin happy birthday. I went over to the bed and hugged him. I had planned to get him a birthday card while I was out. I left Kevin in the guest room. I let Tony know I was gone. My girls were waiting patiently to go to the swap meet. We were going to have a fun day together.

Time had gotten away from us. Indeed, we were having so much fun. Now it was getting dark. I had not called home to let Tony know we were okay. Time flies when you're having fun. I knew he had to be worried. We were gone all day. I gathered up the girls and went to the nearest payphone. When Tony answered the phone, I began apologizing profusely. Tony did not care about my apologies. He kept trying to get a word in as I continued apologizing. "Bunny! Bunny! Listen to me. Come home now! I think Kevin is dead!"

I paused and took a deep breath. "Tony don't be ridiculous. Why would you say such a thing?" I figured maybe Tony was exaggerating the situation just to get me home.

Then with much conviction in his voice, he said it again, "He is dead, Bunny. Please come home."

Now I became concerned and did not want to believe Tony. "He is not dead!" I shouted. "He is just high! Take him to the shower, hit him, and slap him. He will come out of it."

Then it sounded as if my husband was on the verge of crying. "I have done that already. I dragged him and put him in the shower, Bunny. He is not breathing. He is dead. Come home, baby. I need you here. I am alone with him."

Everything Tony was saying finally registered, and I became hysterical. "Oh my GOD! I will be right there." I hung up the phone and ran to the car. I was crying but hoped deep in my heart Tony was wrong. I kept telling myself Kevin was not dead. I asked myself why Kevin would die in my home. I did not tell the children what was going on, but they could sense something was wrong. I just said, "Daddy wants us home and we must hurry."

I drove home as fast as I could. As I ran into the house, I had Damea and Janae grab Tonee and go straight to their rooms. My husband, Tony, was in the room with Kevin. He was standing there looking down as if he wanted to die himself. I put my arms around him and then looked over at my friend. He was just lying there as if he was asleep. "No, Kevin!" I cried as I ran over to him, touching his hand. It was cold and hard. Rigor mortis had started to set in. I broke down crying and said, "GOD, this cannot be happening." Then I knelt beside the bed still holding Kevin's hand and started talking to him. "I told you not to take that many pills." I looked up at Tony and stated, "I told him, Tony. He wanted to die. He did not want to live anymore."

All my brothers had now arrived and rushed in to assist. Tony had called them to let them know what was occurring. Everyone began to cry. We were all sad and felt Kevin could have been either one of us. They began to pray and cry out to GOD. We all joined hands and prayed for Kevin's soul. Chico, always the spiritually sensitive one, began singing a song that came straight from his heart. GOD had given it to him in this very moment. Soon there was a knock at the door, and it was the police and coroner's Office. Tony had also called them. They were there to pick up Kevin's body. I watched them as they took out a green bag and placed Kevin's remains inside. Then they zipped it up.

The gravity of the situation hit me, and I lost it. I had seen dead bodies on TV before but never up close and personal. I started screaming because it seemed so cruel. "Do not put him in there! What are you doing? Stop it! Do not put Kevin in that bag!"

My husband and brothers started grabbing me as I cried and reached for Kevin. The coroner carried my best friend out the door and out of my life forever. Everyone was stunned into silence as I cried. Tony began discussing what happened. He kept going over how he had dragged him to the shower but he was already dead. Tony did everything he could to revive him. I did not understand why Kevin had to die. He was a beautiful person and so full of life. Perhaps he just gave up, I thought. He did not want to live any longer. It had not even been a year since we lost Renee. I just kept thinking to myself he did not want to live anymore.

Just then, I thought about the letter he was writing to Michele. "He was writing Michele a letter," I stated. I asked Tony, "Did Michele ever call?" Tony looked at me and stated, "Yes, she did. I went tell him she was on the phone. He said he would call her back. I told her he was asleep and to leave her number."

"Where is her number?" I asked. "I have to call her."

I followed Tony into the kitchen to retrieve the number. On the countertop, I saw an envelope. It had Michele's name written on it. He had drawn a beautiful rose on the outside of the envelope. He had sealed the envelope so I could not open it up. However, I was tempted to do so. I wanted to know the contents of the letter. Tony then handed me a piece of paper with Michele's phone number scribbled on it. I dialed the number. After a few rings, a man answered the phone.

"May I speak with, Michele?" I asked.

The man on the phone sounded a bit annoyed. "I believe she is asleep," the man answered. I then explained I was her friend from Los Angeles and my call was an emergency.

"One minute," he replied and I could hear him call for Michele to come to the phone.

The next voice I heard was Michele. "Hello, Bunny," she stated. She was already concerned because the call was late. "What is going on?" she asked.

"Michele, did you talk to your husband today?" I asked.

"No. He was resting when I called, and Tony said he would call me back. What is wrong, Bunny?" she asked me again.

"Kevin is dead, Michele. We believe he overdosed." Michele grew silent. I then told her there was a letter he had written her on my kitchen counter. I told her everything I knew about the circumstances surrounding his death. Michele said she would call back and to hold on to the letter. The boys hung around for a while before they all decided to head home. I promised them I would be in touch after I found out more information.

I needed to talk to GOD because I needed answers. Therefore, I cried out to GOD as I prayed. I poured out my heart to Him. As I did, I knew He was there with me and heard my cry. I did not have to scream out. He was there, and I felt His Presence. I needed to cry, and I needed to feel Him. I opened my mouth and talked to Him. I poured out my heart to him and revealed everything:

Lord, things are happening all around me, and you have spared me. I am doing just as much sin as everyone else. I hang with sinners and indulge in unrighteous things. Why have you spared me, Lord? You have spared us all. You have spared my husband and my children from death. It could have been me, Lord. Why was it not me, Lord? I feel and see Your Favor upon my life. I do not deserve it, Lord. I have taken You for granted. I am so sorry, Lord. I miss You so much, and I am not happy where I am in life. Everything seems so false to me. I am living something which is not me. I am not comfortable having to walk seductively across a stage to show off my beauty. I miss lifting my voice to You. I am lost and lonely here. This is not my purpose for living. I am here to serve You. You will get the Glory out of my life. I know 'only what you do for Christ will last.' I sang this song as a child and it is written in my heart, and now it haunts me. I am in trouble, Lord. It is as if I cannot help myself anymore. I need Your help if I am going to make it. My brothers are in trouble too. We all need you,

Lord. It has been so long since we have sought Your Face. Thank You, Lord, for covering us despite all we are doing. Thank You for loving us anyway.

I prayed Kevin's soul was with GOD. I prayed for Michele. I prayed that wherever she was in life, she would get through this moment. I realized there was a call upon her life too. I knew GOD spared her for a reason. I asked GOD to protect her and bring her through her dark moments. I cried and let GOD provide me comfort. I felt His loving arms around me. His Holy Spirit overtook my high, and I began speaking in the Holy Language to my Lord. I lay in my bed in His Presence until I went to sleep in perfect peace. It had been a while since I had GOD on my mind. I had not talked to GOD for a long time—at least not concerning my salvation. I was always praying for the salvation of others. This time around, I prayed for myself. I was in trouble and needed the Lord to help me. His Word, fully vested on the inside, was speaking to me.

I woke up the next morning in good spirits, declaring to Tony we were going to beat drugs and do better in life. I told him I wanted to find a church home. What I really wanted was to return home. I wanted to be a part of my home church. I really wanted a change. Nevertheless, we were in Los Angeles and needed a church right here.

CHAPTER 44

BEGIN AGAIN

Tony and I started breaking down our intake of the pills. We were only taking enough now not to get sick. We began the process of weaning ourselves completely off the drugs. The boys were doing the same. We were getting ready for the Apollo performance and wanted to be at our optimum. My life was changing. I was no longer looking for the next high. I was hard at work trying to stop using drugs altogether. I missed Kevin and Michele and prayed Michele was okay. They were both gone from our lives. As fast as they had come into our lives, they were gone. I had no idea where Michele lived. I did not hear from her again. We had no idea what happened with Kevin's body nor did we hear anything regarding his funeral. I am sure his remains ended up in his home state of New York.

Tony and I planned to visit Grand Rapids for a while after the Apollo appearance. I wanted to see Uncle Bill and I wanted to enroll in a drug rehab program there named Teen Challenge. It was a spiritually-based program and I wanted to be filled with the Word of GOD as part of my recovery. Uncle Bill had talked to me about the program. I was willing to consider it and would let him know my decision once I arrived in Grand Rapids.

It was now time for us to head to New York. My girls stayed with a good friend who used to be my next-door neighbor. When we arrived in New York, we rehearsed for an entire week before the actual show.

El was also rehearsing his solo act—Jackie Wilson's "Lonely Teardrops." Everyone was there—Stevie Wonder, George Michael, Boy George, Smokey Robinson, and many more dynamic artists. Berry Gordy was there as well. The night of the show, we were all in a big tent that was put up for the artists. Everyone was busy getting their makeup touched up and getting dressed in the latest fashion. DeBarge got our makeup done and went back to our trailers and finished getting dressed. Next thing we knew, someone rushed in and wanted us to turn on the TV. We were told that an important news bulletin had just come across the screen. We turned on the TV, and there was a picture of our brother Bobby. The newscaster read the prompt: "Bobby DeBarge, from the Motown recording group DeBarge, was arrested today at Chicago's O'Hare Airport. The Motown recording star claimed he had a bomb. The airliner was on its way to Los Angeles. It appears Robert DeBarge Jr. told the man seated next to him he had a bomb in the suitcase he was carrying. Other passengers on the plane heard him say this as well and became scared. It was said loudly where others on the plane heard it as well. The plane, just taking off, had to turn back to the airport where he was then taken into custody. It was found to only be a hoax—something he said as a joke."

There were bomb threats all over the United States at the time. Now, here was a picture of our brother Bobby on television looking like a terrorist. We shook our heads because we knew our brother, and we knew what prompted his actions. We started to laugh, but it really was no laughing matter. Bobby was in trouble, and he had been detained. Therefore, El got right on the phone with Mama to see what happened and what we needed to do next. Apparently, Bobby was on his way back to Los Angeles. He had been in Grand Rapids to clean up his act. Uncle Bill helped him enroll in Teen Challenge. He only managed to stay in the program for a week. Bobby was ready to leave the program and head back to Los Angeles.

Bobby managed to score some pills while in Detroit. He was feeling relieved since he had enough pills to last him a while. As he was heading back to Los Angeles, he was high. The man seated next to him thought he was acting odd and stared in his direction. Bobby caught the man staring at him and blurted out, "What are you looking at? Yeah, I've got a bomb!" In hindsight, he let us know after he made the statement, he asked himself why he let something like this come out of his mouth. He said other people on the plane began to act strange toward him. Next thing he knew, an announcement came over the speakers saying there was an emergency and they had to go back to Chicago and land. He figured out that the chain of events had something to do with him making a real foolish comment, and he was probably in big trouble. Bobby was correct. The FBI was there waiting on the ground to take him into custody immediately. Bobby said he had pills in his suitcase he was able to get rid of before they took him away. Everything he had explained was just as we had suspected. Of course, we never thought for once he had a bomb. However, we knew he was high for sure.

Bobby ended up getting two years' probation and had to drop for the court whenever they requested. If he were caught with dirty urine, he would have to do time in prison. I figured this was harsh for someone making a joke about a nonexistent bomb. We all felt relieved after touching base with Mama and getting the whole story. Once we found out Bobby was okay, we were able to perform our set at the Apollo without worrying about his fate. After the show, we made jokes at Bobby's expense by referring to him as Bobby Kaddafi. I mean, Bobby did look a lot like the images of terrorists we had seen on the news.

After the Apollo performance, we all went our separate ways. Tony and I flew to Grand Rapids, and I got the chance to attend church. It was just what I needed. I went to the altar for prayer and rededicated my life back to the Lord. It felt good being at my home church where I first felt a connection to GOD. Everyone greeted me with open arms. It was beautiful to hear Uncle Bill's anointed voice. His voice always moved me spiritually. Tony and I had not taken any pills since we left California and were doing quite well. I was so proud of us both.

Finally, it felt as though we were on the right track for once. Therefore, I decided not to go to Teen Challenge. I truly felt I had the drug demon beat. I arrived back in California with high hopes of staying one with GOD. Once back in Los Angeles, we found a church home in the Valley named the Church on the Way. Tony, the children, and I began attending every Sunday.

CHAPTER 45

EL SPLITS

THINGS SEEMED TO BE GOING well at home for the most part. I was finally happy. DeBarge was supposed to be finishing up our fourth album. We were waiting to hear from El to let us know when we were needed in the studio. The movie *The Last Dragon* was also finished. There was a big party held for everyone affiliated with the movie. Bobby attended the party with us. He was sober and was a different brother. He was not taking any chances of getting high since the threat of prison loomed over his head. As a condition of his probation, Bobby had to stay clean. So far so good, and he looked and sounded amazing. He began writing music again and looked forward to securing a new contract. Sadly, the boys were still getting high and living on the wild side.

Chico's star was on the rise. He was recording demos and searching for a contract. Motown was interested in signing him. In the meantime, El was recording DeBarge's latest album by himself. He had not requested our presence in the studio yet. We had no idea when studio time was scheduled for the group. One day, I turned on the TV, and there was El on *Solid Gold* performing our song by himself. I tried to get in touch with him to figure out what was going on to no avail. When the group finally confronted him, he brushed us off. He did not offer an explanation. I knew the boys were still using drugs, and El and Motown had grown weary of their addiction. They were hearing about the wild parties and the crazy antics. El had a lot on his plate. He was now going through a divorce and not taking it very well. He was hurting and had turned cold toward the world. We were dealing with a different El—one we barely even knew. Not to mention Motown had built him up to believe he no longer needed us and could succeed on his own. However, I was maintaining my sobriety at the time and did not understand why I was being pushed aside.

I had not spoken to El. I had no reason to believe our relationship was anything except cordial. I might not have known what was going on, but I had no reason to believe El harbored any ill will toward me. I had a phone, and my number had not changed. I hoped our relationship was such he would call me if he had any issues. I then thought about the wedding and how he had let me down. Once this reality hit me, I decided to begin working hard on my own songs. I was going to surprise El and have them completed. The only thing left would be for us to record the songs as a group. I met two men working with Chico on his demo for Motown. They were gracious enough to let me work out of their studio. Their names were Galen and Ralph. I wrote my own songs as well as recorded songs they had written to showcase to other artists. I was working on recording "A Woman in Love," the song I had written for my brothers. I knew El was busy and figured having the song at least halfway finished would be a great idea. Writing kept me busy while I waited for El to summon us into the studio.

Motown was now interested in offering Chico a solo deal. I was not sure if Chico's deal was the impetus behind El wanting to strike out on his own. Nevertheless, we had no idea what was transpiring behind our backs, but it did not feel good. The boys already had bad vibes and were acting out as a result. They felt El was Motown's favorite and was still giving him a hard time. It appears they were deliberately sabotaging the group whenever we came together. James and Randy even showed up to an important engagement high. Our performance during the Smokey Robinson special was a complete disaster. The public may not have known, but the boys were high out of their minds during the entire show. They no longer cared who knew that they were indulging. Upset with how Motown was handling their career, they rebelled in every way. To them, the writing was on the wall. Therefore, why make things easy for El?

El had now begun doing everything without the group. Worried about my future with Motown, I decided to give El a call. I wanted to know what was happening with the album. He informed me that the album was finished. He then stated our presence would be needed soon for a photo session. El claimed he had to rush to get the album completed due to a tight time schedule. He kept insisting I had nothing to worry about and all bases were covered. I had no reason not to trust my brother. As far as I was concerned, he had no real gripes about me in the group. He had always come and talked to me about everything going on, and they mostly entailed the boys. He knew I understood and sympathized with him. Plus, he seemed to value my opinion. If he had issues with the other boys, I would act as the mediator. Therefore, I figured all was well on my end.

El called and told us we had a photo shoot scheduled. We showed up and acted as if nothing was amiss. El was not talking to us, and we were silent toward him as well. Once the album cover was released, to our surprise, there were four tiny pictures of us in the bottom corner of the album. However, El's picture was big and bright as the day. One entire side of the front album cover was devoted specifically to El. To make matters worse, the album title read, *DeBarge Featuring El DeBarge*. We were outraged. Nothing Motown or El said made any sense. Now we knew for a fact that something was not right. El finally broke his silence and explained that Motown wanted him to record a solo album. He still mentioned nothing about wanting to leave the group. In the meantime, I continued recording songs with Galen and Ralph. I took for granted El would tell me if he were planning to leave the group or if Motown was going to drop us altogether. He would certainly not hang us out to dry. I was no longer using pills and was focused and doing well. El would not keep me in the dark if anything was going to happen regarding our fate at Motown, I surmised.

Everyone began tripping. Still, we were certain El was not leaving the group. We just assumed he was doing a solo project and would return to the group for the next album. None of us wanted our brother to leave DeBarge. We were family and wanted to continue singing together. It was the magic we shared from being together all the time. Every person brought something special to the table, and it worked like magic. Our individual and collective talents made DeBarge a success. We were going through a lot of growing pangs. So far, we had managed to survive a troubled childhood, make it as starving artists, successfully battle bad management, and overcome a horrible contract. We had grown in the industry together and felt we should stick together through thick and thin. This was the story of our lives since we were children—always looking out for one another and picking up one another's slack. This division sowed by Motown was new and was not making our interactions with each other any better lately. Decisions from the top came swiftly, and El reacted by becoming even more distant and cold. The album cover broke everyone's heart and did not make our relationship any better. There were arguments between El and his brothers, which drove them farther apart.

Motown was looking out for their best business interest. Truth be told, they were a business first, and they had to protect their investment. Therefore, El was deemed reliable so it was no secret they were in El's ear. They were badgering him by saying only he could save the ship. He was told he could always come back and pick up with the group once business matters improved. El was easily influenced by Motown since the boys were beating him down mentally and emotionally. They did nothing to help smooth over things and regain their brother's confidence. He had to grow a cold heart in order to turn on his family. Also, the hurt he was feeling from losing his wife did not help matters either. He was having to give up his wife and his family simultaneously. It was too much to shoulder at one time.

El was now showing up solo more frequently on TV performing DeBarge songs. He was also promoting the album solo. We would see him on *Soul Train* and *Solid Gold* singing "Who's Holding Donna Now," and it was devastating. We were still considered Motown recording artists. No one had stated otherwise. I finally could not take it anymore. I was hearing through the grapevine that the group was over, El was solo, and Motown was working out the terms of his and Chico's contracts as solo artists. If this was the case, what were they going to do with the rest of us? By this time, I had four songs I had recorded at Galen and Ralph's studio. They wanted to prepare my demo in case Motown had any thoughts of dropping me. If Motown did drop me, I would have material to shop with another record label. Galen and Ralph knew the group's breakup was a touchy subject with me so they were careful how they presented the scenario to me.

After realizing El was not going to come around and say anything, I panicked. I became furious and planned to find him and make him talk to me. I was hurt and confused. I had calls in to him stating I needed to talk to him and it was important. He was ignoring my calls and did not return one. I decided to go straight to his home and demand he talk. When I arrived at his home, El was leaving. I caught him just as he shut the door. "El, I need to talk to you. I just need a minute."

My brother looked at me and stated coldly, "I do not have time for this, Bunny. I have things to do."

I was hurt by the tone of his voice. It was very patronizing. "So do I. You're not the only one who have things to do. My life is just as important as yours even if you might not think so. What is really going on, El? Why haven't you returned any of my calls? All this time I was asking you what was going on. I wanted to know what you and Motown were considering doing with the rest of us, and you led me on."

El answered matter-of-factly, "We have turned the page, Bunny." Then he walked away. I was shocked and started crying. My tears were not for the loss of the group but for the loss of my brother. El was always the one with such a caring spirit. I started walking toward him. It felt like a love affair and I was losing the man I loved.

"You could have told me, El!" I shouted between tears. "I thought we were better than this mess. We have always talked about any and everything!" El was ignoring me, but I was determined he would hear my every word. "You know I just bought a home and need my job. Had I known the group was breaking up, I would not have bought a house. You knew all this time! You could have at least warned me, El. You could at least have told me not to buy a house. You could have talked to me."

El said nothing else to me. He just walked away, hopped into his car and drove away. I was dejected. My brother had no feelings at all about what Motown had done to his family. I could not believe his callousness. I kept hearing in my head over and over: *We have turned the page, Bunny.* It was a new chapter in my life indeed. I guess this is what my brother was trying to convey. I did not know what to do or what would happen next. I was worried sick and hurting. As fast as my life had finally come together, it was now being torn apart.

I was not upset about El's decision to leave the group. I certainly understood the pressure he was under to produce a product that would sell. At the end of the day, this is the only thing that mattered to record companies. My pain and devastation came about because he did not feel the need to talk to any of us about his decision. I am his big sister, and I felt he owed me this courtesy. I would have understood and been able to prepare myself differently. I have always stood on my own. El knew this about me. I just needed him to be fair enough to level the playing field. Keeping an important component of our future with Motown a secret and pretending as if he had our best interest at heart was disingenuous. If I had to take control of my own career, then fine. I did not need to be in a group with my brother. Rather, I wanted my brother in my life despite the group.

Although I struggled with many insecurities, I wholeheartedly embraced my gift as a singer as well as in my ability to succeed as a solo artist. However, there was an unmatched beauty I cherished being able to come together as family alongside my brothers and create beautiful music. Motown had convinced El we needed him and he did not need us. This was not true. We were all talented, and we could go on our own with the right motivating factors behind us pushing us to succeed. Unfortunately, the focus was on El, and Motown put all their energy and resources into him succeeding as a solo artist. El was playing the game right along with them.

CHAPTER 46

BOBBY'S SECOND CHANCE

I WAS GLAD TO HAVE ventured out and recorded a demo. I had no plans to become a solo artist, and I really did not want this for myself. However, I was on my own now and had the faith needed to succeed. I was concerned about the boys. To say they were devastated would be an understatement. We were all uncertain about our futures. Was Motown dropping us, or were we expected to go on as a group without El? I had songs for however the situation turned out. At least I had a game plan. Meanwhile, Bobby was doing phenomenally. He had impressed the court by adhering to the terms of his probation. He ended up being released early from probation. Bobby looked like a star again and was also writing songs and recording them in Galen and Ralph's studio. Bobby heard what had gone down with El and Motown. He took his position as big brother trying to save the ship.

We called a meeting and decided that since Bobby was doing so well, we would include him in the revamped group. Bobby would take El's place as lead in the group. Tony Jones was in the meeting as well. He was able to witness a witty, confident, and sober Bobby. We were all so proud of Bobby. Tony Jones was convinced he was well and ready to head into the studio. He believed Motown would love the idea of him taking over as lead singer of DeBarge. Tony felt Motown really did not want to give up on the group—especially if Bobby was doing well again. It would be beneficial for them to simply add Bobby rather than disband the group. Bobby was still a strong energy in the industry. With him doing well and back in tune with his creativity, he could take the group even further. Therefore, they were willing to shop the idea to Motown. I was relieved. If need be, I was willing to go solo. However, being a family group was still very appealing. Plus, Bobby and I had always worked well together during his days with Switch. Bobby was confident again. I was in his corner all the way. Tony Jones went back to Motown and shared with everyone how great Bobby looked and how well he was doing. The powers that be were willing to consider the group with Bobby in place of El.

It was early the next morning when my phone began ringing. It was my brother Bobby on the phone. "Hey, sis," he stated. "How are you today?" Bobby sounded like he was in a great mood. I exchanged pleasantries then asked him what was up. Bobby went on to say he had just talked to Lee Young at Motown, and there was a meeting scheduled for later in the day. He wanted me to go along with him. He said the others did not have to show up. I thought nothing of leaving the boys out of the meeting. It was not unusual for Bobby to want me to tag along to one of his business meetings. Bobby and I were the oldest, and we often did things together that did not include our younger siblings.

The meeting would be held at 3:00 PM, so I had plenty of time to prepare. Bobby stated we would meet in the lobby of Motown. After hanging up the phone, I thought Bobby was really in his element. He was still clean and sober and able to articulate his points. I was sure it would be a good meeting and we would accomplish a lot. We would discuss a new direction for the group and how to bring Bobby into DeBarge when many knew him from Switch. There were no worries about anything going wrong—at least not yet.

Bobby and I arrived at the same time and parked on a side street since we did not want to pay for parking. Bobby parked first, got out of his car with his briefcase, then waited for me to park. After I parked, I walked over to greet him. We stepped out into the street, and before I knew it, Bobby grabbed me and threw me back toward the curb. He started cursing at a car driving down the street. I shook my head and thought his behavior was a bit odd and awfully familiar. I knew well the overly dramatic Bobby whenever he was high. "He was going to hit us—that fool!" he yelled. "Are you all right?"

I looked at him, puzzled because the car was nowhere near us. Yet Bobby was standing there being melodramatic. It was the first sign of my brother not being sober. "Are you okay?" I asked as I gave him a knowing look.

Bobby knew this look and immediately became defensive. "I am fine," he said and then rubbed his nose.

"Oh my GOD!" My heart dropped to my stomach. "Bobby, you look like you are high."

"No!" he shouted. "I am not high!"

Regardless of what he was saying, I was not convinced. "I hope not, Bobby," I stated in a worried tone. I was too scared to go into the meeting knowing the truth about Bobby's state of mind. Red flags were everywhere, and I did not want Motown to notice his erratic behavior. I hoped Bobby was not lying and perhaps his anxiety was just getting the best of him and not the drugs. However, deep in my heart, I knew the truth. If Bobby went into this meeting high, he would mess up any chance to revamp our career. We still had a few minutes before the start of the meeting. We decided to stop at the coffee shop on the first floor of the building.

We ran into Rockwell, one of Berry Gordy's sons. We started a lively discussion about his new single, "Somebody's Watching Me." Michael Jackson worked with him on the song, and he was excited about the hype. As we talked, I could tell that Bobby's high was increasing. He had not eaten, and the effects of the drugs were strong. He was clearly out of his mind. I waited until Rockwell left and confronted Bobby again. "Bobby, you are high! You cannot fool me." Now I was angry and concerned. Knowing Bobby, he was bound to be extra and over the top at the meeting. I start whispering a silent prayer.

We finished our coffee, and off we went to meet Tony Jones, Lee Young, and the rest of the legal department at Motown. Bobby's high was beginning to come down, and he was sure he had it all together. He was not listening to anything I had to say. Bobby was not portraying the calm, confident man he was the day before, and it was obvious he was not okay. It was easy to notice something was off. However, in his mind, he had it all together. I have never felt so helpless in my life as I watched my brother make a complete fool of himself.

During the meeting, he was dramatic and carried on a one-way conversation with the team. He was not letting anyone get a single word into the conversation. As he was talking and scratching, he went to open his briefcase, and pills spilled all over the floor. I was embarrassed, and I could do nothing to stop this train from running off the track. I knew Bobby had blown it for himself and DeBarge. However, Bobby was oblivious to what was transpiring. He believed the meeting had gone well. My nerves were shot.

When we were left alone, I tried in vain to tell Bobby they knew he was high and he had blown this opportunity. Convinced he had outsmarted the team, he kept implying they knew nothing and he was not worried. Sadly, he was sure of himself and pleased with the meeting. He left the meeting thinking it was a go with him joining the group. I knew otherwise. I saw the looks on each person's face. I figured it was best to just say nothing else to Bobby. When I arrived home, my phone rang as I walked through the door. It was Tony Jones on the line. "Hi, Tony," I stated, defeated. I already knew what he was going to say, but I listened anyway.

"Well, you know Bobby blew it for you guys. You know it is so sad," he began, "after all the talking I did to convince Motown he was doing well. They knew he was high at the meeting. Then he goes and drops pills all over the floor. I am afraid Motown is going to drop the whole group, Bunny."

I was not surprised. I already felt it in my spirit. There was nothing I could do about what took place at the meeting. I told Tony I was going to shop my demo elsewhere with the songs I had recorded. "I think you should," he stated. "But why not start with Motown? Why not try to make something happen here for Mrs. Bunny?" he asked. Tony was trying to lift my spirit. "I listened to your songs, and I like them. You have been working hard, and I would like to take the demo to Motown and shop you a solo deal. Do not be dismayed—I really think we can work something out here. If not, I would be willing to help you shop it elsewhere." Now *this* conversation was finally going somewhere. It was just what I needed to hear. I gave Tony the go-ahead to shop my demo at Motown.

Tony Jones was enthused and was sure he could strike me a solo deal with Motown. I had no other choice except to go out on my own. I had a family to take care of, and I was determined not to lose my home. I finally gathered the strength to carry on—even if I had to do so myself. I gave myself a little pep talk. Full of motivation and inspiration, I wrote a song called "I Will Never Let Die." It inspired me to go on with my life. I was hurting but was determined not to let my dream die. I went on knowing I could make it if I put my mind to it.

CHAPTER 47

BUNNY DEBARGE: IN LOVE

It was not long before the boys learned Motown had dropped them from the company. Bobby blamed the whole fiasco on me. He told a different story than what occurred, and the boys believed him. It did not make matters any better since Tony Jones had talked Motown into accepting me as a solo artist. Bobby had put out a rumor whereas I supposedly had gone to Motown bad-mouthing everyone. Allegedly, I was telling everyone's business, looking out only for myself and not wanting the boys to have a contract. I was furious! Bobby knew exactly why the boys were dropped from Motown. Rather than come clean with the boys, he chose to spread a vicious lie on me—the one who always had his back even if he was in the wrong.

My brothers were very angry with me and it hurt. I called them one by one and told them the truth. Then I called Bobby and asked him why he lied on me. He argued me up and down, saying I told Motown he was high when he was not. Even after calling my brothers and confronting Bobby, he chose to hold fast to his lie, and the boys believed him over me. Tony Jones knew Bobby had lied and told me to simply ignore him. I tried hard to move past the vicious lie, but I loved my brothers and wanted them to know the truth. I would never betray them in such manner. Deep down inside, I felt they knew the truth, but it was easier for them to believe a lie. I would have no problem standing by any decision I made if it involved the truth. But the rumor Bobby started was not the truth.

Truth be told, Bobby was ashamed so he led the boys into believing a lie. Once again, we had found a way to hurt one another. There was nothing more I could do if they wanted to believe Bobby over me. I felt so alone. The little DeBarge kids who were always together found themselves at odds with one another yet again. It was a never-ending saga since we came into the industry. We vowed to stick together no matter what came our way. Now we were comfortable spreading lies and believing those same lies. How did this happen? It hurt to see what was going on in our lives. We had always been such a loving family. Our love for one another was special, and everywhere we went, people felt it. Hurting people were drawn to us. We would comfort them, yet we could no longer comfort each other. The world turned us cold toward one another, and I hated it with a passion. Not only was our love for one another special, but so was our ability to forgive. We have had to forgive some significant trespasses. Forgiveness was second nature to us. Now we seemed unwilling or unable to forgive one another. All we knew now was the pain of hurting one another. The pain had grown so bad we began staying out of one another's way. We were hurt children in an adult world doing everything possible to destroy one another.

I could still hear Uncle Bill's voice teaching about the five fingers and telling us to stick together at all costs. Now, we were five broken fingers whose hand no longer functioned. We needed one another but resorted to looking for outside entities to fulfill us. We were no longer seeking GOD during this tumultuous time. We were clearly self-absorbed and caught up in our own ego. We were not acknowledging Him, and He was not directing our path. We were not trusting in the One who blessed us with the gift of music. We were not seeking help, and we had no spiritual direction. However, GOD can turn our lives around and work everything for our good. There was a call on our lives, and I knew GOD was aware of everything going on. He was the Author of the book of our lives. I had no idea where our lives were headed or when we would come out of this fog. One thing I knew for certain: we belonged to Him, and we were the Kept Ones.

Motown hired Galen and Ralph to produce some of the songs for my album. They had been working with me already, and Motown liked the direction of the songs. Other producers came in to work on the album. There was Robbie Buchanan and Jay Gray who produced a couple of songs. Then Jellybean Benitez, Jerry Knight, and Aaron Zigman also had songs on the album. Of course, good old faithful Diane Warren joined the team and wrote the song "Fine Line." All these individuals joined forces for my solo album *Bunny DeBarge: In Love*, and they were phenomenal.

The album was a labor of love, and I was determined to make it happen. But I missed my brothers terribly. Being in the studio without them was not the same. I did not have the same joy as when we were all together. Doing this album really became work for me. Before, it was such fun working with my brothers. We understood each other creatively, but now we were divided. I imagined us all feeling the same way. Something was missing. Not just GOD—we were missing one another. We could feel what one another felt without even asking. Somehow, we just knew because we had such a strong bond and connection. Unfortunately, when we hurt and our emotions are too involved, we cannot talk to one another. We end up talking at one another, and the breakdown in communication tends to make matters worse.

We were working and trying to do our own thing, but it was not the same. We needed one another's ideas, which we were sadly keeping to ourselves and not sharing with each other. I was so lonely doing my album without my brothers' input and ideas. I needed their blessings and validation. They came around every now and then. I would share my progress with them, wanting to hear their feedback and longing for their approval. They would give their blessings, but it did not seem sincere.

The boys secured a record deal with a company called Striped Horse Records. Two men, Joe Tanis and Ed Wright, became their manager and helped them land a record deal. Bobby was added to the group. They were back in the studio working on their album. Motown had kept three of us as solo artists: El, Chico, and me. We were hard at work on our albums as well. Chico finished his album first. He was going on different TV shows promoting his album. I finished my album next. Chico and I had release dates for our albums. El had not yet begun his solo project because he was still promoting *The Rhythm of the Night* album.

CHAPTER 48

TOMMY AND DUCKIE

ALL DEBARGES WERE WORKING EXCEPT Tommy. Tommy was in trouble at home in Grand Rapids. We heard rumors that his drug problem had gotten worse after he received money from the accident, and he was not handling it very well. Tommy was supposedly getting high all the time. He had the money to fund his drug habit so it was no surprise. The drug dealers were swarming around Tommy like vultures, and he allowed them to take advantage of him. With the money, Tommy and Duckie married and bought a home. Tommy also bought a brand-new sports car he would often lend out for drugs to the drug dealers. Mama was sickened by all the money Tommy was spending on drugs. She did not like the fact he was squandering his financial windfall on drugs. However, there was nothing she could do to stop his self-destruction. Tommy was grown, and it was his money to blow. Mama hated the fact she could not control Tommy's recklessness. It must have made her upset to see the drug dealers have access to money she felt could be put to better use.

Despite Tommy's destructive lifestyle, Duckie was happy to be his wife. She now carried his last name and was mother to his three children—two boys, little Tommy and Christian, and a little girl named Marina. I had never seen Duckie so happy before. She now had her own place, and she could decorate it as she saw fit. No longer did she have to rely on Mama or the benevolence of family. She could now buy whatever she wanted for herself and her children. Duckie was always into fashion. She just never had the money to buy what she wanted because of Tommy's addiction. However, she could spout off the names of all the popular designers and brands at the time. She was into fashion magazines and books. She also loved to decorate other people's homes. Fashion and decorating were her thing. Now she could do both—buy the latest fashion for her and the children as well as decorate her own home. She could cook in her own kitchen and have her own Christmas tree and decorate it as she saw fit. Finally, she had everything she had waited for in life. It meant a lot for her to have means of her own.

Duckie was now reaping the benefits of being the mother of Tommy's children. She was a good mother, and she often told me she would never leave her children or give them away. She had felt neglected by her mother and often expressed her mother was wrong for leaving when she was just a child. Duckie loved her children very much, and this was why she was still around putting up with Tommy. She needed help raising them. Duckie had a few odd jobs here and there she was not able to keep. She had no one to watch the children while she worked. Tommy, being on drugs, would be gone all night and sleep all day. Therefore, Duckie would find herself having to quit job after job after job. Her only hope was for Tommy to jumpstart his career and make it in the music business. She stood patiently by his side, watching his siblings work hard to make it in the industry.

Tommy was steadily spending the insurance settlement on drugs. Duckie was smart enough to open her own account so she could have access to the money as well. She allowed Tommy to use some of the money, but she ensured the bills were paid. Duckie did not intend to go out in the world backward. I talked to her from time to time, and she would tell me she had a plan for keeping their home and never being put in a position to depend on anyone else again. However, Tommy was looking bad. He was in the streets and spending lots of money on drugs. Mama was furious and felt the need to intervene. She went behind his back and got people to sign a petition saying Tommy was a drug addict and incapable of handling his own financial affairs. She tricked Tommy into coming to court. He had no idea what was going on. He thought he was going for a ticket when he was there to have his money snatched from his hands.

Duckie was blindsided by Mama's actions, too. It did not make any sense why Duckie should not have been the sole conservator of the money. After all, she was his wife and did not have a drug problem. However, Duckie did not know how to speak up on her own behalf. Everything Mama had planned was kept a secret and Duckie was none the wiser. The judge questioned whether Duckie was also on drugs. He asked if she would be able to handle the money. Mama then told the judge Duckie and Tommy had been together for years. Even though she was not on drugs, she was weak when it came to Tommy. She convinced the judge Duckie was incapable of managing the money because of her devotion to Tommy. Therefore, the judge granted Mama conservator of the money.

Tommy came home upset and told Duckie the news. She just listened to him and said nothing at all until he was through. Then she asked Tommy why she did not become conservator since she was his wife and not on drugs. He told her he had no idea what Mama was planning. He even believed Duckie may have been in on the scheme. Duckie then told him she knew nothing and was surprised as well. Tommy finally told her she did not get control of the money because Mama convinced the judge she had a weakness for him.

Duckie did not argue the point with Tommy nor did she argue the point with Mama. However, I believe this was the day Duckie gave up on her happily ever after. All those years she waited to have her own life. She finally had the means to control her life, and it was snatched away. Control of her life was back in the hands of the woman she did not have the heart to fight—Our mother. Duckie was right back at square one: depending on Mama for her day-to-day existence. She now had to ask Mama for money for herself and her children. She watched Mama dish money out to her only if she deemed it necessary. I am sure Duckie was dying on the inside.

We all knew Mama was not a good steward of money herself. She had her own problem with spending money and keeping tabs on what she did with the money. The only thing that set her apart from Tommy was the fact she did not use the money to buy drugs. However, money was Mama's drug, and she had an entitlement mentality when it came to her children's money. Duckie continued feeling some type of way about being Tommy's wife and not being able to control their finances. It was her and Tommy's money to do as they pleased. She never voiced her frustration to Mama. Rather, she took it out on Tommy. She became bitter toward Tommy and no longer wanted to lie with him sexually. Tommy often talked about their lack of a sex life to anyone and everyone who listened. Tommy, hurt by Duckie withholding her affections, went deep into his sorrows to express it. This would become his whole conversation when he would get high. Instead of Tommy understanding why his wife was bitter, he took it as if she wanted to be with other men. Sadly, his demons led him to believe he would be in control if he set her up with men and watched her act out sexually.

By this time, Tommy persuaded Duckie to get high and be with other men so he could watch her have sex. Perhaps this is what he felt she wanted since she was uninterested in him sexually. They were both suffering. For years, Duckie had dealt with Tommy begging her to get high and do sinful things sexually. Somehow, she was able to remain clean and not give into his wild desires. Now, she had seemingly given up on a life of bliss with Tommy. I feel she wanted to get back at Tommy for all the hurt she was feeling inside. Eventually, she grew vulnerable and started indulging in drugs as well as giving in to Tommy's need for voyeurism.

Duckie had never done drugs with Tommy in all the years they had been together. She finally gave in and dived headfirst into drug addiction. With Duckie now indulging, all hell broke loose. Tommy's woman was doing drugs with him and living out his lewd fantasies. It broke my heart and shook me to my core. The children were already suffering from their father's drug addiction. The only stabilizing force in their life had been their mom. Now she was also strung out on drugs. Duckie began doing whatever she could to get drugs for herself and Tommy. It was so sad to watch.

CHAPTER 49

DEBARGES ON SEPARATE STAGES

DURING THIS TIME, I WAS doing well and no longer actively battling addiction. Since the demise of the group, I had not used any drugs. I was off into my new solo career and promoting my new album. However, I was extremely unhappy. The loneliness I felt not having my brothers by my side was crippling.

The boys along with Bobby had finished their album and were shooting photos for the cover. I was scheduled to perform on *Soul Train*. It would be my first solo performance on stage alone and I was terrified. I was not a good dancer and needed to quickly learn some steps to move about the stage. A dear friend, James Walker, promised he would come over and teach me some steps to go along with my single "Save the Best for Me." We worked every day leading up to the *Soul Train* performance. James talked the boys into surprising me by coming down to the *Soul Train* studio as a show of support. I was so glad to see my brothers. Everyone was there except El.

The boys being there helped me get through the show. Their presence made me happy. I pranced around the stage with confidence. However, something about showcasing myself in this manner did not sit well with my spirit. I never had any issues when I sang solo in church. I never had to dance and prance around in front of the congregation in order to share my gift of singing. The focus was never on me—it was all about Jesus. Performing on *Soul Train* was a much different task than singing for Jesus. Though triumphant, I did not like the feeling at all. It was not fulfilling. I could easily perform when my brothers were by my side. But now I was alone, and the focus was solely on me.

The song took me out of my element. The song was not from my heart. Someone else wrote it, and I was not used to singing other people's songs. I preferred writing my own lyrics and coming up with my own bass line. My songs were written about my life and would be written from my heart. "Save the Best for Me" was a promotional stunt Motown believed would help gain traction for the album. I would have rather sang "A Woman in Love" or "Never Let Die," the songs I personally wrote for my album. Nevertheless, this was my job now. I had to quickly learn to take the bitter with the sweet. It was difficult performing a song I did not even believe in. I got through the show somehow. Deep down inside, I knew this avenue was no longer for me. It lacked purpose. I was not a solo artist—not in this sense anyway. I did not want to be promoted as a sex symbol. If I were to be a solo artist, it would be for Jesus and not singing "Save the Best for Me." Nevertheless, I pretended to be happy in order to not make any waves.

The day after the show, all the boys headed to Los Angeles to buy some pills. Tony and I found it hard not to join them and indulge. The temptation was too great. We promised to do it this one last time and not indulge again. We all went together and scored some pills. The boys ended up hanging out at my home for a while. We sat around all night and talked. Little did Tony and I know we were fooling ourselves. It did not take long for us to be back in the throes of addiction. We did not go back right away. However, we started using every weekend, and it progressed from this point.

It was summer, and my two oldest girls, Damea and Janae, were in Grand Rapids. We only had little Tonee with us at the time. I was doing interviews with more scheduled. When the weekend came around, Tony and I would go on a drug binge. We visited some friends of ours while we were in the Los Angeles area before returning home to the Valley. Margie and Marvin were a couple we had recently befriended. They had been wanting us to stop by their new apartment for quite some time. Since we were in the area, we decided to pay them a visit. We called to let them know we were on our way. The couple had a daughter named Tarrice. She was a couple of years older than Damea. She wanted me to leave Tonee with her for the weekend. I took her up on her offer since it would give Tony and me some time alone.

When we arrived at their apartment, Margie surprised us with dinner. Margie was a great cook, and we all loved her cooking. As the day turned into night, Tony and I became higher and higher off the pills. We decided we should probably stay with Margie and Marvin until morning. They had a guest room with a waterbed and offered us the room for the night. I had fallen asleep with my legs hanging over the wood frame of the bed. When I awaken the next morning, both of my legs were cramped. When I went to stand, I could only stand on my left leg. My right leg was numb and had no feeling at all. It crumpled as I tried to stand. I figured this was only temporary, and I would regain feeling in my leg within a few minutes. However, this was not the case. I tried putting on my shoe, and it would not fit either.

I was scared and told Tony I should go to the hospital. I then told Margie what was happening. Tony took me to the hospital where I remained in the ER for hours. All kinds of tests were conducted to determine what was wrong with my leg. Finally, they diagnosed me with a blood clot and wanted to admit me and drain the blood to get it flowing through my leg again. I called my manager, Tony Jones, to let him know what was going on. He suggested I get a second opinion. He found a doctor I could see right away. We left the hospital and arrived at the doctor's office. The doctor ran all kinds of tests. He stuck pins in my leg and used all kinds of medical instruments to see if there were any reflexes. I felt nothing, and it was scaring me. Finally, the doctor was able to tell me I was suffering from a pinched nerve. I had damaged a nerve in the back of my leg while sleeping on the waterbed. The doctor did not know if it was permanent or not. "Let's give it a couple of months. If it is not permanent, you should start to get feeling back in it again. Once the feeling comes back, it will be painful. However, thank

GOD for the pain. At least you will have feeling in your leg again," the doctor explained.

I was laid up for a couple of months recuperating. I called my sister-in-law Kathy and told her to come get Tonee. She agreed to keep her the entire summer. Despite being on bedrest, I still had promotional events for the album. I had to show up to radio stations for interviews. Motown also scheduled magazine interviews at the headquarters. Tony had to carry me from the car into the building for the appearances and interviews. He never once complained. After about two months, I started to feel pain in my right foot. I started shouting," Thank you Jesus for the pain!" I knew then the loss of feeling was not permanent. I was praying for the day GOD would restore feelings in my leg. He spared me once again, and I was grateful.

By this time, I was hearing through the grapevine that Motown really did not want me on their roster. The only reason they signed me was to keep me from joining another label and competing with my brothers. Motown believed this would conflict with what they wanted to do with Chico and El's solo career. Therefore, I was only signed to stay out of the way. They had no interest in putting money into promoting my album. I was practically left on my own to promote my debut solo album. This hurt me especially hearing it from my brothers. I finally gave up. I became scared and started getting high regularly again. This time, I did not go to any lengths to hide my reoccurring addiction from Motown.

With my life in turmoil, Tony and I were involved in a car accident, and I happened to be the driver. I had dropped some pills while stopped at the traffic light. When the light changed to green, the car in front of us did not move. I stepped on the gas and ran into the backend of the car. By the time the police arrived, I was not yet feeling high. The pills had not worked their way through my system. However, by the time we filled out papers and went through the motions, I began feeling the effects of the pills. The officers were getting ready to send us on our way when I nodded out right in front of them. They (rightfully) suspected I was under the influence.

The officers searched my car and found pills and placed me under arrest. I had never been to jail a day in my life. I was high out of my mind and scared to death. I began crying hysterically, and my behavior spun out of control. While the arrest was going down, someone contacted Motown. My husband ended up going to the bondsman and bailing me out of jail. Now I had to appear in court. It frightened me to be in trouble with the law. Driving under the influence was the charge. I would be receiving a letter in the mail regarding my court appearance. After the arrest, I only did a few promotional events. I believe my arrest gave Motown a good excuse to just say forget it. They only had a few more months before the option was up anyway.

When the day came, Motown did not pick up the option to fully sign me. I was no longer on salary, and we were living off our savings. Because there was no money coming in, we quickly drained our savings. We were spending it on drugs. Our addiction had worsened. I did not even try to pick myself up this time. I just wallowed in it.

CHAPTER 50

NO MORE DENIAL

TONY AND I WERE IN trouble. We had started getting high every day. Our children were with family so we only had to focus on ourselves. It did not take long for us to fall behind on the mortgage and car note. Every dime we had went toward supporting our pill habit. We decided to remain in the house until we could no longer stay. Afterward, we planned to move back east and considered Steubenville, Ohio, where Tony could easily land a job. The thought of going to Steubenville made me sick to my stomach, but we did not have many options.

During this time, El was on tour, and we wanted to see him perform. He was set to appear at Magic Mountain. We had already seen him on TV performing by himself but had not yet seen his live show. What an embarrassing experience it would end up being for us all. Before we arrived at the venue, it was confirmed our tickets would be waiting to be picked up in the ticket office. We were reassured we would get into the venue with no problem. After all, we were family, and we were members of DeBarge. El would perform songs we all had contributed to while in the group. Therefore, everything should have gone smooth, right? Wrong! We had trouble right off the bat starting with getting into the venue. To make matters worse, there were no tickets set aside for us, and we had to argue in order to be let inside. It was a humiliating experience. As if this was not bad enough, we ended up with the worse seats in the house.

Everything continued to go downhill from this point. Perhaps we had not done ourselves any favor by showing up. We sat there watching El and his hired background singers singing our songs. I sat there in a daze. The reality of the situation hit me like a ton of bricks, and it was the most miserable feeling in the world. We were treated as outsiders, and it did not feel good. We set aside our pride and tried in vain to pretend as if we were so proud of El. Truth be told, I was deeply offended. Once the show was over, we wanted to go backstage and see our brother. However, we were not allowed backstage. Security treated us as though we were nobodies. They had to get permission first because they did not know if we were El's sister and brothers. We were furious, hurt, and demeaned. We were finally allowed backstage, and El seemed genuinely happy to see us. He introduced us to his band and background singers. They were singing our praises and telling us how much they were fans and loved our songs. Yet we were forced to watch them be paid while we did not have enough money to purchase a pack of cigarettes.

We left the venue more broken than before we came. Background singers were getting the glory for our hard work. Lyrics we had written from our heart and background vocals we had harmonized so beautifully were being credited to others. They were all smiles and being praised for singing the melodies we created—and they were being paid for it. I was crying inside and reflecting over our experience at the concert. Why were we overlooked and did not get tickets? Why were our seats so far from the stage? Why were we treated so harshly when we tried to go backstage to see our brother? It did not seem to matter to anyone that we were members of DeBarge. I was conflicted. I loved my brother but did not know how to feel about him. It was a weird vibe, and I wondered if he cared how we were feeling. I doubt he did because El began to believe he had been DeBarge all by himself.

Just like other times when we were unable to cope with disappointment, all hell would break loose in our lives. We no longer had a career, and El had gone on with his life. We spiraled completely out of control. Tony and I were now very heavy into doing drugs—not just pills. By this time, we started smoking cocaine as well. The car had been repossessed, and our home was now in foreclosure. The worst part was hearing how bad we were being talked about in Grand Rapids. My children were being fed plenty of misinformation about their mom and dad. They were not with us to see what was happening. However, they were old enough hear the gossip and feel the backlash of the horrible things being said about their parents. It did not matter if what they heard was true or false. They were old enough to form opinions based on all they were hearing on the home front. This bothered me and was hard to accept. Before my girls left to stay with family, we were still managing to hold our lives together. Therefore, they did not actually get to see how bad life had become for me and Tony. Family members painted a dire image in my children's minds, and I was too deep into my addiction to stop the onslaught.

I was sick of life, and I did not want to be with Tony another day. It would not have mattered to me if I ever saw him again. I wanted out of the marriage, and I voiced it at every opportunity. We did not know how to go our separate ways at the time so we remained together and planned to head back east. I grew tired of feeling sorry for Tony. He did not deserve my empathy. Though we were husband and wife, we had no sex life and was not sleeping in the same bed. I wanted out!

We managed to sell most of the items in the house and pretty much used all the money on drugs besides enough to eventually get back home. We remained in the house until we had to practically be thrown out. Even with nowhere to go, we were still not ready to head back home. Our reality was sad. We could not bring ourselves to accept that our days in Los Angeles were practically over. Randy invited us to stay with him and his new girlfriend, Wendy, and we accepted. We could have stayed with either of the boys since they all lived in the same apartment building (Randy, James, Bobby, and Chico along with our cousin Alvin). Mark and El lived elsewhere. It was wild in the apartment community to say the least.

El picked his days to come around. However, Mark came over every day. We were in and out of one another's apartments, and it was no big deal. Bernd Lichters also had an apartment in the same building. We all were getting high off pills and cocaine. The boys had an endless stream of girls running through their apartments. They loved to party. It would be nothing for them to party all night long. Bobby, believing he was the boss, would be able to put up with the boys' party antics in small doses. Afterward, he would grow weary of their silly little ways, and an explosive argument would ensue. He partied with them then throw his own parties. However, as the one who liked to call order when he felt it was needed, he would demand the boys to tone it down. I guess Bobby never grew out of believing he had to keep the boys in order.

Chico started getting high off pills, but he was not indulging in cocaine. It was a nonstop party in the apartment building. I was trying my hardest to get rid of Tony. I wanted him to go back home to Ohio, and I would just return to Grand Rapids. We got into a heated argument, and I told him I wanted to break up. After a couple of days of arguing back and forth, I was able to convince him to leave. He finally had his mother send him an airline ticket to return to Steubenville, Ohio. My girls were living in Ohio with their aunt Kathy. Tony decided to go and spend time with them before they returned to Los Angeles. Once the girls returned, we would go and live with El. Mama was also in Los Angeles at the time visiting for the summer.

The morning Tony was to leave, I told him we would only be separating for a while. I told him we both needed time apart. I convinced him we would probably get back together if he gave me some space. I had to say this for him to leave. I really had no idea what I wanted to do about our marriage. I just wanted to be alone. For Tony to feel good about leaving at all, I had to give him hope we would get back together in time. I told him what he wanted to hear so he would agree to leave. He was scheduled to leave later in the day, and we needed to make a phone call to his mother. Randy did not have a phone so I went to use the phone in Bobby's apartment.

I knocked repeatedly on Bobby's door. It took him a few minutes to let us inside. I could tell he was not in a good mood. I did not think nothing of it. Bobby was hardly ever in a good mood. You just got used to it. In fact, I chose to just ignore his attitude. I was never intimidated by Bobby, and his mood swings did not unnerve me like they did the boys. It was easy for me to stand up to Bobby and not allow him to talk to me any old way. I would get back with him and let him know I had a mouth too. Bobby was irritated and mumbled his naughty little words but handed me the phone anyway. Then he went to sit down in a chair. I could tell he was high and probably still tired from the night before. However, I was in a happy mood. Tony was about to be out of my hair, and I was able to talk with my girls on the phone. They were at my mother-in-law's house when I called. Just hearing their voice meant the world to me. I guess my happy mood disgusted Bobby. He began to huff and puff, hem and haw as I talked with my girls. After he could not get a reaction out of me, he began to voice his frustrations.

"I wish you would hurry up and get off my phone," he stated, visibly irritated. "Don't nobody feel like hearing all that silly shit you are talking." I ignored him and continued talking. Of course, Bobby thinks that when he speaks, the world should stop and listen. By me ignoring him, he started to lose it. "How are you going to ignore what I'm saying in my house—on my phone? Get off my phone now, Bunny!" he shouted.

I looked at Bobby and stated, "Look, Bobby, I haven't done anything to you. I am not your brothers, and your attitude don't scare me!" I continued talking to my girls.

Bobby forcefully grabbed the phone out of my hand and yelled, "Bitch, get out of my house!" Then he pushed me hard and shouted, "Tony, get your bitch ass out too!" Tony noticed that Bobby had pushed me down to the floor and told him to keep his hands off his wife. Bobby then got in Tony's face and asked him what he was going to do about it. Next thing I know, Tony punched Bobby with his fist. I screamed for them to stop and grabbed Tony, trying to pull him away from Bobby and push him out the door. I looked back to see if Bobby was all right, and I saw a huge lump on his head. He was enraged and cursing at Tony. He was threatening Tony and yelling this was not over and he would see about him later. I was upset with Tony and told him he should not have punched Bobby. I understood Bobby forced his hand, but I did not like to see my brothers and my husband fight one another. Thankfully, Tony was on his way to Ohio and would soon be taking the city bus to the airport. I figured he would be long gone before Bobby could plot his revenge. Hopefully, by this time, Bobby would have taken a nap and gotten over what happened. We went back to Randy's apartment to gather up his belongings then said our good-byes.

A couple of hours had passed since the blowup between Tony and Bobby. I felt everything was okay and the incident was now water under the bridge. I stayed inside the apartment as Tony went to wait for the bus. I did not feel like waiting with him. As Tony waited at the bus stop, James and Marty visited Bobby's apartment and noticed the lump on his head. They inquired about what had happened. Bobby, with his tendency to revise history, went on to tell them Tony had hit him with a belt buckle. He failed to mention how he had instigated the incident by pushing me to the floor and referring to me as a bitch. Marty happened to be looking out the window and noticed Tony still standing at the bus stop. He motioned for James to come out on the balcony then let James know Tony was still outside. James and two of his friends leaped over the balcony and ran up on Tony. Marty stood back as he watched James move in on Tony and start beating him. The other two guys decided to join in. After seeing Tony was outnumbered and unable to fight back, Marty tried to stop the fight. It was too late.

By this time, they had broken several of Tony's ribs and blackened both of his eyes. Tony tried to come back to the apartment to let me know what just happened. However, Mama had just pulled up. She saw Tony and noticed his condition. She ended up taking him to another bus station so he could get to the airport from there.

Meanwhile, as all this was going on, I was in Randy's apartment, oblivious to what had just taken place. Nobody said anything—not even Mama. The boys came inside and acted as if nothing happened. The only thing out of the ordinary were the boys being overly kind to me. They waited on me hand and foot. Whatever I asked them for or asked them to do, they obliged. I found their behavior quite odd but figured they were being nice because they knew Tony and I had broken up. They continued to pamper me, and I was none the wiser. Everyone knew about my husband being attacked except me. Everyone kept quiet and continued giving me their undivided attention.

James Walker came over to hang out with me. He was like family. He felt bad and could no longer keep up the charade. James Walker felt it was unfair that everyone was talking about the beat down yet keeping it from me. He finally broke down and told me what transpired earlier in the day. He told me the boys and two of their friends jumped my husband. James Walker went into the gory details of the fight. I felt my heart jump out my chest. I was visibly upset and beyond hurt. Now it all made sense why my brothers had been acting so nice to me. I ran looking for them. When they saw me coming, they knew the cat was out of the bag.

James Walker was hot on my heels. I found James and Marty first. "Why would you do that?" I screamed at them both. I had no idea about Tony's condition. I started bawling.

James Walker then pointed toward the other two men who had also jumped my husband. "There's the other two that jumped in," he stated without batting an eye.

The boys stood looking silly. They were upset with James Walker for spilling the beans. I ran over to the two men and started hitting them. I was crying, "Do you even know my husband?" I shouted. "You had no right jumping in something you knew nothing about!" I was hitting them with all my might. My brothers ran over and grabbed me. They apologized profusely to the two guys then asked them to leave. They were upset with James Walker and continued saying he was wrong for telling me. However, James Walker kept saying, "She is my sister too! She needed to know. Bobby blew it up and he lied. He made it seem like Tony had hit him with something and that he was innocent."

The next morning, I received a call from my children. They were on the phone distraught. They asked me why I let their uncles beat up their daddy. It broke my heart to hear my baby Janae crying, "They broke my daddy's ribs, Mommy! I hate them! I do not care what they say! They hurt my daddy, and I don't want to speak to them again! I hate them, Mommy! I hate them!" My poor baby did not understand why her daddy had been so viciously attacked. There was nothing anyone could say to make her understand. It was her daddy who was hurting, and I could relate to the pain she was feeling. I told her Mommy did not know anything about it and I had nothing to do with it. I agreed with her it was wrong. He was my children's father, and he did not deserve to be attacked. My children had to see their daddy hurt. I thought to myself Bobby was a grown man capable of fighting his own battles. He did not need James or Marty to fight his battles. If they wanted to beat Tony up for something worthwhile, it should have been when he touched my baby Damea. After all, Bobby came to the house the same night I discovered he had molested Damea and did nothing except give me pills. Also, neither of the brothers did anything to Tony when Peaches, their baby sister, said he touched her inappropriately. Yet they were ready and willing to beat him down over a grown man telling a bald-faced lie.

Bobby had no remorse about what he had done, and this bothered me a great deal. The boys realized they were wrong. Initially, they seemed to have some semblance of remorse. We all knew how Bobby operated. The thing with Bobby, he could make things out to be something it was not. He was a diva and melodramatic. However, the boys found a way to excuse themselves from culpability. The damage was done, and they decided to move on from the incident. I had to deal with my daughters and their hurt. Janae seemed to be the most affected. She loved her uncles and always had a close bond with them. But what they did to her father is something she continues to carry with her even today. They hurt her daddy. I thought about the pain I felt when my daddy got beat up by my uncle, and I could relate to my child. History was repeating itself again. Now my daughter could relate to my feelings. The generational curse was manifesting again in our lives, and it was only just the beginning.

CHAPTER 51

UNWELCOMED HOMECOMING

It was not long before my girls were back in Los Angeles. Mama had since returned home to Grand Rapids, and I would soon follow. My plan was to live with her for a while. I decided not to move to Steubenville, Ohio, with Tony. Before Tony left Los Angeles, we hired a moving company to drive our belongings back east. Everything we owned was now stuck in Pittsburgh, and we needed money to get our belongings to Michigan. The drive and storage cost a few thousand dollars, and we did not have the money to cover the expenses. I became worried. I needed to find a way to get our belongings to Michigan. It was everything I had left in this world besides my children—my gold albums, family pictures, and other valuables that were irreplaceable. I did not want to lose my life's work. However, I had no idea how I would get the money, and the cost was going up daily. To complicate matters, I also needed money to return home. This was going to be costly as well. I asked El if he would help me return to Grand Rapids, and he agreed to think about helping but had not yet given me an answer. While waiting for a response, I could not bring myself to ask him for the storage money. I was now faced with losing my belongings, and the anxiety was killing me. It felt as though my life was hanging in the balance.

It was time to return home. I could not stay in Los Angeles another day. There was nothing left for me in the city. I felt like a hollow, empty shell with a dark overcast cloud following me around. I was lonely and had nothing. I did not have my brothers, I did not want my husband, and I did not want to live in Steubenville. At the time, all I wanted was my mother. I needed her, and I wanted to go home. I needed family and friends in Michigan to just love me and support me unconditionally. It felt like the place I needed to be at this time in my life. I was lost and in a very poor mental state. I felt unloved and like a failure.

My intentions were never to come to California and fail. I never intended to return home downtrodden either. I came to California to pursue a music career and build a musical legacy. What happened to me? What happened to us? We came to California a close-knit family—caring and loving one another to the point we always knew what was going on in one another's lives. We were always concerned for one another's well-being. This started when we were children. If one of us was hurting, we all hurt. We would then rally around each other to make sure they got what was needed. In the beginning, everyone accepted the idea our closeness was the only way to survive the industry. We believed in one another and provided each other unconditional support. Somewhere along fame's twisted path, we took a wrong turn.

My mind drifted to happier times. I thought about our first promotional tour and the tour with Luther Vandross. How did we become so fractured? We stopped caring about one another's place in life and where we were going with our careers. We began hoarding ideas and not sharing them with one another. We became suspicious and looked at one another as stealing our individual ideas. The only thing we seemed to do successfully and effortlessly was get high. This was not in our plan and certainly not our purpose.

Thinking back to our childhood, all we had to hold on to was GOD since we experienced the childhood from hell. We learned about heaven, and we desired to go there when it was GOD's timing. We learned about GOD and had a chance to know Him personally. If we did not have GOD, we would not have had any hope for the situations we were now facing. We were out in the world living a life of hell. The only thing real in our lives was GOD.

I found the people in Los Angeles fake. They lived in a complete fantasy world. Everybody knew somebody who knew someone famous either through social or familial association. It was nothing to wear the finest outfits, drive the fanciest cars, yet live out of a post office box. To me, Los Angeles was where lost angels congregated. It was a totally different world than Grand Rapids, Michigan. It now felt so far away from where I wanted to be in life. Fame was no longer appealing. All I had left from my time in the spotlight were broken dreams. I needed to be home. The hope and optimism I felt when I first arrived were gone. Since then, my eyes were wide open, and I learned so much about the city I once loved. Now, nothing about the city was real to me. Maybe the never-ending sunshine made sin so plentiful. The city was flooded with people desperate to fulfill their dreams. Sadly, there were just as many broken dreams. My dreams were now among the broken ones. I was miserable and wanted to feel like a child and be comforted by my mother. Yet my faith remained, and I figured GOD could bring my life full circle. I just did not know how or when. My hope was still steadfast in GOD.

El ended up coming through and gave me the money needed for my children and me to fly home. I would be leaving the following day. The girls and I took the bus to the airport. I felt sad leaving my brothers behind. I did not know what would happen to them. They were all in trouble—including El. He looked to be okay to anyone not close to him. However, my brother was miserable along with the rest of us. Neither of us were living in our purpose. I was in so much emotional turmoil and also feeling my brothers' emotional pain. It was hard to carry their burden, so I knew I needed to let go. But I did not know how to at the time. I would have to fall on my face a few more times before life showed me how to stop living for my brothers.

As the girls and I entered the plane, tears were in my eyes. I had such beautiful thoughts when I first came to Los Angeles. I had such big dreams and high hopes. Most of all, I was confident. My brothers and I had favor when we first arrived. If not for GOD's favor, we would have been starving artists much longer. We were in California without money or a car. At times, we did not know where we would lay our heads. A person can really get lost in California while pursuing their dreams. I saw many fold under pressure. At least we made it to the top, I thought. We landed somewhere. Although we did not sustain our success, at least the stars aligned in our favor. Many changes happened in our lives. Many things were still going on. Nevertheless, we were still being kept. We were the Kept Ones and did not realize how close GOD kept us to Him.

At this very moment, I stopped and gave thanks to GOD. I remembered He is the same yesterday, today, and forever. Therefore, in my heart, I could leave my brothers behind and know they would be all right. There was no reason for me to worry about them. GOD was keeping us all covered. I stepped onto the plane and said my farewell to Los Angeles.

We arrived home to Grand Rapids! I did my best to hide the pain from my children. I sensed they knew I was sad. They had been there with me and seen it go all the way up then all the way down. Scared to death and not knowing what would happen next, I gathered up my girls, hopped into the cab, and headed to my mother's house. There was no one to greet us at the airport. There was no warm reception at home. No one was there cheering for and making a fuss over the fallen star Bunny DeBarge.

CHAPTER 52

CHAOS AND CONFUSION

MAMA'S HOUSE WAS IN AN uproar when I walked inside. Tommy and Duckie's children were there, but the parents were nowhere in sight. Mama was nearly in tears as she told me Duckie had left Tommy and the children. She did not think Duckie was planning on coming back. "She should have been back," she stated through tears. "I have not heard anything. I begged her not to leave these kids on me."

I looked around, and the children were all over the place playing without a care in the world. Mama was carrying around the baby, Little Chico, on her hip. The house was small—only big enough for Mama, her husband Papi, my sister Carole, and her twin Darrell. I wondered where my children and I would sleep. *This is unfair*, was my first thought. I needed Mama right now for what I was going through. Duckie and Tommy have always had Mama. I needed to be here now, and Duckie should have taken her children with her if she wanted to leave. Besides, Duckie has her own mother. This is my mother. I was in bad shape and needed help. I needed somewhere to live with my children. It was my turn, I thought. Enough is enough with Duckie and Tommy! I was furious! I could not wait to hear from them and give them a piece of my mind.

Mama was worried sick about Duckie. She said it was unusual for her not to call. "When Duckie left, she told me the kids were just as much Tommy's kids as they were hers, and it was time for Tommy to keep them. She said Tommy had money now so he could do it. She said once she found a job, she would send for them."

I would reach out to Duckie the next time she called. I knew how she felt about her children, and it was unlike her to leave them behind. Truthfully, Duckie was not herself anymore, and she was tired. But why now? Why when I needed to be home with my mother? I had no idea what to expect once I returned home. However, I did not expect to return to a madhouse. I did not feel at home in my own mother's house. I was not welcomed because Duckie and Tommy had put an enormous strain on the household.

I had been home a couple of weeks before Duckie finally called. Mama was not there so I was able to talk freely to Duckie. She was glad to hear my voice and wanted to know what was going on with me. I explained to her I had returned home for good and needed my mother's help. I asked what was going on with her and if she was going to come back to get her children. She told me she had to get a job, and it was over between her and Tommy. She went on to explain how she was unable to care for the children and her mother could not help because she worked full-time. "The kids are better off with Tommy," she stated.

I jumped right in on her. "The kids are not with Tommy," I said. "He is not here, Duckie. The children have been put off on Mama, and you know this, Duckie. Tommy is nowhere around. He is in the streets."

Duckie's response surprised me. She did not seem to be the least bit concerned about my comment. "I cannot help that, Bunny. They are his kids too. I am not leaving them on your mother—Tommy is. I do not have any money to take care of them—Tommy does. Your mother has his money so she does not have to worry about the money to take care of them. I have no rights to anything—she has it all. This is why I left the children there. I cannot take care of them." Everything Duckie said was valid. There was nothing I could say to counter her argument. My whole attitude toward her swiftly changed. Suddenly, I understood perfectly. I told her I wanted her to be okay because she was going through a struggle. I shared my pain and how desperate I was to get myself together. I felt lost and needed to live with Mama. I begged her to come home as soon as she could and get her children. I understood her not wanting to take Tommy back though.

Duckie did understand my point of view. In fact, we both understood each other's pain firsthand. She had lived with our family for years. Duckie was both easy to communicate with and easygoing. She agreed to come get the children when she could afford them. Otherwise, she did not see herself coming back for good. She had found a new love life and was being wined and dined. Duckie had found love, support, and affection in the arms of a woman. She was being taken care of now, and she missed having security in her life. I could not be upset with her no matter how hard I tried. I knew her life struggles. Before hanging up the phone, I reassured her of my love and asked her to please be careful. I heard happiness in her voice, which made me happy. However, after ending the call, I looked at her children and mine. They were all suffering.

Duckie had to make a decision. I knew it was hard for her to walk away from her children. She loved her children, and I believed she would eventually get to a place whereas she could be their mother again. Duckie was caught up in meeting her own needs at the moment. She had to figure out life, which was understandable. Her approach might not have been the best. However, she would have to figure out the consequences of her actions. She had lived within the confines of our family for so long. It was now time for her to spread her wings. Duckie really had nothing to lose, which was not lost already. In Grand Rapids, she had no life and no money. Why should she sit back and allow someone else to dish her husband's money out to her? She was finally going for her own. I gave her my blessings.

Mama was sorry she had missed Duckie's call and wanted to know our entire conversation in full detail. I found it hard to tell her anything. "When is she coming back?" she asked. "Did she say, Bunny?" Mama already knew Duckie was not coming back. I guess she hoped for me to have said something to change Duckie's mind.

"She's not coming back, Mama," I stated point-blank. I looked over at my mother. She looked to be in distress. I began to wonder if Mama really understood why Duckie had left. If she did, she was not voicing it. Mama was devastated. She had raised her children. All her babies were adults. The twins had graduated high school. Now, she was saddled with the responsibility of caring for Tommy and Duckie's small children. She did not mind being a grandmother; she just did not want to raise her grandchildren. Even though the children were with Mama most of their lives, Duckie was there to take off some of the pressure. Mama had gotten used to supporting Duckie. She did not mind helping her out. However, four small children at her age was a bit too much. Little Chico, who was only six months old, was a mama's boy and cried out all the time for his mother. Marina was two years old. Christian and little Tommy were not much older.

Mama had tears in her eyes as she asked why Duckie would do this to her at her age. I genuinely felt sorry for my mother and Duckie too. It was a no-win situation. I forgot all about myself needing my mother. I could not put any more on Mama. Even though I was in trouble myself, I would help her as best as I could when I was around. However, I had to leave Mama's house. It was too small. I was in dire straits. I had to reconsider going back to my husband when I was not ready to do so. I dreaded my decision. It was not what I wanted, but there was no other choice.

CHAPTER 53

TRYING TO REBUILD

I WAS DISAPPOINTED NOT BEING able to stay with my mother. I had no other choice except to swallow my pride and call my husband Tony. I told him to come get us and take us to Steubenville. Tony was glad to hear from me. He used his mother's car to pick us up. My in-laws owned rental property in Steubenville. They let us live in the upstairs apartment over the day care. They gave us some furniture, which we fixed up, and I enrolled the girls in school. Tony began seeking a job. Since we did not have to pay rent, we would use the money to get our belongings out of storage in Pennsylvania. I did not care to be in Steubenville, but it was better than the alternative. At least we had our own place.

The world seemed to fall apart around me, and my spiritual life seemed dead. I had not been fed spiritually since I had no church to call home. There was a church in the city I was interested in attending. The pastor was someone I knew very well. He was from my home church back in Michigan. I was so glad to see him as pastor of a church in Steubenville. His name was Elder Richard Young. He was a good friend of our family and had ministered to me as a child. I felt it was a great blessing to be in Steubenville along with Elder Young. However, my father-in-law was also a pastor and with a church in the same city. He would have been insulted if I attended another pastor's church. I did not want to cause a commotion especially since my in-laws were helping us get back on our feet. Therefore, I felt an obligation to become a part of their church. I was upset about my dilemma though. I did not mind going to my in-law's church whenever we came for a visit. However, their church would have never been on my radar if it were not for familial ties. Therefore, I rebelled and chose not to attend church at all.

I have always been a very friendly person. As a result, I had no problems making new friends. Tony and I befriended a couple who lived nearby. We had a lot in common with the couple. Tony happened to have known them from his school days. We visited them often just to get away from our own lives. We also did drugs with them from time to time. They did it recreationally, and it was always on the weekend. Both seemed very dedicated to their jobs, which helped to control their drug usage.

Tony and I were now freebasing. We had learned how to cook cocaine. We were not doing the pills as much because we had a hard time finding them. However, Bobby found a place in Detroit where we could cop them. Whenever we had the money, Tony and I would take a ride to buy a supply. Getting drugs now was unlike when we lived in Los Angeles where we could get our hands on pills practically every day. Detroit was a four-hour drive and just too far away. Our love life was still not the greatest. I only came back to Tony because I felt I had no choice. I still could not bring myself to sleep with him. He would sleep in the bedroom, and I would sleep on the couch.

There was a young man Tony had grown up with who was also into music. He was smitten by the fact I was Bunny DeBarge. He was in town and wanted to get something started musically. He wanted to form a group and do some gigs around the Ohio area. He would come by often and talked about his ambitions. I was not motivated and felt he was just playing around. However, he had gone around and used my name to promote his endeavors. Apparently, he did end up finding someone to promote some gigs in the area. He came over to let Tony and I know he had found us a promoter. I was not doing anything except passing time. I decided why not. It was not as if I had anything else to do at the time.

My namesake was more of a big deal to everyone else than it was to me. People were really excited about the prospect of seeing me perform. Musicians from everywhere showed up to audition and become a part of my band. Watching everything come together, I began searching for background singers. I guess my name was getting people enthused. But I was not thrilled. It seemed as though the spark I once felt when it came to performing and sharing my musical gifts had been extinguished. I decided to just go through the motions and get through the gigs. We rehearsed every day then would get high every night. Finally, Tony and I found a way to maintain our drug habit in Steubenville.

I worked the band pretty hard so they could learn all of DeBarge's songs. The band ended up sounding very polished, and I was proud of their quick progress. It did not take long to secure management. Excited about the prospects of managing an established group, they began looking for more lucrative gigs. They also wanted to work with the rest of the group since neither of us had a contract or management at the time.

I eventually talked to the boys and asked them if they would be interested in doing some shows. If they were willing, management would send for them. The boys were excited. At the time, they were not engaged in any musical endeavors and saw it as a chance to make some fast money. Management sent for Randy, Mark, and James. We all ended up staying together at our managers' ranch in Cambridge, Ohio. We started rehearsing daily with the musicians who were allowed to stay in the guest house.

I was no longer with my husband Tony. We had gotten into a terrible argument. I decided enough is enough with our marriage. The morning after the huge blowup, I just woke up and left him. I then drove the children to Grand Rapids. It was summertime, and my children were not in school so everything worked out perfectly. I could no longer tolerate the state of our marriage. Tony and I had lost our physical and emotional bond a long time ago. It was time to end the charade. I was unhappy being married to him and grew tired of putting on a mask. It was not fair to either of us.

Everything was going as planned once the boys arrived. We told management about our brother Bobby. We wanted him involved in the group's revival as well. Management was all in and asked us to get him on the phone. I called Bobby right away, and they talked to him about their plans for the group. Bobby agreed to come but put terms on his involvement. He laid out a list of demands. Management obliged, and Bobby was on his way to Cambridge, Ohio, to join the rest of his siblings.

When Bobby arrived in town, he began to dominate and run the entire show. The managers quickly grew very fond of Bobby, and he was getting anything he wanted. They trusted Bobby's ability to get the work done. Bobby wanted to add a couple of band members to the group. He had met some boys in Rap Town he worked with from time to time. He was comfortable with them, and they knew all his Switch music. Bobby just had to have them on the team. Robert, one of the managers, ended up flying them to Cambridge to join the band. Their names were Dan Richardson and Chucky Myers. Dan played the keyboards, and Chucky played bass. We ended up with two keyboard players and two bass players. Bobby talked management into keeping both.

We rehearsed every day, and the band was sounding more and more polished. Management was on their job securing gigs. They found some promotional things for us in the city so we could test the waters. Bobby made sure we were all paid. Bobby also insisted we be allowed to return home after the performances. He wanted to make sure we had breaks in between the gigs so we would not tire out. He made sure management followed through with giving us time off.

We had a show scheduled in Los Angeles, which was planned before we moved to the ranch in Cambridge, Ohio. It would pay extremely well, and we wanted to do it. After the show in Ohio, we got paid, and off we went to Los Angeles. The musicians in Ohio took a break and went back to their respective homes. We had other musicians awaiting our arrival in Los Angeles. Once we arrived, James Walker was at the hotel to do our hair and makeup. I was so glad to see him again. He caught me up on all the juicy gossip going on in the city.

El came to the Los Angeles show. It was so special because all of us were together except Tommy. After the show, we went to get pills and cocaine. We had a party in our hotel rooms. We were to check out the next day and head back to Ohio. Chico came later and joined us. His single was hot and climbing the charts. We were so proud of him.

We did not get any sleep while in Los Angeles. We were too busy getting high. Before leaving, we made a call to our managers. We asked if we could bring James Walker back to Cambridge. We convinced them we needed him to do our hair. They agreed and paid for his ticket to Ohio.

We were having a ball. We returned to Ohio high and had enough pills for the days ahead. None of us were taking our time in Cambridge seriously. It was just something to pass the time. I think after the disappointment with Motown and the group breaking up, we no longer had the hunger needed to make it. We were on the wild doing whatever we had to do to maintain our high. I was now one of the boys. I was hanging with my brothers and not facing any consequences in life.

Rev. Jesse Jackson had come into town campaigning for president of the United States. Management made plans for us to perform a song before his speech. We were to sing it a cappella. We came together and quickly wrote a song. Later on at the rally, we sang the song. The news was there and caught footage of us singing.

We were all set to go on our next gig. This time, we would stay at an expensive hotel until it was time to hit the road. It was a plush hotel, and we were able to order room service. There were no limits placed on what we could order. Everything seemed to be going smoothly up until a certain point. Something was going on behind the scenes, and we were clueless. Management took us to buy new clothing for some promotional tours at the local schools. They even placed us on a daily per diem. We had no reason to believe anything was amiss. As far as we knew, management was doing their job by taking care of our needs as performers.

Early one morning while still at the plush hotel, the hotel manager paid us a visit. He told us we could not use the phone anymore nor order room service. We were taken aback and had to use the front desk phone to call our managers. They pretended as if they did not know what was going on but reassured us they would fix the misunderstanding as soon as possible. After the call, the hotel manager told us we had to leave and could not take any of our belongings. We were now fuming. Nothing the hotel manager was saying to us made any sense. This all seemed like a bad dream.

We were forced to leave the hotel with nowhere to go. The hotel manager put us out on the streets. We tried in vain to contact our managers but to no avail. Here we were, in the streets with nowhere to stay and very little money. I had grown close to one of the guys in the band. Luckily, he had enough money to purchase a motel room. We had been talking on the low and had taken a liking to each other. We decided to hang close to each other throughout the day and night. The boys managed to call home and get money for a hotel room. We had no means of getting money for the next night and just decided to take it one day at a time.

We were still trying to get in touch with our managers. We wanted to retrieve our belongings and head home. Some of the band members were from Ohio. They had cars and were able to just drive home. However, one of the band members was from Michigan. Like us, he was stuck with no money and no way to get home. Everyone's belongings were still at the hotel waiting for the tab to be paid.

The tab was in the thousands of dollars. We had no idea how to pay for it. The managers were nowhere to be found. They began ignoring our phone calls. It became apparent our managers had no money and were having financial problems. In our last conversation with them, we were advised they would get a loan and take care of the matter. We knew nothing beyond this and were left on our own to figure out this fiasco. We all needed tickets to get home. No longer able to count on management, we had to look to other sources. The guy I was with paid my way home. Ed Wright and Joe Tannis, who had been managing the boys before this trip, got enough money together to get them back to Los Angeles. Sadly, we could not take any of our belongings.

When we returned to our respective homes, Bobby began working hard to get our belongings back. He was in Los Angeles trying in vain to get in touch with management who were in Ohio. Bobby kept in touch with the hotel manager. The hotel manager agreed this fiasco was something beyond our control and was willing to help return our belongings for an even exchange. Since we were a known group and had a sibling with a hit record at the time, they wanted us to do a show at Cedar Point and include both El and Chico. This would pay for the tab, and our belongings would be returned. We were between a rock and a hard place and had no other choice except to agree. First, we needed to figure out how to get El and Chico to say yes to the hotel's terms.

Bobby talked to El and Chico and informed them what was going on. They both agreed to do the gig. Bobby secured dates from hotel management so El and Chico could work it into their schedule. The hotel sold tickets to the upcoming show. All we had to do was show up and perform. Six weeks would pass before it was time for the show. As time for the show drew near, Bobby called to remind me about the show. I did not know if I wanted to go. I had been feeling a bit under the weather and could not shake it. I told him I would let him know if I was coming. When time came for the show, I was still not feeling my best. Plus, I did not want to go back and face another potential fiasco. I told my brother to get my belongings for me and ship them to Grand Rapids.

I was beginning to feel sick every morning and hoping it was the result of withdrawals. I had formed a habit again and did not have access to any pills. So either I was sick from withdrawal or I was pregnant. Did my one-night escapade lead to me getting impregnated? I realized I had not had a menstrual cycle. It dawned on me I might very well be pregnant. However, I was hoping it was just sickness from not taking the pills anymore. I was totally ashamed of myself for the indiscretion. If I happened to be pregnant, I decided not to keep it. During this period in my life, I was not proud how I was conducting myself. I was no longer with Tony and pretty much doing things I would not have ordinarily done. At least my marriage to Tony sheltered me from a lot of poor decisions I was now making.

The day of the performance at Cedar Point came. DeBarge showed up along with Chico and El. The band members were there as well. Everyone collected their belongings after the show. Ed Wright announced he had an engagement for DeBarge abroad. We had a chance to perform in France and make some money. There was no way

I was missing this opportunity. I had heard so much about France, and it was somewhere I always wanted to go. I was still having morning sickness and realized I was indeed pregnant. However, I had no plans to tell anyone since I had already made up in my mind to have an abortion. I was ashamed of this decision. But I had no real feelings for the person who impregnated me and was not about to have his child. I planned to have the abortion upon returning from France.

CHAPTER 54

FRANCE

BEFORE HEADING TO FRANCE, WE had gigs scheduled in Los Angeles. I noticed that Bobby's voice was sounding different. Lately, he had been hoarse to the point he would have to pass the microphone for me to sing his high notes. This was unlike Bobby, and I could tell he was getting worried. I told him he needed to see a doctor. He brushed me off and said he would when we returned from France. I believed Bobby because this appeared to be more than just a common sore throat. He had never suffered with hoarseness. Now, his voice was going in and out, and he had no explanation as to why.

Thankfully, DeBarge already had passports from the time we went overseas with Motown. However, Ed Wright had to get passports for Bobby and James Walker. We decided to take James Walker with us to France. Not only was he a part of our family, we also wanted him to do our hair and makeup. It took Ed no time at all to get Bobby's and James's passports, and we were soon on our way to France. The flight would be long. Therefore, we all took fours and doors to help ease the fatigue associated with the long flight.

We were now in the air, and the pilot had turned off the seat belt light. We were all seated in first class except James Walker. He had a coach ticket and was seated at the rear of the plane. James Walker thought this was unfair. After the seat belt light was off, James walked to first class where we were all seated. "It's not fair. You all get to sit in first class and I have to sit in coach like a sardine."

Before anyone could say anything to ease his frustrations, Bobby went in. "Excuse me, James, *you* are not a DeBarge. *You* are just a hairdresser. Do not start that sissy shit. And . . . you are sardine . . . and fish!"

James Walker just stood there with his mouth agape, stunned by Bobby's abrasive language. I could see that James's feelings were hurt, and Bobby felt no remorse. James was part of our family, and we loved him very much. However, sometimes Bobby would become jealous of our relationship with him. He was always reminding James Walker he was not related to the DeBarges. He would point out to James how we were sisters and brothers and this did not include him. Tired of Bobby going in on our friend, I jumped to James's defense. This upset Bobby, and he became livid. Before I knew it, all hell broke loose in the friendly skies.

James Walker, seeing the situation spinning out of control, returned to his seat in coach. I started out trying to keep peace and explained to Bobby what he said was not right. I told him he was cold and always hurting people's feelings. I asked him how he would like it if someone hurt his feelings. Bobby did not appreciate me defending James Walker, and he lashed out. He said since I had such a heart for James, then why not give up my seat and go to the back of the plane? The boys noticed the exchange between Bobby and I heating up and decided to move out of the way and into another seat. They knew there was no stopping either of us now. I was seated between Mark and Randy. Once Mark moved, I was able to get closer to Bobby. "You did not have to say it like that," I stated. "That was cold, Bobby."

Bobby was determined to let me know he meant every word he had spoken. "I said what I meant. Now the sissy is gone after he done started all this mess. He ought to be glad he is here. I mean, really . . . and he's got the nerve to complain. You guys can spoil him—I'm not," he stated without flinching. "He is not a DeBarge, and I meant that!" After getting his point across, he made a statement about me keeping my mouth shut.

"Excuse me," I said while picking up one of our promotional pictures. "Do you see your face on here?" It was a picture of the group DeBarge, and of course, Bobby's image was nowhere to be found. In hindsight, I should not have said such mean words to my brother. I was just tired of him being mean to people and wanted him to understand how it felt to be humiliated. This made Bobby even angrier. Before I knew it, he referred to me as a *bitch*. That was it! I was no longer going to stand for Bobby's coarse words toward me. We engaged in a back-and-forth verbal tirade whereas we hurled insult after insult at each other. Our argument grew so loud the pilot announced we were about to have an emergency landing. Both Bobby and I thought we had caused the emergency landing because of our argument. We quickly shut our mouths and put on our seat belts. Bobby vowed never to talk to me again, and I told him I could not care less. I guess we were no longer sister and brother according to Bobby. At the moment, I did not care. We gave each other the silent treatment the remainder of the flight and resorted to throwing eye daggers here and there. Once we were allowed to remove our seat belt, I quickly moved away from Bobby.

France ended up being beautiful and the food simply amazing. However, I was too sick to fully enjoy it. I was too sick to do much of anything and wanted to return home. I had matters that needed to be taken care of and soon. James Walker wanted to go home as well. He had had enough of the abuse from Bobby. Bobby would not let it go and amped up the argument once we landed in France. James Walker and I returned home, leaving the others in France.

CHAPTER 55

NOT MY BROTHER EL!

WHEN I RETURNED HOME, I followed through and had the abortion. It was not long before I was myself again. Tony was calling all the time wanting to know my plans for our marriage. I did not want to go back to him. Again, I felt there was no other choice and did it for the children's sake. Tony worked and I needed help. The thought of reaching out to Social Services in Grand Rapids was not fun. I was Bunny DeBarge, and everyone knew me. It was an embarrassing situation.

I put off going back to Tony as long as humanly possible. I was back staying at my mother's house. Mama's situation with Tommy's children did not help my situation. Duckie was not coming back anytime soon, and school was about to start. I needed to find a place to live and fast. Yet I had no money and was not about to go on welfare. Tony was willing to move to Grand Rapids since I did not want to remain in Steubenville and get a job. I finally gave in and told him to come. We would stay in Mama's basement until we got our own place.

I enrolled the girls in school, and Tony quickly landed a job. It did not take long for us to begin looking for an apartment. We found a place on the northwest side of town. It was a small apartment, but it was ours. We fixed it up to our liking. All three of my girls were now in school. Tonee was in a Head Start Program, and the bus picked her up each day. Damea and Janae were both in junior high school. I was miserable living in Grand Rapids and hated being back with Tony. We both were using pills and cocaine more than ever. The pills were hard to come by though. Every so often we took a trip to Detroit to cop some pills. We were fast becoming cross-addicted.

I was missing California like crazy. At every opportunity, I would go for a visit. It was the month of March, and Bobby and I had birthdays coming up. James Walker also had a birthday in March. He was good friends with the singer Cherelle who also had a birthday in March. A birthday party for Cherelle was being planned, and I wanted to be a part of it. James Walker wanted all the "March babies" to celebrate birthdays together. He was sending a ticket for me to come to Los Angeles where I would stay at Cherelle's house. I had never met her before and only knew her as the artist who sang duets with Alexander O'Neal.

It was a beautiful party, and everyone who was anyone was present. Cherelle knew many famous people who all showed up to celebrate her special day. El and Chico showed up in a limousine. I showed up with James Walker and Cherelle's sister, Rhonda. We stayed for most of the party then left and had our own party. We got high and partied the remainder of the night. The next day, I linked up with Bobby. He had been at the party but not when I was there. He came after I had already left. We did a recap of the night. Bobby went on to mention he may have started something he might regret. I asked him what he meant. He stated El was high at the party last night. This startled me, and I could not believe what I was hearing. "Not my brother El! He would never do such a thing," I stated.

"Yes he was, Bunny." Bobby seemed very concerned and disappointed. "Apparently, someone had given him some coke to snort, and he was wired up. He was running his mouth about it and acting all silly. I was mad about it and asked him who gave it to him. He was tripping. I had to give him some pills to calm him down. After the pills hit him, he started saying, 'Damn, I been missing it. Why didn't you all tell me it was like this? I have been missing this all the time.' He was like a little kid, Bunny, and he liked it."

I shook my head in disgust. "Of course, he liked it, Bobby! Don't we all?" I stated. "This is not good news." I then began to worry about El.

"He's all right," Bobby stated. "I was with him all night. I talked to him and told him he did not want to start getting high. I told him to look what it is doing to the rest of us."

Although Bobby and I were heavy drug users, we did not want El to get involved with drugs. A part of me wished I had never started. "I just hope he listens to you, Bobby," I stated, very concerned. Bobby then goes on to tell me El was lonely and was no longer happy being in the music business without his family. It was getting to him, and he was on the wild side. I knew this in my heart to be true. I remembered being onstage alone without my brothers, and it was a very lonely experience.

El had just finished his album entitled *Gemini*. He was leery of Motown and wanted out of his contract. For a while, my brother was not writing his own stuff. He was not even producing, and this was so unlike him. He had been under so much pressure from Motown to leave the group during the *Rhythm of the Night* album it stifled his ability to write and produce. I was proud of his *Gemini* album. I felt he had some good material on it. At least he began writing again on this album. However, in my heart, I knew El would never be as big as he was when we were together as a group. It was not the same. The anointing was on the family. Being solo was not the way it was supposed to turn out.

GOD knew what He was doing. I believed deep in my heart we would be together again and sing for His Glory. We would be onstage again as Children of GOD. We would sing praises to Him while glorifying His Name. I held this vision close to my heart. I did not know how He was going to do it, but I believed He would in due time. I felt El knew this as well, and he was simply going through the motions. He was breaking bread with many who recognized the uniqueness of who he was but could not visualize the true vision GOD had for him. Now my brother El was getting high and enjoying it. I knew he was in trouble just like the rest of us. He had begun to cover his pain with drugs.

El on down to the twins (which included James, Chico, Carole, and Darrell) were the last five children between Mama and Daddy. Fortunately, they did not experience the hell the first five children did with Daddy and Mommy. They were too young to understand what was going on. However, they caught the repercussions of the fallout—especially James. James was caught up in Bobby's madness resulting from his childhood abuse by Daddy. With James being Daddy's favorite, Bobby targeted him relentlessly. James did not understand Bobby's wrath and found it hard to deal with at times. The younger siblings were witnessing our pain being played out. We were living out the repercussions of childhood abuse. Unfortunately, El could no longer escape the aftermath no matter how hard he tried. He was a part of the five fingers and was hurting too.

After his divorce, El must have vowed to never allow a woman to overtake his emotions. He was vulnerable with Roberta, but this seemed to be a thing of the past. He never loved a woman fully and completely again. El had truly loved Roberta, and all she did was break his heart into a million tiny pieces. He became a notorious womanizer and went through women left and right. They were not hard to find. There were groupies hanging around constantly fighting for his affections. The groupies would go from an encounter with one brother to an encounter with the next. For the boys, it became a contest to see how many of them could sleep with the same girl. Once the boys' hearts were involved, they would want the girl to become their one and only. However, they would have to contend with knowing another brother or brothers had also been with the woman they now loved. In their dysfunctional way of moving on, they would offer forgiveness without the other brother ever asking for it. With them behaving in such manner, they were never able to regain one another's trust. Their promiscuous ways brought so much division between their brotherly bond. There was a lot of animosity among them. They preferred to gossip behind each other's backs rather than talk it out among themselves. My brothers were hurting each other badly. They were betraying one another using women. They carried the pain of betrayal around, never dealing with it properly. Because of their closeness, they would start back hanging around each other while hiding what they truly felt about the other. Honestly, they never enjoyed hurting each other. But never learning to simply apologize for their indiscretions created a vicious cycle whereas they did harm to each other's egos.

I learned if you do not give someone the opportunity to at least apologize, the proverbial slate is never clean. You cannot begin the journey of rebuilding trust. You also do not allow the person a chance to forgive themselves and grow from the experience. Subsequently, they will hurt you again. Sadly, this was the story of our lives. We would forgive almost on instinct whether the person deserved it or not. We would roll out the red carpet and allow them back into our lives with relative ease. Our hurt began to be compounded because our way of thinking was so dysfunctional. We were taught to simply forgive and forget. This line of thinking was unrealistic and definitely not rooted in truth. It was yet another Scripture we had misinterpreted due to false teachings in the church. You forgive but you do not forget until the person asks for forgiveness. You cannot allow the person back into your life until they get real and show contrition. In the meantime, you love from a distance. This gives them the opportunity to realize what they have done and forgive themselves in the process. It cleans the slate. If this does not occur, you open yourself to more hurt. It then becomes easy for people to transgress against you because they faced no consequences for their actions. Nothing is settled, and trust is never regained.

Because we did not know any better, we would hang around toxic people and be hurt again and again. We would allow them back into our lives with no questions asked. We would act as though nothing had occurred and treat them with the same respect as someone who had never caused us harm. As a child, I learned to shoulder the burden of people hurting me—even my loved ones. Indeed, we teach people how to treat us. My siblings and I had no idea how dysfunctional we were in our understanding of forgiveness. Our ability to give a million and one chances with no questions asked stemmed from our childhood. It began when we would return to living with Daddy and be forced to act as if nothing happened to force us to leave. We would try to live this happy family life. It was forced vulnerability. Mama taught us her version of forgive, forget, and move on as though nothing ever happened. Daddy never cleaned the slate with his children. He was never made to, and this seemed perfectly fine in his mind. As far as we were taught by Mama, we were doing the right thing by not holding Daddy responsible for his abusive actions.

The boys were voicing their disdain for one another to me. They loved one another and would still hang around one another.

Unfortunately, they needed each other to validate they were okay. To them, there was no one else in the world like them. They could only relate to one another since they all had the same dysfunctions and struggles. They walked lock step with each other. They shared the same fears. They needed one another to better understand themselves. They also needed one another to cover their wrongs. No matter what they did to hurt one another, they did not stay away from one another too long. Sadly, I could not exclude myself from this sad reality. Though I was their sister, I was just like them. Being a female, though, I did not fit into their world of the bro code. It was hard, and sometimes I wanted simply to be a brother without having to actually be a boy. I admired their love and closeness and how they would be there for one another covering for one another no matter the cost.

As time passed, I started to see what we were doing. I began to resent them covering for one another's wrongdoings. They gave one another the freedom to carry on in their individual debauchery. There was never a clean slate. I would voice my concern, but they did not value my opinion. I was not a brother. This would hurt my feelings. Though just like them, I was not actually one of them. Being left out was hurtful. I would have alone time with each of them from time to time, and they would express their ill feelings for one another. They would reveal what one was doing to another. I would intervene and act as a peacemaker. I wanted them to keep the lines of communication open and talk instead of bicker. Whenever I would bring them together to talk about their concerns, they would bail on me every time. I would be left looking foolish while they carried on as though they did not have any ill will toward one another.

Maybe they just wanted to use me to get it all out of their hearts and minds. Perhaps they just wanted me to act as a listening ear and not try to fix their relationship. Obviously, they had figured out a way to not hold grudges. I just loved them all dearly, and each one of them were so precious to me. My only prayer was for them to continue loving one another and come together in the good times and the trying times. "Just be real to each other," I would preach. Somehow, they found it hard to be completely honest about their feelings. I worried about their relationships much more than I worried about myself. It was so sad because I had children, and they were beginning to face their own trials in life. It seemed as though I was more into what was going on with my brothers than my own household. I was treating my brothers as if they were my children. I had my own life and was not dealing with personal obstacles. Perhaps it was easier to focus on their shortcomings rather than face my own.

Mama would be there doting on them only when they picked themselves up and began to shine. She would parade them around like a proud mother bragging about their success. However, when they would fall and be at their worst, they would become my problem, and I would have to nurse them back to health. No one was there to nurture and care for me when I stumbled. I was in trouble myself yet still making my brothers a top priority. To be quite honest, even if someone had offered to help me, my pride would have probably not allowed me to readily accept it. Yet I was crying my eyes out and complaining because I felt unsupported and alone in my fallacies.

I was silently screaming HELP ME! If anyone did reach out to help, I ran. It is difficult to love someone who has no clue how to love themselves. I did not know self-love existed for a long time. All I knew was how to selflessly love others—mainly my brothers. I was silently screaming and begging others to love me without uttering a single word. Everything I was feeling about my brothers, myself, and others were dysfunctional. However, no one cared enough to tell me to stop the madness. Therefore, I carried on living a life of hell while inflicting hurt upon myself and allowing others to do the same.

It would always be hard for me to leave Los Angeles whenever I visited. I had lived most of my adult life there and hated the thought of returning to Grand Rapids. I would be in Michigan wishing I was back in Los Angeles with my brothers. I missed my brothers so much. I missed our camaraderie. I longed for them and our love for one another. Now I was with them, and we were all getting high together—including El. I was only supposed to be there for the weekend and ended up spending two weeks in Los Angeles being unproductive. Cherelle's birthday party was over, yet I was still in party mode and not wanting to leave my brothers. Tony called daily for me to return home. Each day I promised him I would catch the flight. However, each day I would not board a single plane. Finally, after two weeks, I was worn out and tired from running around and getting high. The drama between my brothers, paired with the endless supply of drugs, became overwhelming, and I knew it was time to leave.

As I prepared to leave Los Angeles, I was worried about Bobby. The hoarseness in his voice was getting worse, and he neglected going to the doctor. I tried to take him to the doctor before I left. He made promises each day he would go the next day. When the next day came, he would not follow through. At this time, Bobby was off into other things. Both he and Tommy lived dangerously. I worried every day about getting a phone call that one of them had died. Now, Bobby had added an extra layer to my concern because he refused to care for his throat. His appearance was also very concerning because he did look sick. It just did not feel right leaving him without knowing what was wrong. If Bobby had plans to go to the doctor, I would have been the one to ensure he actually followed through. He would never go on his own volition. Nevertheless, I had to return home to care for my own children in the midst of a failed marriage.

On my last night in Los Angeles, I asked Bobby to promise he would take care of himself and go to a doctor. He made a promise, but I knew if he had not gone by this time, he probably would never go. It was bittersweet. I was leaving Los Angeles worried about Bobby as well as my other brothers—especially El. He was new to the drug game and was quickly being swallowed up. I was in bad shape myself. Perhaps they were equally worried about me. It seemed crazy how we worried about the next sibling more than we worried about ourselves. We were willing to do for the other one what we were unwilling to do for ourselves. This was another DeBarge family dysfunction: I have your back and you have my back. We never had to worry about our own "backs," so to speak, because it was the other sibling's responsibility. This was how we functioned, and it eventually took its toll on us in the worst way.

To be continued . . .

The Third And Final Volume Of "The Kept Ones" Coming Soon!

Thank you for reading "The Kept Ones: DeBarge, The Fame Years!"
Please share your feedback on social media using our hashtags & handles:

Instagram.com/BunnyDeBarge |@BunnyDeBarge

Facebook.com/officialBunnyDeBarge | @OfficialBunnyDeBarge

Twitter.com/BunnyDeBarge | @BunnyDeBarge

Youtube.com/BunnyDeBargeOfficial | @BunnyDeBargeOfficial

Hashtags (TAGS) | #debarge #thekeptones

Official Website & Press Kit | OfficialBunnyDeBarge.com

For Booking & Media Requests Contact Management

Sally B. Waller, Artist Manager & Publicist

VocalzMusic & Publishing (VMP)

Sallyb@VocalzMusic.com | VocalzMusic.com

Bunny DeBarge is available for public speaking, music performances, public appearances, interviews and of course book signings.

If you enjoyed this book, please consider writing a review with your honest impressions on Amazon, or the platform of your choosing. Your feedback is incredibly valuable for helping independent authors like Bunny DeBarge to reach a wider audience.

Made in the USA
Columbia, SC
18 October 2024

44265795R00213